BEYOND POST-COMMUNIST STUDIES

BEYOND POST-COMMUNIST STUDIES

Political Science and the
New Democracies of Europe

TERRY D. CLARK

M.E. Sharpe
Armonk, New York
London, England

JUN 10 2003

Copyright © 2002 by M. E. Sharpe, Inc.

All rights reserved. No part of this book may be reproduced in any form
without written permission from the publisher, M. E. Sharpe, Inc.,
80 Business Park Drive, Armonk, New York 10504.

Library of Congress Cataloging-in-Publication Data

Clark, Terry D.
 Beyond post-communist studies : political science and the new democracies of Europe /
by Terry D. Clark.
     p. cm.
 Includes bibliographical references and index.
 ISBN 0-7656-0980-0 (alk. paper)
   1. Democracy. 2. Democratization. 3. Post-communism. 4. Europe, Eastern--Politics
and government--1989– 5. Europe, Eastern--Research. 6. Political science--Study and
teaching. I. Title.

JC423.C584 2002
320.947--dc21   2002020622

Printed in the United States of America

The paper used in this publication meets the minimum requirements of
American National Standard for Information Sciences
Permanence of Paper for Printed Library Materials,
ANSI Z 39.48-1984.

BM (c) 10 9 8 7 6 5 4 3 2 1

Contents

Preface ix

Chapter One: Going Beyond Post-Communist Studies 3
Post-Communist Studies and Democratic Consolidation 3
Paradigms in Communist Studies 8
Democratic Consolidation 11
Democratic Consolidation's Research Agenda 14
Looking Ahead 15

Chapter Two: The Study of Post-Communist Politics 18
Stateness 19
Democracy and the Market 20
Bringing the State In 25
   Strategic Choice and Post-Communist Studies 26
   Path Dependency and Post-Communist Studies 28
   Institutionalism and Post-Communist Studies 29
Contributions to the Agenda 35
What We Are Not Asking 40

Chapter Three: The Missing Agenda 42
Bringing Society Back In 42
   The Distribution of "Democratic" Values 43
   Civil Society 46
   Social Movements 48
The Rule of Law 49
A Usable State Bureaucracy 50
Issue Areas Outside the Agenda of Democratic Consolidation 52
   Principal-Agent Problems 52
   Local Government 55
   Institutional Development 57
What Is To Be Done? 57

Chapter Four: Reformulating Democratic Consolidation 59
Transition Theory 60
Toward a Theory of Consolidation 64
A Theory of Democratic Consolidation 66
   Weakening and Increasing Competing Forces 69
   Increasing Institutional Involvement 71

v

Further Explicating the Theory 73
Implications 75
Applying the Theory 77
    Russia 78
    Lithuania 79

Chapter Five: Imagining Post-Consolidation Studies 84
Fundamentals of Rational Choice 84
Spatial Analysis 86
The Median Voter Theorem 87
Legislative Roll-Call Vote Analysis 89
Legislative Committee Systems 92
Relations with a President 94
    Presidential Vetoes 94
    Presidential Appointments 96
The Courts as Political Players 97
Analysis of the Party System 99
Rules Matter 102
Principal-Agent Problems 104
    Committee Systems 104
    Legislative Oversight 105
Implications 107

**Chapter Six: Further Extending the
    Post-Consolidation Agenda** 108
The Majority Cycling Problem 108
Legislative Agenda 110
Cabinet Formation 118
    The Portfolio Allocation Model 118
    Explaining Lithuanian Cabinet Formation, 2000–2001 121

Chapter Seven: Some Further Theoretical Considerations
    (with Jan Weiss) 128
Toward a Formal Model of an Unconsolidated Democracy 129
A Formal Model of Democratic Consolidation 134
A Concluding Word 138

Notes 139

**A Short Bibliography of Rational-Choice Literature
    Arranged by Subject** 163

Index 169

List of Tables and Figures

Figures

Figure 4.1	The Process of Democratic Consolidation	73
Figure 5.1	Preferred Defense Budget for a Hypothetical Lithuanian Voter	85
Figure 5.2	Notional Preferred Defense Budget for Parties and a Lithuanian Voter	87
Figure 5.3	Notional Party Preferences on the Defense Budget in the *Seimas*	88
Figure 5.4	Spatial Illustration of Party Preferences on Economic Issues	90
Figure 5.5	Spatial Comparisons of a Status Quo Bill (SQ) with the Policy Preferences of a Committee (c*) and the Parent Legislature (C)	93
Figure 5.6	Spatial Comparisons of the Status Quo (SQ) with the Policy Preferences of the *Seimas* (L) and the President (P)	95
Figure 5.7	Spatial Comparisons of the Policy Preferences of the *Seimas* (L), the President (P), and the Constitutional Court (CC)	98
Figure 5.8	A Notional Party System	100
Figure 5.9	Effect of Party Shifts on the Notional Party System	101
Figure 5.10	Spatial Comparisons of the Ideal Points of a Bureaucratic Agency (B) and the Median Voter in the Legislature (L)	106
Figure 6.1	Notional Spatial Illustration of Party Preferences on the Defense Budget	114
Figure 6.2	Spatial Representation of Lithuanian Political Parties on Economic (X-axis) and Defense Spending (Y-axis), 1997 Budget	117
Figure 6.3	Estimated Party Positions on Economic Development Model, 2000	125
Figure 6.4	Estimated Party Positions on Defense Policy, 2000	126

viii LIST OF TABLES AND FIGURES

Figure 7.1 A Graphic Display of the Relationship between the Payoff (c) and the Proportion of the Vote (x*) for Any Contestant in a Presidential, President-Parliamentary, or Majoritarian Party Parliamentary System   132
Figure 7.2 A Graphic Display of the Relationship between the Payoff (c) and the Proportion of the Vote (x*) for Any Contestant in a Presidential, President-Parliamentary, or Majoritarian Party Parliamentary System under Conditions of Imperfect Information   134
Figure 7.3 A Graphic Display of the Relationship between the Payoff (c) and the Proportion of the Vote (x*) for Any Contestant in a Premier-Presidential or non-Majoritarian Parliamentary System   136
Figure 7.4 A Graphic Display of the Effect of Requiring Super-Majorities (z > .5) for a One Hundred Percent Payoff (y* = 1) on the Relationship between the Payoff (c) and the Proportion of the Vote (x*) for Any Contestant in a Premier-Presidential or non-Majoritarian Parliamentary System   137

Tables

Table 5.1 *Seimas* Roll-Call Vote Outcomes on Economic Bills, 1997   91
Table 5.2 Use of the Veto by Lithuanian Presidents   96
Table 5.3 Comparison of Election Results Based on Plurality and Majority Rules in the *Seimas* Single-Mandate District Races, 2000   103
Table 6.1 Party Preference Orderings for Three Notional Lithuanian Voters, 2000 *Seimas* Elections   110
Table 6.2 Winners in Head-to-Head Pairings of Parties in Table 6.1   110
Table 6.3 Party Preferences on Three Privatization Plans (A, B, and C)   111
Table 6.4 Winners in Head-to-Head Pairings of Privatization Plans in Table 6.3   111
Table 6.5 Party Preferences on Three Privatization Plans (A, B, and C), Changing "Right" Party Preferences   113
Table 6.6 Winners in Head-to-Head Pairings of Privatization Plans in Table 6.5   113
Table 6.7 The Decisive Structure of the 2000 *Seimas*   122

Preface

It has been my good fortune that my academic career began on the eve of the collapse of communism in eastern and east-central Europe. I, along with my colleagues, have had the privilege of studying the profound social, economic, and political challenges that have attended that collapse. In contrast to those who labored before us, we have had access to rich repositories of data of all types and descriptions, as a consequence of which we have been able to pursue a greater universe of questions. Nonetheless, despite both the energy and excitement that all of this has generated, I must confess to one frustration. Almost ten years after the collapse, we still do not have adequate theories capable of guiding research in many major areas of concern.

Perhaps the fact that I received my Ph.D. in political science from the University of Illinois at Urbana-Champaign helps explain why I am even concerned about theory. I remain grateful to the excellent faculty at that institution, who challenged me to think theoretically. However, to be honest, I have not always been convinced of the utility of models and the like. In fact, in my early years as a scholar I was deeply committed to an area studies approach, focusing on the richness of context. At best, I was ambivalent to the claims of political scientists, such as Alexander J. Motyl[1] or Philip G. Roeder,[2] that theory is central to the research enterprise, finding myself decidedly more at ease with attempts to expand our substantive knowledge of the region.

My conversion, if that is the proper word, occurred over an extended period of time during which I grappled with the reform process in Russia and Lithuania, the two countries for which I was best prepared to conduct research. To my mind, history and culture failed to adequately address why the latter was experiencing far greater difficulties, particularly in its efforts to create a democratic state. Equally disconcerting was the overly optimistic literature on Russian public attitudes and institutions, a literature with which I found myself in profound disagreement. (The literature became decidedly less sanguine following the ruble collapse of 1998. However, well into the mid-1990s, it was difficult to find a journal willing to publish articles expressing any degree of skepticism about the Russian democratization process.) I slowly came to the conclusion that the underlying problem with much of this work was that it was explicitly idiosyncratic and contextual and therefore not comparative. Hence, all institutions were judged "democratic" as long as they conformed in *form*, but not necessarily *content*, to those in other political systems.

I ultimately became convinced that the meaning of democracy and democratic institutions could not be contextually dependent. If such phenomena are unique to every political system, then they are useless categories. One can simply declare that all political systems are ultimately democratic and that all political institutions perform democratic functions as long as they conform to the meanings of those concepts as imbedded in the particularities of the given culture. Theory presented itself as the way out of this morass by providing a common set of concepts, categories, and linkages. I have come to the conclusion that theory is equally important for other reasons as well. Without it I am at a loss to understand how we might compare cases by juxtaposing what has been discovered elsewhere—as represented in the theoretical constructs that are informed by that knowledge—with the "facts" in the particular case before us. Indeed, absent this process we are forced to rediscover the wheel each time we engage in research. Worse, we can not enter into the exchange of ideas and information that permits any degree of accumulation of knowledge. And perhaps most important, we can not truly know the answer to the question "why?" In short, aside from theory, I am not sure how one goes about making progress in expanding our substantive knowledge. None of this, however, argues that we should naively employ theories without regard for context. That would permit the accumulation of neither substantive nor theoretical knowledge.

The best-developed project addressing the issue of democracy theoretically is *democratic consolidation*. Not surprisingly, given the field's area studies tradition, the response to the application of the theory in post-communist studies[3] and calls to expand its application[4] have been generally less than enthusiastic. The most common protest is that the context in which post-communist democratization is taking place is simply too different from that of Latin America, the region whose experience provided the basis for developing the theory, to permit comparison.[5] The unfortunate consequence, however, of rejecting democratic consolidation is that scholars of post-communist Europe fail to offer a constructive critique of the theory that permits them to engage political science as a discipline.

I have concluded that the better approach is to engage in research efforts to revise shortcomings and oversights in democratic consolidation theory.[6] That is one of the purposes of this book. In the first two chapters I review the research on democratic consolidation in post-communist Europe. In the third chapter I consider the issues that we are not adequately addressing. In the fourth chapter I put forward a proposal for tightening the theoretical linkages in democratic consolidation, a proposal that is predicated on a rational-choice definition of a consolidated democracy.

A second and related purpose of this book is to demonstrate how rational-choice approaches can be meaningfully applied to analyzing political processes in some of the democracies of post-communist Europe. A small but significant number of states in the region are already consolidated democracies. These states provide an excellent "test bed" for rational-choice theories. In chapters five and six I use selected examples drawn from Lithuania to demonstrate the utility of these theories. The book, however, is not about Lithuania. It is about moving beyond the set of theoretical tools currently employed to analyze political processes in post-communist Europe.

As an author, I offer this book in the hope that it will contribute to the ongoing conversation that constitutes the life of a discipline. Toward that end, I have two goals in mind. First, I envision that the theory the book offers of the consolidation phase of democracy will contribute to a much-needed discussion on how we can more meaningfully determine the end of the democratization process. Just as important, I hope that it will serve as a catalyst for a debate concerning which post-communist states are consolidating, regressing, or consolidated. My second goal is to apply rational-choice perspectives and approaches to post-communist states in a broadly systematic manner intended to suggest a fundamentally new research agenda for the discipline. The fact that the agenda proposed in this book is theoretically based will hopefully make a much needed correction to the current debate, in which those who criticize the paradigmatic dominance of democratic consolidation often fail to offer an alternative set of approaches and theories (other than traditional, atheoretical case studies).

In the end, however, I confess that I will be satisfied even if the book accomplishes none of these goals. I have taken great pleasure simply in writing it. The process has been an exciting one. Frequently, I have found myself awestruck by the sudden discovery of answers to puzzles that in some cases had eluded me for years. At the same time, it has constituted an amazingly relaxing experience. On more nights than I can recall, I have found myself enjoying the escape from the cares of life that it has brought me. Indeed, I have "felt God's pleasure" in the very writing, and for that I am grateful.

BEYOND POST-COMMUNIST STUDIES

Chapter One

Going Beyond Post-Communist Studies

Post-Communist Studies and Democratic Consolidation

The collapse of Communist Party rule in eastern and east-central Europe held out the promise that scholars studying the political systems of the region could escape their isolation from mainstream political science. Much of that promise has been realized. The previous dominance of area studies emphasizing idiosyncratic explanations rooted in historical and cultural understanding has given way to a diverse array of social science approaches. Statistical analyses, comparative assessments, and in some cases even explicitly theoretical pieces have emerged alongside of and complemented the more traditional case studies approach. In the process, post-communist studies has had a much closer relationship to political science than did the former soviet studies and communist studies.

Despite this, political scientists studying post-communist systems have yet to fully integrate with their discipline. This owes largely to the fact that democratic consolidation as a paradigm dominates the study of the new regimes of eastern and east-central Europe. The fact that a paradigm controls a field of inquiry is not inconsequential. Paradigms matter. They matter because they establish the vocabulary and the concepts that permit scholars to communicate with each other. They matter even more so because the structure of reality that these concepts construct focuses scholars on particular sets of problems and particular approaches to unraveling those problems. In so doing, paradigms contribute to progress in understanding the human reality. Without them we would be hopelessly lost trying to comprehend an infinite universe of knowledge. However, the corollary to this defense of paradigms is equally important. Paradigms also blind us to issues and approaches and thereby reduce our comprehension of reality.

Given the authoritarian nature of the former communist regimes as well as the normative preference of most scholars for democracy, the dominance of the democratic consolidation paradigm is not at all surprising. Indeed, since the collapse of communism, scholars overwhelmingly have been concerned with the possibility of the emergence of democracy in the region. A great majority of the analyses of post-communist politics focus on the development of democratic political institutions, the strategic choices of elites, and threats to the survival of democracy.

While not surprising, the paradigmatic dominance of democratic consolidation has nonetheless substantially retarded the field's integration with political science. Democratic consolidation is a curious amalgam of behavioralist and new institutionalist approaches. Of the two, behavioralism, with its emphasis on culture and socialized behavior, is the more familiar to a field previously rooted in a largely humanistic, area studies tradition. Consequently, statistical analyses of value systems and participatory behavior have emerged as a growth industry of sorts. On the other hand, while students of post-communist systems have also used institutionalist approaches, their use has often been informed by notions of the restraining effect that historical and cultural legacies have on alternative paths available for political development.

Much of political science, however, has moved largely beyond behavioralism's focus on the effects of history, culture, and values on political behavior. Many of the dominant paradigms and approaches are now explicitly premised on rational choice. Starting from the assumption that political actors are motivated to achieve their private interests, however that interest may be defined, rational-choice approaches seek to determine the possible range of outcomes resulting from competing interests. The more sophisticated of these approaches recognize the constraining effect of institutions on the choices available to salient political actors. This literature comprises what is most often referred to as the new institutionalism, an explicitly rationalist school. In contrast to many of the approaches included under the rubric of democratic consolidation, the new institutionalism is a coherent body of theory. It argues that the institutions themselves are the result of bargaining among political actors for political advantage. They are not culturally or historically predetermined. Nor are they irrevocably fixed. They can be discarded when they no longer serve the interests they were intended to serve. (We shall consider new institutional approaches in considerable detail in chapters five, six, and seven.)

Rational-choice approaches and the new institutionalism in particular were developed to explain political phenomena in the developed Western democracies. Many would therefore argue that they can not be appropriately applied to the states of eastern and east-central Europe. The argument rests on the assertion that the region is still transitioning to democracy. In reality, however, the states of post-communist Europe are a good deal more diverse than such an assertion admits. Among the countries included in the region are Albania, Bulgaria, the Czech Republic, Hungary, Poland, Romania, Slovakia, the former Yugoslavia, and ten of the fifteen republics of the former Soviet Union (excluding the five republics of Central Asia)–Armenia, Azerbaijan, Belarus, Estonia, Georgia, Latvia, Lithuania, Moldova, Russia, and Ukraine. Not all of them are experiencing democratic consolidation to the same degree. Hence, we must disaggregate the states of the region and apply the proper approaches and paradigms to each set of states.

Democratic consolidation—as a paradigm encompassing a broad set of approaches addressing democratization—is clearly the most appropriate for understanding the political processes occurring in countries such as Bulgaria, Croatia, Estonia, Latvia, Montenegro, Romania, and Slovakia. However, in other countries it is questionable if democratic transformation is even occurring. Belarus is the clearest case of a state that is making no progress toward institutionalizing democracy. It is also debatable as to whether Armenia, Azerbaijan, Georgia, and Serbia are transitioning to democracy. And, Russia and Ukraine are "stuck." At best, they are encountering considerable difficulties in establishing democratic norms and institutions.

In a small but significant set of countries, however, including the Czech Republic, Hungary, Lithuania, Slovakia, and Poland, democracy is arguably already consolidated. These countries are beyond the scope of democratic consolidation. As a group they raise similar issues to those in consolidated democracies. Hence, they permit us to use the more mainstream paradigms and approaches in the discipline of political science. If these countries are different, we should ask why and how they contribute to the development of theory. If not, we should use theory to understand them. In short, this set of countries presents us with the best opportunity to integrate post-communist studies into mainstream political science.

This book is about going beyond post-communist studies. It is about exploring new possibilities for studying the consolidated democracies of east-central Europe. It explicitly argues for disaggregating the post-communist states of Europe and analyzing the consolidated democracies within the context of processes in normal, Western-style democracies.

Failing to do so, we not only risk properly understanding them and the processes occurring in them, we reduce our contribution to theoretical developments in political science. I am, however, not arguing that we should give up more traditional idiosyncratic case studies. Such studies have value. They give us context and provide the gist for more general, broad-gauged analyses. My argument is much more modest. There is too little of the latter—particularly theoretically informed studies.

The organization of the book is as follows. I begin by making the point that post-communist studies, like communist studies before it, is dominated by a paradigm. I then turn to a careful consideration of that paradigm, democratic consolidation. My purpose is first to lay out the issues on which the paradigm has focused us and second to identify where we might meaningfully give more consideration. It is at this point that I make the case that democratic consolidation's major problem is a general failure to coherently tie the process of democratization to a definition of the goal of the process itself, democracy. As a consequence, democratic consolidation does not permit us to consider that the process may well be complete and a democratic regime has consolidated. We are predisposed by the paradigm to assume that whatever political system we are studying is in a perpetual state of transition. I then propose that the solution to the problem is to import an explicitly rational-choice perspective. The perspective not only postulates an end to democratization as a process, it allows us to continue studying the newly consolidated democratic regime. In the book's final chapters, I build on this argument to demonstrate ways in which rational choice, a dominant paradigm in political science, permits us to study consolidated democracies in east-central Europe. Of course, it is not possible to identify all of the issues that we might usefully consider, but I focus on a few that seem most illustrative.

Throughout the book, I use political processes in Lithuania to demonstrate my points, particularly as they relate to how we might profitably study the consolidated democracies of post-communist Europe. I do so for the pragmatic reason that this is the country with which I am most familiar. There is, however, an even better reason for doing so. Given the proposition that there is a small set of consolidated democracies in post-communist Europe, Lithuania is the one about which there is most likely to be disagreement. If we can demonstrate the utility of theoretical approaches developed in consolidated democracies in the Lithuanian case, we make the case for their applicability to the remaining states.

My more direct response to those who raise concerns about the utility of Lithuania is that I can find no well-grounded empirical argument that Lithuania is not a consolidated democracy. The country's democratic system most certainly meets the most commonly used definition, a political system in which democracy is the only game in town, no salient political forces pursuing or suggesting any alternatives for resolving political issues other than democratic norms and procedures.[1] It is true that in the immediate aftermath of the 1992 elections to the *Seimas*—which brought the former communist party, the Lithuanian Democratic Labor Party (LDLP) to power—some elements of the *Savanoriai*, the country's voluntary reserve defense force, engaged in activities suggesting they might overturn the election results by force. However, any such designs were quickly abandoned as political leaders across the spectrum distanced themselves from this threat to the constitutional order.

In fact, there are no salient antidemocratic or anti-systemic political parties in the Lithuanian political party system, indicating elite acceptance of democratic rules.[2] The very small group of individuals comprising a would-be fascist party remain unregistered, and while the country's second largest city elected a populist mayor in the local elections of 2000, he was not anti-systemic or extremist in any sense. In his short term in office, he continued to support contention for power by democratic means and he did much to make democratic participation more open. Further, while the public expresses low levels of trust in some democratic institutions,[3] this appears to be connected with dissatisfaction with the performance of these institutions rather than with democracy in general. The *New Baltic Barometer II*, for example, found that Lithuanian citizens, not surprisingly given the hardships of the post-communist era, rated the Soviet economic system as better than the current economic system. Nonetheless, less than 1 percent of the respondents were categorized as strong supporters of an authoritarian system and another 7.7 percent as only moderate supporters. The remaining respondent population supported democratic means of governance.[4]

Further supporting the contention that Lithuania is a consolidated democracy is the *1999 Regular Report from the Commission on Lithuania's Progress towards Accession* (to the EU).[5] In its general evaluation, the report states, "Lithuania fulfils the Copenhagen political criteria." Finally we should take note of the fact that the country's political democratic system has passed the "two turnover" test.[6] Power has been successfully and peacefully transferred on not two, but three occasions as the result of democratic elections. The first time was the election of a Democratic Labor Party majority in the 1992 elections to the *Seimas* replacing the *Sajudis* majority elected in 1990. The second occurrence was in 1996 when the Conservatives and the Christian Democrats gained a majority. The third occurrence was in 2000 when a bloc of centrist parties achieved a majority. There were no serious discussions or efforts to stop any of these changes in power by anything other than electoral means.

Paradigms in Communist Studies

A central premise of this book is that paradigms have shaped both communist and post-communist studies. In so doing, they have contributed to our understanding of the political systems of eastern and east-central Europe. Nonetheless, they have also impeded us in some important ways from properly understanding political processes in those very same countries. Indeed, the monumental failure of communist studies was the inability to foresee the collapse of communism. This owed to the conservative nature of the dominant paradigms, all of which presumed the durability of the system. Similarly, post-communist studies, dominated by democratic consolidation, assumes a virtually endless process of democratization. As a consequence, scholars are seeing democratization where it does not exist. In the same vein, they are unable to argue that the process is complete and a consolidated democracy is now in place. One task of this book is to address ways to resolve the latter issue.

The centrality of paradigms to communist studies is a relatively easy case to make. For most of the cold war, scholars studying the Soviet Union and the communist states of eastern Europe were largely engaged in a debate over which model best fit these political systems. In the early part of the era, the prevailing view was that communist systems were hierarchically structured and ideologically informed. Maintaining a monopoly on the mass media and political organization, the Communist Party stood at the pinnacle of a mobilized society. The will of the party leadership was embodied in every aspect of state and society as party and state organs faithfully executed the directives of these political elites. Scholars employing this totalitarian model[7] viewed citizen activity as largely conformist, the cost of dissidence either being so high that few were likely to engage in it or the socialization of the masses and control of sources of information so complete that dissidence was unlikely. Political change was explained only in terms of changing leadership.

With the death of Stalin and the emergence of the thaw during the Khrushchev era, many scholars began to challenge the totalitarian model. Viewing citizens of communist countries as more participatory, they argued that a pluralist model better depicted the relationship between leaders and masses. While the Communist Party held a monopoly on political and economic power, there was considerable room for debate within broadly established limits. Just as important, the party was not monolithic. Rather, it was composed of bureaucratically structured entities with divergent interests. The pluralist nature of these political systems was reflected in the competition for resources between government ministries, budgetary negotiations between localities and the center, and the frequency with which citizens petitioned local governments or engaged in writing letters to the press.

In contrast to scholars employing the totalitarian model, pluralists viewed Soviet and East European political systems as dynamic. Hence, they employed approaches focusing on change. Despite this, all of the pluralist models assumed that the communist system was highly durable and generally impervious to collapse. Among the pluralist approaches were interest-group theory, the bureaucratic model, and modernization and development theory. Interest-group theorists focused on the existence of competing views within these systems, which frequently found expression in professional journals and at times even newspapers. Jerry Hough[8] extended the initial arguments of H. Gordon Skilling,[9] contending that competing interests were institutionalized in party and state structures. Various state-sponsored and organized interests were represented by any number of government ministries and party activities. The essence of Hough's model, which he labeled institutionalized pluralism, is that politics in Soviet-type European communist systems is a bargaining process between these various interests, one in which party leaders serve as brokers or mediators. Hence, change emerges from interaction and bargaining among interest groups rather than as a consequence of leadership renewal.

Scholars employing the bureaucratic model viewed the communist countries of eastern Europe and the Soviet Union as comprising one large bureaucratic entity organized and administered by the party.[10] In contrast to the totalitarian model, however, the party was only loosely united by overarching goals. In the day-to-day activities of governance, the individual entities and activities of the party exercised a significant degree of latitude in carrying out their functions. While state and society were coordinated, outcomes were neither rigid nor uniform. Change resulted from the interaction between bureaucratic entities within the party.

Modernization and development theorists employed a system-level approach explicitly focused on political change to explain communist systems. The essence of the model was that the scientific-technological revolution had placed demands on sociopolitical systems for fundamental restructuring. In order to compete more effectively in the economic realities created by the new technology, countries were compelled to encourage the free flow of information and the distribution of new ideas and methods. This necessarily involved the opening up of society and the introduction of certain civil liberties associated with Western liberal democracies, foremost among them freedom of the press and speech. The logic of the argument led some to contend that communist systems would tend toward convergence with the West. In a parallel argument based on the ideas of Harold Lasswell, other scholars contended that the expansion of education required by the new global technological developments leads to the emergence of a class whose vested interest is in the free exchange of ideas and information. It is this class and not the requirements of the technological revolution itself that pressures for fundamental political change.[11]

In an effort to combine the strengths of both the totalitarian and pluralist approaches, some scholars attempted to use corporatism to analyze communist political systems. First employed in the Soviet case by Bunce and Echols[12] (and later rejected by Bunce as lacking empirical content) corporatism treats the state as a unitary actor that regulates socioeconomic order through the agency of private and public associations. Since the state views itself as the representative of the overarching interests upon which the harmony of the whole of society rests, it acts to implement policies to achieve the general interest by efforts to negotiate between the competing interests represented by the associations. When necessary, it applies force to repress those interests that can not be accommodated without disrupting social harmony or denying the attainment of the general interest. Despite the intent to meld the repressive traits of the totalitarian model with the interest-group activity addressed in the pluralist model, in its application corporatism was often indistinguishable as a concept from much of the pluralist literature, particularly that associated with advocates of institutionalized pluralism. McCain used corporatism to assess the "relations between specialist elites and the party in policy-making." He found some institutionalized groups more influential, most notably the Procuracy.[13] Similarly, Ziegler employed the corporatist model to analyze the involvement of elite-dominated interests in environmental policy.[14]

At times the debate between pluralists and advocates of the totalitarian model was heated if not downright uncivil. In hindsight, it would have been strange had it not been; for what was at stake was no less than establishing the prevailing intellectual framework structuring scholarly thinking and research about these systems. Hence, in a Khunian sense, the debate represented a contest between paradigms. In essence, the prevailing model structured the research agenda as well as norms and standards for the entire community of scholarship focused on politics in the communist systems of Europe.

Democratic Consolidation

The collapse of communism created a paradigmatic vacuum for scholars studying eastern and east-central Europe. That vacuum was quickly filled by democratic consolidation. This is not at all surprising for a number of reasons. First, there is a general scholarly consensus, expressed by Valerie Bunce, that democracy is the most important issue in the region.[15] Second, students of post-communist Europe possess an overwhelming normative preference for democracy. Third, the collapse of communism has contributed to the widespread acceptance of the view that democracy (in any number of forms) may be the only viable political regime in the present era. This is not to argue that we have arrived at the "end of history." While interstate conflict may continue over any number of issues, particularly those related to economic wealth or cultural identity, the only remaining political issues concern how to best encourage and facilitate the trend to democratization. The "democratic peace hypothesis" that democracies are less likely to engage in conflict with each other has given further impetus to this view.

Democratic consolidation as a paradigm has its genesis in the analyses of the breakdown of authoritarian rule in southern Europe in the 1970s and Latin America in the 1980s. By the late 1980s and 1990s the phenomenon had become globalized, extending to eastern and east-central Europe, Asia, and parts of Africa. Recognizing the historical significance and proportion of the collapse of authoritarianism as well as the potential it created for democratization to occur on a global scale, Samuel P. Huntington labeled the phenomenon the "Third Wave."[16]

What concerned scholars most was not only whether the newly emerging democracies would survive, but whether they would mature. In other words, scholarship came to be increasingly concerned with the durability of the new democracies of the "Third Wave." Early scholarship of the phenomenon focused largely on preconditions for democracy, identifying inventories of static factors thought necessary for democracy to take root.[17] The most common of these was Seymour Martin Lipset's proposition that democracy is not possible in the absence of high levels of economic growth.[18] Others included the minimalization of socioeconomic disparity, avoidance of extreme class polarization, a political leadership dedicated to the democratization project, the widespread public acceptance of democratic values such as tolerance and compromise, the instauration of democratic institutions, the existence of a civil society, and a military under civilian control.

By the mid-1980s a second, more dynamic approach was adopted by scholars studying democratization under the auspices of the Woodrow Wilson Center.[19] The project identified a two-stage process. The first stage, which focuses on the breakdown of the authoritarian system, was mislabeled the transition to democracy. The second stage, democratic consolidation, occurs in part concurrently with the collapse of the regime; however, it carries on well afterward until an ideal end-state is achieved. The end-state is a political system in which no salient political forces (among elites or the public) seriously question the legitimacy of the democratic regime. In essence, democracy becomes the only game in town.[20] The process by which this is achieved is one in which both the elites and the public are habituated to democratic rules and norms. It is a reversible process, a possibility that those focusing on static factors largely ignored. Further, there is no inevitability to democratic consolidation. Simply achieving a prerequisite level of economic growth or adopting democratic institutions in no way guarantees that democratization will even occur.

A number of approaches for studying the process of democratic consolidation have been employed. The most common are strategic choice, institutionalism, and preexistent conditions. Scholars of the breakdown of authoritarian rule have had a profound influence on analyses of democratic consolidation. This is not at all surprising given that it follows the breakdown of authoritarian rule. These scholars argued that the process is contingent on the choices taken by political actors at strategic moments.[21] The approach has been adopted by a number of influential studies of democratic consolidation.[22]

The new institutionalism, premised on the assumption of the rational individual, has become an extraordinarily powerful approach in the discipline of political science in the last twenty years. We should therefore expect that scholars would attempt to use it to study democratization. However, the form in which it has been adopted is weakly related to the theoretical underpinnings of the new institutionalism. Institutions are essentially analyzed in isolation from one another. Lacking theoretical coherence, these studies are primarily concerned with testing ad hoc hypotheses about the impact of institutions on democratization. Among the most commonly considered institutional designs are the party system and the structure of executive-legislative relations (whether parliamentarism or presidentialism is adopted).[23]

Preexistent conditions has been the approach of choice for many studying democratic consolidation in post-communist systems. This approach focuses on the legacies of communist rule, the mode of transition from communist rule, and an array of static factors. The legacy of the communist past can refer to political values still resident in the population or residual effects of the period of communist rule. Such effects have addressed any number of issues, including explaining the availability of an alternative to the former nomenklatura as a function of the degree of repressiveness. Scholars analyzing the mode of transition from the communist system have contributed to a burgeoning literature on path dependency. Such analyses generally argue that the way in which political systems exited from communist rule conditions and restricts the available paths to democratization.[24] Still other scholars have focused on the existence of a set of static factors as necessary to democracy.[25] The most common of these factors are economic development, a military under civilian control, a democratic past, and the existence of well-developed political institutions such as political parties or a legislature.

None of this, however, makes the case that democratic consolidation is inadequate as a paradigm. Multiple approaches to studying a phenomenon suggest that a wide array of methods and theories can be adapted to the agenda bounded by a paradigm. Further, conceptual "fuzziness" seems to be in the very nature of paradigms. For example, realism's central concept of power is an extraordinarily vague concept with multiple uses. Yet few would contend that the paradigm in its current form, neorealism, has not established itself at the center of international relations as a discipline. We may well better understand a lack of conceptual clarity as reflecting a paradigm's capacity to accommodate an expansive set of issues, without which it would be less capable of bounding a discipline or field of study.

Democratic Consolidation's Research Agenda

The research agenda bounded by democratic consolidation is indeed an expansive one, with scholars focusing on any number of arenas within which to seek explanation for the success or failure of the democratization project. Some scholars stress economic factors as the key element in the process. Similarly to the modernization theorists, they frequently relegate political institutions to a secondary role or contend that economic development is best undertaken by an authoritarian regime. Only after a substantial degree of economic development is achieved can the choice for democracy be made. Other scholars follow Samuel Huntington's contention that both successful economic development and democratization require the creation and development of political institutions capable of successfully managing each transition.[26] Still others insist that democracy is not possible in the absence of a citizenry actively engaged in a wide range of private associational activity outside of state sponsorship.

The most ambitious effort yet to establish the limits of the paradigm is Juan J. Linz and Alfred Stepan's tome, *Problems of Democratic Transition and Consolidation: Southern Europe, South America, and Postcommunist Europe*. Linz and Stepan lay out five interacting arenas that mark consolidated democracies: civil society, political society, rule of law, a usable state bureaucracy, and economic society. Additionally, they add *stateness* (the willingness of people and groups to be citizens of the nation-state exercising sovereignty over the territory on which they reside) as a necessary precondition. Perhaps their most important contribution is the point that no one arena among the five is more important than any other. Progress must be made in each of them if democracy is to consolidate.[27] It is interesting to note that Valerie Bunce, among the most vocal critics of the utility of theories and approaches developed in other regions of the globe, has identified virtually these same five arenas as the focus of concern for scholars of the post-communist world (representative government, rule of law, a Weberian bureaucracy, some dispersion of economic resources, and civil liberties guaranteeing the participatory rights of citizens).[28]

Civil society is understood to comprise a web of private associational activity autonomous from the state. It is through this medium that citizens are able to press demands upon state institutions. Political society comprises the set of institutions and rules by which elites contest for political office. These include the core institutions of democracy: political parties, elections, electoral rules, and a legislature. The rule of law refers to the pervasive acceptance on the part of both elites and the general public that democratic rules must be followed. It is supported by a system of laws, an independent judiciary, and a well-formed legal culture. A usable state bureaucracy provides the state with the means to effectively carry out policy without which democratization itself is not possible, while an economic society refers to "the norms, institutions, and regulations which mediate between state and market."[29]

Looking Ahead

This chapter has argued that the collapse of communism in east-central and eastern Europe created a paradigmatic vacuum that was quickly filled by democratic consolidation. In the next chapter we turn to a consideration of how democratic consolidation has informed the research agenda of post-communist studies. I will demonstrate that a rich research agenda within post-communist studies has emerged within the framework of several of the arenas identified by Linz and Stepan.

The focus that a paradigm gives a discipline necessarily means that some questions are ignored. Even issues that the paradigm itself would suggest as important topics for research can go unnoticed or underdeveloped. Chapter three addresses issues to which post-communist scholars have devoted inadequate attention. These include three of the arenas of a consolidated democracy (civil society, the rule of law, and a useable state bureaucracy), principal-agent relations—in particular those involving the legislature and committee systems and the legislature and executive agencies—and local government.

Given that each of these issues has a self-evident connection with democracy, it seems strange that scholars of democratic consolidation have paid so little attention to them. Chapter four begins by identifying the lack of a coherent theory as the primary reason for this. It then goes on to discuss a related problem: The lack of theory has contributed to our inability to identify how or when a political system has become a consolidated democracy. In essence, we are led to assume a virtually endless process of democratization. As a consequence, scholars are unable to see that the process is complete and a consolidated democracy is now in place. Lacking the means to distinguish between the states of post-communist Europe, we are treating them as if they were similar. This is a mistake. Some of these political systems are already consolidated democracies, while others are not even democratizing.

Chapter four develops a theory of democratic consolidation intended to resolve this problem. It does so by linking what is essentially a set of rational-choice explanations with an explicitly institutional definition of the outcome of the process. The chapter concludes by applying the theory to Russia and Lithuania. The exercise makes the case that Lithuania demonstrates the theoretical criteria of a consolidated democracy, while Russia does not.

Since some countries of post-communist Europe, such as Lithuania, have achieved a stable democracy, democratic consolidation is no longer an appropriate paradigm for analyzing political processes in these countries. We need to use theories and approaches more appropriate to these states. Rational-choice theories suggest themselves, since they were developed in the context of consolidated democracies. Chapter five considers some issues encompassed by the rational-choice paradigm that appear particularly appropriate for analysis in the post-communist states. The primary approach used to consider these issues is single-dimensional spatial analysis predicated on the median voter theorem. Among the issues considered are legislative roll-call analysis, the impact of committee systems on legislative outcomes, presidential veto powers, presidential appointments, constitutional court decisions, and changes to the party system.

Chapter six further elaborates on the potential research agenda that rational choice offers for studying stable democracies of post-communist Europe. The chapter begins by noting that the institutions discussed in chapter five all function to reduce the number of policy options. In most cases they leave political actors with only two choices. For instance, a committee system operating under a closed rule gives the parent legislature a choice of either the committee's proposal or the status quo. Similarly, exercise of the veto or the presidential power of appointment leaves the assembly with a choice between the presidential or legislative preference. When there are only two choices between which political actors may select, a majority will clearly emerge around one. The problem is considerably more complicated when the number of choices is not confined to two. Chapter six is devoted to considering these issues, in particular setting the legislative agenda and the cabinet-making process.

Chapter seven returns to the theory developed in chapter four and reconsiders the notion of an equilibrium between political elites that defines a consolidated democracy in light of the rational-choice approaches and concepts demonstrated in chapters five and six. The chapter's primary goals are, first, to summarize the theory by formulating a mathematical model of this equilibrium and, second, to consider the implications of the mathematical model. It concludes with a summary of the book's main points and a subject listing of the rational-choice literature most applicable to post-communist states.

Chapter Two

The Study of Post-Communist Politics

While most scholars would agree with the present focus on processes of democratization in the post-communist world, they do not necessarily agree that democratic consolidation should be the reigning paradigm in the discipline. Criticism is largely directed at the utility of approaches and theories employed by some students of democratic consolidation. Among the concerns most often expressed are that the complexity of the transition process in post-communist systems requires that they be treated as a separate class of states.[1] In essence, the post-communist transitions are so unique that they defy comparison with democratization projects in other regions of the globe.[2]

Despite these reservations, democratic consolidation informs much of the scholarship in post-communist studies. While some generalizations derived from experiences with democratization in other regions may not be applicable to the political systems of the region, the paradigm nonetheless bounds the set of issues with which post-communist studies as a discipline is overwhelmingly concerned. This is what paradigms do. This chapter will make the case for the pervasive influence of the paradigm by reviewing the myriad of studies of post-communist systems that focus on the agenda established by democratic consolidation. I will approach the task by discussing the scholarly contributions in several of the arenas that comprise a consolidated democracy.

As I do so, I will further make the case that the paradigm permits a rich mix of behavioralist and institutionalist approaches, a point I made in the preceding chapter and one I will come back to in the next chapter. The behavioralist approaches, focusing on the causal relationship between attitudes and values on one hand and political behavior and outcome on the other, are preferred in post-communist studies, a field traditionally more comfortable with historical and cultural analyses. The institutionalist approaches are more clearly at the center of mainstream political science; however, within the democratic consolidation paradigm they are employed to test largely ad hoc hypotheses with no direct relationship to theory premised on rational-choice assumptions. Consequently, dominated by a paradigm that permits a diffuse set of approaches, much of which is either atheoretical or at odds with rational-choice theories, post-communist studies remains largely outside the mainstream of political science.

Stateness

Scholarship on the issue of stateness may well comprise the most dynamic research program in post-communist studies. The concept refers to the willingness of people and groups to be citizens of the nation-state claiming sovereignty over the territory on which they reside. It is identified as a necessary precondition of democracy in separate works by Rustow[3] and, later, Linz and Stepan.[4] Whenever a significant proportion of a citizenry refuses to recognize a state's claim to sovereignty, the state is likely to experience considerable social and political turmoil. Dahl addressed the problem of stateness as one of legitimacy, arguing that democratization becomes more difficult in its absence.[5] Offe labels the development of stateness as one of three parallel challenges facing the region, the other two being marketization and democratization itself.[6]

Scholars of post-communist systems concerned with stateness problems have focused largely on nationalism and ethnic violence. The basic argument is that these factors contribute to fragmentation of the state and a consequent reduction of the likelihood of democracy emerging. The relationship between a lack of state legitimacy and the failure to habituate citizens to democratic norms and procedures is quite straightforward. Citizens who do not wish to be part of the state in which they reside are not likely to engage in the democratic process unless their basic demand for separation or dissolution of the state can be achieved by doing so. They are certainly not likely to view the state as legitimate. Under such circumstances, the state's very existence is threatened. It is equally threatened if citizens refrain from the process because they perceive that they are more likely to achieve their goals by working against the system. In such a case they are more likely to engage in anti-system activity aimed at undermining the state. The result is either state repression or citizen violence, or both.

Neither ethnic identity nor nationalism need be a destructive force. They may well contribute instead to the development of an integrative state, which in turn can help lay the basis for democratization.[7] The danger of course lies in the emergence of exclusivist nationalism. Given the violence associated with the breakup of states in parts of the post-communist space, this has been one of the major issues addressed by scholars. Particular attention has been given to the causes for nationalist and ethnic violence. While more recent scholarship has called for an eclectic approach,[8] the debate generally divides scholars into essentialists and contextualists. The essentialists' argument is strongly rooted in behavioralist notions. In essence, its adherents contend that complex historical, religious, and social factors lie at the roots of ethnic conflicts. Such conflicts are often irrational and not amenable to solutions based on calculations of economic self-interest.[9]

The contextualist position, on the other hand, argues that ethnic and nationalist tensions may exist for a considerable amount of time without exploding. What is necessary to ignite them is the emergence of a political, social, or economic structural impediment to one group or another being able to achieve its interests.[10] While at first glance the argument appears to be predicated on rational-choice assumptions, more careful analysis reveals that it is peculiarly behavioralist in its focus on groups and group interest. Rational choice maintains that groups do not have interests, only individuals do. A slightly modified contextualist argument is somewhat more rationalist, asserting that political leaders incite nationalist discord and violence in order to pursue their own interests. In essence, they perceive they have more to gain by doing so.[11]

The contextualist position has drawn the largest number of advocates. This owes among other reasons to the fact that it permits discussion of institutional means for resolving the problem of stateness. The most commonly discussed institutional structure is federalism. While some view this as a solution to ethnic discord and fragmentation of the state,[12] not all agree. In their view federalism can serve to undermine stateness under certain conditions.[13]

Democracy and the Market

Turning to the arenas of a consolidated democracy, there is a rich literature on the link between democracy and the market.[14] Indeed, given the observation that there are no nonmarket democracies anywhere on the globe, it would appear that democracies require a market economy.[15] Nonetheless, as the experience of much of the third world and more recently the People's Republic of China demonstrates, the emergence of a market is a necessary but not sufficient condition for democracy. This has established the basis for one of the main issues on the agenda of democratic consolidation. Under what conditions does the market facilitate democratization?

One major line of inquiry has focused on the link between economic growth and democracy. Lipset is generally credited with advancing the argument that democracy is associated with high levels of economic development.[16] The problem is how to achieve the requisite level of development if, as Lipset and others contend, rapid economic growth can destabilize nascent democracies.[17] Those studying post-communist systems, however, have not found this to be the case. What seems to be more detrimental to democratization is economic crisis.[18] To the degree that rapid economic growth helps to overcome economic crisis, it contributes to the consolidation of democracy.

Another line of inquiry has considered the relationship between a class system and democracy. Economic growth creates new opportunities by diversifying an economy. This in turn leads to the emergence of classes with distinct interests. Among the most important of these for many scholars is a middle class of property owners. Barrington Moore, among others, has made the point that it is the middle class that insists upon limiting the state and political elites in order to secure its own economic interests; he goes so far as to state that democracy is not possible without a bourgeoisie.[19] Pursuing a similar line of reasoning, Richard Ahl[20] contends that economic reforms in Russia have produced little basis for social cleavage. This is reflected in the relative homogeneity of public opinion toward economic reform. Comprising the rules and institutions for mediating social conflict emerging from social cleavage, the logical rationale for democracy is consequently weakened by the near absence of such conflicts.

Closely associated with the emergence of a class system is yet a third major line of inquiry: the degree to which socioeconomic disparity impedes the emergence of democracy. Larry Diamond argues that such disparity must be reduced before democracy can take root.[21] Muller and Seligson provide empirical evidence for Diamond's position with their findings that income inequality is negatively correlated with democracy.[22] Adam Przeworski et al., however, maintain that democracy can be sustained if income inequality is reduced over time,[23] while Ross Burkart argues that economic disparity is a problem only in the middle stages of democratization. It may in fact facilitate the process in early and even later stages.[24] Those analyzing transitions in post-communist settings remain divided on the issue as well. A number of scholars contend that the costs and benefits of economic reform must be relatively evenly shared across the population. When they are not, notions of fairness and equity are violated, and support not only for the market but even for democracy itself is jeopardized.[25] M. Steven Fish, however, has found no statistical evidence that socioeconomic equality is a predictor of democracy in post-communist states.[26]

In addition to focusing on the major economic issues addressed by democratic consolidation, scholars studying post-communist systems have made some original contributions to the agenda. Perhaps the most important of these is whether democratization can be successfully accomplished concurrently with other major transitions. The post-communist systems are collectively undergoing a transition on more than one dimension. Most are attempting to democratize at the same time that they are engaging in marketization (the transition from a Soviet-style command economy to a market economy). Still others are simultaneously engaged in forming an identity capable of unifying the country after the collapse of communism. The complexity of a multidimensional transition has led many to question whether it is possible to carry out democratization concurrently with marketization.[27]

The issue is related to an argument among students of democratic consolidation as to whether authoritarian regimes are more efficient in generating economic growth.[28] However, the explicit focus on the dynamic interaction across two arenas of a consolidating democracy—the economy and state institutions—represents a significant departure. The economic reforms, which are often enacted under conditions of economic crisis in post-communist systems, themselves further exacerbate the crisis and increase the economic stress endured by the general population. Under such conditions, citizens are likely to vote against continuation of market reforms. To avoid this, political elites may choose to insulate themselves from accountability to the public. As Adam Przeworski notes, economic crisis brought on by reform attempts may force "democrats to rule undemocratically."[29] In either case, popular legitimacy for the new democratic institutions is undermined by the failure of the economy to meet the self-interests of the mass of citizens. Hence, the public is less likely to accept the new rules, and democratic consolidation is retarded.[30]

It should be further noted that the concern of post-communist scholars with the interaction across multiple dimensions of the reform process also has led them to address economic reform in its broader, institutional context. Here they have pointed out the necessity of a legal and regulatory infrastructure to the success of economic reforms, and they have been among the first to stress the importance of state institutions and political actors to the functioning of that infrastructure.[31]

In yet a second major contribution to democratic consolidation, the concern with public support for market reforms has contributed to the analysis of public opinion by scholars of post-communist studies. These studies are essentially behavioralist in their approach. Questioning the persistence of antimarket values among post-communist publics, a number of scholars have considered whether these publics are becoming more supportive of economic reform. The research findings have been inconclusive to date. Raymond M. Duch is among the foremost of those considering the issue. Using data collected in the European portion of the Soviet Union in 1990, he contends that, owing to their opposition to the Soviet command economy,[32] Soviet citizens were likely to continue their support for economic reforms despite worsening personal financial situations. In a later article, Duch extends this argument to post-Soviet Russia, contending that Russian citizens, remembering the negative experience of the recent past, blame both personal hardships and downturns in the overall economy on the failures of the Soviet centrally planned economy. To the extent that economic performance influences public attitudes, it does so by effecting support for specific office seekers without dampening overall support for institutional reform.[33] Hence, both one's personal financial situation and negative subjective evaluations of the economy are laid to blame on the Soviet past and not the reforms. In essence, memories of the failures of the Soviet economy have provided the reforms with a "reservoir of popular support."

The analyses of other scholars, however, do not support Duch's relatively optimistic arguments. Those analyzing public support for reforms in east-central Europe have generally found that subjective evaluation of the economy and one's personal financial situation are closely linked to support for continuation of the reforms.[34] Looking again at the situation in Russia, Robert J. Brym argues that the continued economic crisis has led to a significant decrease in support for economic change.[35] Reflecting this, analyses of voting behavior and party identification demonstrate a clear relationship between personal financial situation and opposition to reforms.[36] Kullberg and Zimmerman further qualify the argument with their finding that it is not short-term economic hardship, but subjective assessment of the long-term opportunity structure that explains support for reform.[37]

Other scholars seeking to uncover the connection between orientations to political and economic reform have also touched upon the relationship between subjective evaluations of economic performance and attitudes toward reform. Such studies have measured these attitudes by focusing on locus of responsibility (whether the state or the individual is primarily responsible for social well-being), a key economic value affected by the market reforms and the deconstruction of the Soviet socialist system. In one such study, Finifter and Mickiewicz concluded that beneficiaries of change were more likely to be the strongest supporters of reform. Further, they found that those who were most satisfied with their current life situation were most opposed to the reforms, the inference being that those with a positive retrospective evaluation of their personal economic situation would be more likely to support the status quo.[38] Reisinger, Miller, and Hesli's analysis (which focuses on reevaluating Finifter and Mickiewicz's findings concerning the link between locus of responsibility and support for change) also differs from that of Duch. They find no statistically significant relationship between evaluations of the overall state of the economy and support for reform. Further, they find a strong positive relationship between evaluation of one's personal financial situation and support for change.[39]

Thus, the literature is contradictory on the link between subjective economic evaluation and support for reform in Russia. Are Russians sophisticated, continuing to support economic change in spite of the economic hardships that they are experiencing, or have they turned against the reforms in favor of a more efficient socialist economy? The question is far from insignificant given the continued decline in the standard of living being experienced by many Russian citizens. Indeed, while some economic indicators are positive, prospects for the majority continue to be poor. Further, insofar as support for economic reform is linked with support for political democracy, the issue is even more critical. Do citizens in transitioning political systems evaluate democracy based on a rational calculus of economic gain or do they judge democracy on its own terms independent of the market? The answer to the question has much to say about whether the economy is indeed the primary factor in the success of democracy, as so many have contended.

Survey research on the issue has thus far been inconclusive. Supporting the primacy of the economy thesis, Bahry, Boaz, and Gordon conclude that those who oppose political reforms do so because they have been hurt by the market reforms.[40] Rose and Mishler find that hope for an economic improvement is correlated with support for political reform.[41] Others disagree however. Waldron-Moore contends that support for democracy is not judged on the basis of either personal economic or political gains, rather it is prized for its moral qualities.[42] Gibson reverses the equation, finding that attitudes toward democracy determine support for the market.[43]

Bringing the State In

A number of scholars have sought to correct a perceived overemphasis on economic development in the democratic consolidation literature by calling attention to the crucial role played by the state. In their view, a weak state is a major reason for the failure to facilitate and legitimate democracy in the face of continuing economic crisis. Ultimately, the effective functioning of political institutions is far more important to the success of democracy than is the success of market reforms, as such institutions are able to mitigate the effects of economic inequities by giving citizens alternative means by which to both protest and redress these inequities.[44] Adam Przeworski argues that economic reform itself may even undermine the state and therefore impede democratization. Market reforms and mass privatization can markedly reduce the capacity of the state to perform its roles, among which are providing for the physical security and social welfare of its citizens as well as ensuring the conditions for effective citizenship. The latter entails the inclusion of all groups and thereby contributes to their acceptance of the new democratic regime. Even more important, it is the state that both formulates and implements a strategy for market reform and democratization. Hence, the weakening of the state that may attend major economic reforms could threaten to undermine democracy itself.[45]

The state is comprised of the institutions and rules by which authoritative political decisions are made, implemented, and enforced. These constitute the primary arena within which salient political elites are habituated to democracy. As such, many scholars of democratic consolidation argue that it is also the most important for the success of democratization.[46] These scholars focus on the institutions comprising the state, the vehicles that political elites use to compete for control of the policy apparatus of the state (chief among which are political parties), and the evolution of elite attitudes toward these institutions. While many of these studies are related to new institutionalism, the dominant paradigm in the subdiscipline of comparative politics, within democratic consolidation they are only loosely tied to the elegant theoretical matrix provided by rational-choice theory, which lies at the heart of new institutionalism. As a consequence, the overwhelming majority of the analyses revolve around testing ad hoc hypotheses lacking any theoretical coherency with one another.

The major approaches have been strategic choice, path dependency, and institutionalism. Early theorists of democratic consolidation focused largely on strategic choice, arguing that the democratization project was dependent on the willingness of political elites to make the decisions to create and support a democratic state.[47] Subsequent theorists have argued that the mode of transition is more critical to the success of democracy. In essence, the prior regime type and the means by which it collapsed are far more consequential as they both condition and limit the range of options open to political elites.[48] The literature on both strategic choice and path dependency has been overwhelmed in quantity by that on institutionalism. Institutionalists argue that the very design of the state (its structures, rules, and procedures) as well as linking institutions between the state and political elites determine the likelihood of the success or failure of democratization.[49]

Strategic Choice and Post-Communist Studies

Many scholars of democratic consolidation have focused on the decisions taken by political elites at key junctures in the transition process. They argue that elites make these decisions based on a cost-benefit analysis of available alternatives. The implicit assumption of most is that political actors seek above all else to maximize the likelihood that they will be able to hold onto political power for the longest period possible. Consequently, while democracy as a value may not be the goal of political elites engaged in bargaining to achieve private interest, under the right conditions it may nonetheless be the outcome of the process. The key question addressed by scholars employing the approach is what conditions might lead to the choice for democracy? However, their primary concern is with the overall process leading to democracy, not the achievement of a set of preconditions or static indicators.

The literature stresses the importance of pacts in the elite bargaining process. Pacts, which define the "rules governing the exercise of power" and defend the most important interests of salient political actors,[50] serve a number of purposes. First, they reduce uncertainty in the cost-benefit analysis undertaken by elites and therefore reduce the likelihood of miscalculation and possible resort to violence. Second, they further reduce the likelihood of violence by guaranteeing the vital interests of the major players. In so doing, they contribute to acceptance of the rules themselves. Third, they permit power sharing and tolerance that can ultimately lead to the acceptance of democratic rules. Fourth, they lay the groundwork for democracy, which is dependent upon the construction of rules for political competition (most often finding their way into a constitution) that are acceptable to all parties and that do not threaten the fundamental interests of any set of political players. The major drawback to pacts is that by guaranteeing the interests of the major political elites, they reduce competitiveness and place major policy issues outside of the reach of the public.

A number of scholars have employed the strategic actor approach to an analysis of democratic consolidation in the post-communist case. The first to do so was Russell Bova, who looked at the series of pacts negotiated among political elites that ultimately led to the collapse of the Soviet Union.[51] Among those using the approach to analyze the transition process in east-central Europe are Helga A. Welsh and Andrew C. Janos. Welsh focuses on the crucial role of elite bargaining and pacts to the outcome of the process;[52] while Janos considers the role of elite bargaining in permitting elites to adapt to the challenges presented by both internal and external factors.[53] In the case of post-Soviet Russia, Thomas F. Remington has employed the approach in its most classic form. He argues that the collapse of the Soviet Union has witnessed the emergence of social and political pluralism to such a degree that no one element of the elites is capable of dominating. The relative balance of forces has essentially forced them to follow the rules and procedures of the current system. Should this continue, over time the rules and procedures will become self-enforcing.[54] Similarly, Michael McFaul argues that two previous efforts to achieve a negotiated settlement among political elites ended in violence (the 1991 August coup and the 1993 storming of the Russian parliament). The third effort, the implementation of the 1993 Russian Constitution, has been more enduring owing to the greatly reduced ambiguity in the balance of forces between the political elites and to the reduction in the number of items on the political agenda.[55]

Path Dependency and Post-Communist Studies

A second approach employed by scholars analyzing political transformation during democratic consolidation focuses on the way in which the authoritarian regime collapsed. Huntington distinguishes three modes of transition. The first, transformation, involves transition from above, in which authoritarian elites essentially take the lead in democratizing the system. The second mode of transition, replacement, constitutes revolution from below. An existing authoritarian regime becomes so weak that it collapses or is subject to a violent overthrow. As a result, the previous regime is replaced by a new, democratic one. In the third mode, transplacement, a new regime emerges as a result of the dynamic bargaining between the old elites and a strong opposition. In Huntington's view, the less violent and the more consensual a transition, the greater the likelihood that democratic consolidation will be successful. On that basis, he rank orders the three modes of transition in descending order of preference: transplacement, transformation, and replacement.[56]

Scholars of path dependency have also focused on the legacy of the prior regime type as a constraining factor in the transition process. Linz and Stepan, for example, distinguish between four regime types—authoritarian, totalitarian, post-totalitarian, and sultanistic. They argue that each regime type limits the possibilities for the mode of extrication from the old regime. In some cases, pacts are not even likely, as the old regime did not permit for the emergence of an opposition with which to negotiate. More important, however, the prior regime type creates a set of difficulties and challenges to democratic consolidation. Sultanistic regimes, for example, lack a civil society and basis for rule of law altogether. Hence, these two arenas must be constructed from scratch.[57]

Post-communist studies have largely focused on the constraints placed on democratization by the prior regime type. Given that the prior regimes in the region were classified in only two of Linz and Stepan's categories (totalitarian or post-totalitarian), these analyses have attempted to identify further characteristics of the old regime that have a significant impact on the course of the transition. Alexander Motyl, for example, considers why democratic consolidation has been more problematic in the region of the former Soviet Union (with the exception of the Baltic states) than in east-central Europe. He identifies two explanatory factors. The first is failure of the prior regime to generate an elite dedicated to radical change (as exemplified by Ukraine). The second is the case in which the prior regime experiences the emergence of such an elite, but it is too weak in the confrontation with status quo conservatives (as exemplified by Russia).[58] Vachudova and Snyder ask why democratic consolidation in east-central Europe has been more successful in some cases than others. They argue that the more successful cases have been characterized by the presence of a counter-elite emerging during the old regime and subsequently winning control of the political agenda, a relatively prosperous economy, and the absence of a significant ethnic minority. The less successful cases are marked by the absence of a strong dissident movement during the prior regime, a relatively weak economy, and the substantial presence of ethnic minorities. In these political systems former communists have been able to retain political power despite continuing economic crises by focusing the public on ethnic and national problems.[59]

Reflecting behavioralist concerns with culture and history, post-communist studies has also considered the legacy of the pre-communist era, particularly in east-central Europe. Most of the countries of the region had an experience with democracy during the interwar period. Scholars have considered how these experiences have influenced the current attempt to democratize. An example of this is provided by Dawisha and Parrot, who edited a volume of analyses of the countries of southeastern Europe. The chapters consider the hypothesis that those countries with a pre-communist tradition of exclusivist nationalism have had a more difficult transition, whereas those countries with a pre-communist legacy of a unified national identity and competitive, multiparty politics have experienced an easier path to democracy.[60]

Institutionalism and Post-Communist Studies

Much of the literature on democratic consolidation has emphasized the role of political institutions, which several theorists consider to be the primary factor in the democratization process.[61] Institutionalists maintain that choices available to political actors are constrained by the rules of the political game. Institutions, in particular, establish the contours of those rules. While historical and cultural legacies of the prior regime may well increase the challenges to democratization, the proper choice of institutions can do much to overcome such difficulties. Among the institutional designs most studied are party systems and executive-legislative relations.

Scholars have long contended that political parties are essential to democracy. Theorists such as Dahl,[62] Duverger,[63] Sartori,[64] and Schattschneider[65] maintain that interest groups insufficiently represent the diverse interests in society. Schattschneider in particular argues that interest groups are biased in favor of elites and minorities possessing superior economic and political resources. In his view only political parties, because they explicitly seek to organize majorities, are capable of organizing and representing the interests of the broad mass of the public.

More recent scholarship has argued that political parties are crucial to the emergence of democracy. Focusing more on party systems than individual parties, the general contention has been that without a strong party system there can be no democracy. Pridham maintains that party systems are crucial to legitimating democracy, particularly in the eyes of the general public. Hence, the strength of the party system is a measure of the degree to which a democracy has consolidated.[66] Powell identifies the characteristics of a party system that are most crucial to helping habituate citizens and political elites to democracy: fragmentation and polarization, and party-group ties.[67] Fragmentation refers to the number of political parties in the system. For most scholars, this is not simply the number of registered parties, but rather the number of parties that can make a difference in the formation of governments or policy outcomes.[68] The preferred number of such parties has been a subject of considerable debate. Most scholars accept highly fragmented party systems (large numbers of "effective" parties) as problematic, since they make forming governments or enacting coherent programs difficult. To the degree such systems contribute to ineffective governance, they undermine public confidence in democracy. Similarly one-party systems are rejected, as they reflect the dominance of a single element of the political elite and deny the existence of any meaningful choice to the public. The debate therefore revolves around whether a two-party or multiparty (three to five parties) system best contributes to the viability of democracy.[69]

Arend Lijphart has provided the strongest challenge to the view that majoritarian, two-party systems of the type found in the United States and the United Kingdom provide more effective and stable governance and therefore lead to more sustainable democracy. Analyzing twenty-one democracies, he argues that while multiparty systems tend toward cabinet instability, the durability of government is not associated with the durability of democracy. Further, multiparty systems can accommodate diverse social interests on a larger number of dimensions. In so doing, such a system contributes to democracy's acceptance to both elites and the public.[70]

The actual number of parties in a party system has long been tied to the choice of electoral system. In the classic formulation of the argument, known as Duverger's Law, proportional representation voting leads to the emergence of multiparty systems, whereas first-past-the-post systems such as those in the United States and the United Kingdom tend to favor the development of a two-party system.[71] Others, however, working from behaviorialist assumptions, have contended that the number of existing social cleavages is far more important than the electoral law in determining the number of parties in a party system.[72] More recent scholarship has found empirical evidence supporting the thesis that both the electoral system and social cleavages affect the number of political parties.[73] Scholars of democratic consolidation have added yet another factor: the timing of elections. Shugart and Carey, among others, have argued that legislative elections held concurrently with presidential elections will likely result in smaller numbers of parties, as those seeking legislative office will seek broader coalitions to avoid being marginalized by effects of the winner-take-all nature of executive elections.[74]

Efforts to test Duverger's Law in post-communist systems have had mixed results. Ordeshook and Shvetsova in their multicountry study found that the choice between proportional representation and single mandate districts affects not only the number of parties. The latter had the further effect of attenuating the trend to a greater number of parties normally associated with ethnic and social heterogeneity.[75] Moser, however, has found that the standard relationship between electoral system and the number of political parties holds in Hungary and Poland, but not in Russia and Ukraine. In Russia, in particular, proportional representation has benefited and strengthened a small number of parties, while the single mandate system has weakened parties and led to their proliferation. He attributes this to the lesser degree of party institutionalization in the two post-Soviet states.[76]

Not only does the literature on party systems stress the necessity to avoid a high degree of fragmentation, it focuses as well on avoiding a high degree of polarization. Polarization contributes to the breakdown of governance by making it more difficult for parties in a multiparty system to cooperate. In the worst case, a highly polarized system would also include extremist parties opposed to democracy itself. Such parties encourage anti-system behavior on the part of both the general public and political elites. Hence, they impede habituation to democratic norms. Such parties can be a particular problem in democratizing systems. Pressing demands that can not be accommodated and encouraging political behavior that is inherently destabilizing, they complicate the tasks of the legislative body as well as executive agencies.

Analyses of post-communist political party systems have reflected this concern with polarization by focusing on former communist parties and anti-systemic forces coming to power. Many of these studies, however, are case studies. While in much of the region the former communists do not represent a threat to democratic consolidation, as they have restructured themselves into a responsible social-democratic party, such is not the case in much of the former Soviet Union. There is particular concern with the Communist Party of the Russian Federation (CPRF), which a number of studies have concluded remains opposed to democratic rules.[77] For this reason there has been considerable analysis of the causes of the electoral failures of pro-reform parties as well. The general consensus is that they have suffered from a proliferation of such parties as well as the failure of the reforms for which the public holds them accountable.[78]

A final measure of the strength of a party system is the degree to which it is rooted in the socioeconomic system. Good elite-mass linkages are strengthened by the existence of group or class identification with differing political parties. Interest group identification with particular political parties indicates growing public acceptance of the new political rules (elite contestation and popular participation). As a consequence, a greater diversity of interests is represented in the political system and legitimacy is enhanced, as a broader spectrum of views is given voice in elections and the legislature.[79] More important, programmatic parties appealing to divergent sectors of society reflect the growing social complexity of a newly emergent or previously suppressed civil society, which some scholars argue is essential to democracy.[80] (We shall give further consideration to this arena of a consolidated democracy in chapter four.)

A number of studies of post-communist systems have concerned themselves with the social basis for political parties. Again, many of the analyses here focus on a single case. Motivating this research is the assumption that party systems organized along a continuum representing diverse, clear interests will contribute to the public's acceptance of the democratic order.[81] The general conclusion is that, thus far, political party systems lack ideological clarity and that they are still establishing ties with specific groups and classes.[82] This largely owes to the lack of a class system under the communist regime, the economic reforms of the post-communist era only now creating the possibility for such a system. Nevertheless, those most hurt by the reforms are voting for socialist and social-democratic parties.[83]

Whether or not the economic reforms are facilitating the emergence of the socioeconomic conditions necessary for a class-based political party system has been a subject of research as well. The general consensus is that they are.[84] However, noneconomic behavioralist dimensions such as ethnic divisiveness, the preference for a strong state, and pre-communist traditions continue to have as much to say about the party system as class identity.[85] Further, as in other matters related to political parties, Russia and many of the states of the former Soviet Union remain problematic, with the base of the parties not clearly differentiated (with the exception of the former communist parties) and the public generally eschewing identification with political parties.[86]

In addition to party systems, much of the literature on the importance of institutional development to democratic consolidation has concerned itself with executive-legislative relations. The key question here concerns whether parliamentary or presidential systems are to be preferred. A number of scholars have argued that parliamentary systems are preferable to presidential systems.[87] Among the failures of presidentialism cited by these scholars are: It encourages zero-sum politics, it lacks flexibility to respond to popular loss of faith in the executive given the fixed term of the president, it encourages executive-legislative gridlock owing to the existence of competitive popular mandates between the two branches, it is associated with minority governments, and it encourages the formation of weak party systems.

Some analyses, however, have failed to find empirical support for the thesis.[88] The most comprehensive of these efforts is that of Matthew Soberg Shugart and John M. Carey, who demonstrate that the dichotomy between presidentialism and parliamentarism is overly simplistic.[89] There are at least four different types of executive-legislative systems in existence in democracies: British-style parliamentarism, U.S.-style presidentialism, French-style premier-presidentialism, and president-parliamentarism. It is the latter that is the most problematic form of democratic governance owing to the ambiguous position of the cabinet, which must enjoy the confidence of both the president and the legislature to continue to govern. As a consequence, such systems are subject to frequent conflict between the executive and legislative branches.

Shugart and Carey further argue that the two other types of presidential systems (presidentialism and premier-presidentialism) can in fact overcome what they view as the most serious problem associated with parliamentarism, the trade-off between representativeness (ensuring a voice to as many interests as possible) and policy efficiency. Indeed, both systems permit a larger number of political parties in the legislature while retaining policy efficiency in the office of the president. Premier-presidentialism offers even greater advantages, as it overcomes the rigidity of the presidential systems (neither the government nor the legislature having fixed terms) as well as the problem of a dual mandate between the president and the legislature (the competition being transferred to one between the president and the prime minister representing the parliamentary majority).[90]

Scholars analyzing various forms of executive-legislative relations in post-communist systems have been as divided on the issue as have theorists of democratic consolidation. Those favoring parliamentarism generally contend that presidentialism is the institutional choice made by relatively consolidated elites. Having emerged from the communist system relatively unified and their grip over the state bureaucracy still intact, these elites use the presidency to maintain their control over the policy process and deny the emergence of a strong opposition. Zielonka finds that presidentialism has contributed to executive-legislative gridlock in east-central Europe and contributed to an intra-elite conflict over power that threatens to undermine democratic consolidation.[91] In the former Soviet Union, Roeder argues that presidents have contributed to the emergence of a number of authoritarian regimes owing to their propensity to usurp legislative prerogatives and place themselves and their office outside of accountability.[92] Easter finds this to be the case in both the former Soviet Union and east-central Europe where the choice for presidentialism has been made.[93]

There are, however, a relatively equal number of supporters of presidentialism among post-communist scholars. Ishiyama and Velten argue that it is not presidentialism, but the choice of a single mandate electoral system that is most prejudicial to democracy in the region, as it denies political voice to significant minorities.[94] Valerie Bunce maintains that there may well be advantages for a presidential system in the post-communist context,[95] and Thomas Nichols identifies presidentialism as the choice to be preferred in systems with low levels of social trust (such as Russia, the subject of his case study).[96]

Some form of presidentialism has been the choice of most post-communist political systems. However, not all chief executives are accorded the same constitutional powers. A question that scholars in the field have asked is how to account for the variation in the degree of powers of the president. (Indeed, this seems to be the real issue distinguishing Linz's dichotomous categorization of parliamentarism and presidentialism from Shugart and Carey's more nuanced categories, which further divide presidentialism into three types.) In one study Shugart looked at the issue and found an inverse correlation between party strength and executive strength. Those constitutions that designed and put into place measures to ensure stronger party systems were more likely to also grant fewer powers to the executive. In his view, the choice was made on the basis of whether political elites believed they held a greater chance of being elected as a member of a party organization or as an individual based on personal reputation. The latter was likely to lead to a constitution providing strong powers to a president.[97] Frye uses a similar rational-choice approach in analyzing variations in the strength of presidential powers across post-communist systems. He argues that the key factors are the bargaining power of the electoral favorite at the time of the writing of the constitution and the uncertainty of the electoral outcome. In all cases, the greater the uncertainty, the weaker the presidency is likely to be. However, in cases where the electoral outcome is thought to be more certain, the constitutional powers of the presidency will more likely be determined on the basis of whether the electoral favorite is able to control the agenda. If so, he/she will create a powerful president whose office he/she expects to occupy.[98]

Contributions to the Agenda

Besides testing the propositions and findings from democratic consolidation in the countries of east-central Europe and the former Soviet Union, post-communist studies has contributed several propositions of its own to the paradigmatic agenda. These have largely concerned the transformation of leftist parties, the development of legislatures, and the values of political elites. Most of these are case studies that test ad hoc hypotheses, many of which are rooted in behavioralist assumptions. This is particularly the case for analyses of elite values.

Given what many considered to be the death knell for the political left in east-central Europe and the former Soviet Union with the collapse of the communist regimes, the interest scholars have shown in the reemergence of socialist and social-democratic parties in the region is not at all surprising. This interest in most of the region, however, is quite apart from any general concern that communist regimes will regain power with the intent of ending the experiment in democracy. Rather, analyses of the "return of the left" reflect the holistic approach of post-communist studies to democratic consolidation by focusing on the problematic of the revival of parties opposed to rapid economic reforms.[99] How will the slower development, or nondevelopment, of an economic society reduce the likelihood of the emergence of a consolidated democracy or degrade developments in other arenas such as political institutions, civil society, or stateness?

In looking to the causes for the revival of the communist parties, scholars have concentrated on structural factors as well as explanations focusing on the effect of the prior regime or mode of transition on the adaptive capacity of the former communist party. Structuralists have considered such factors as the electoral system or the economic hardships endured by the general population. Very little support has been found for the contention that the former communist parties have benefited from the adoption of proportional representation, an electoral system that most of these parties favored fearing they might otherwise be excluded from political power.[100] Even electoral system thresholds do not seem to favor either parties of the left or right.[101]

On the other hand, a number of studies have found evidence that the former communist parties, as well as the political left in general, have benefited to a significant degree from the hardships created by the economic reforms in the region. Committed to democracy and the market, they have nonetheless called for reforms with a more "human face." They have further presented themselves as parties of specialists and technical experts with the experience necessary for managing the reforms, in juxtaposition to the parties of the right that are responsible for the current difficulties due to a lack of competence and an overly politicized approach.[102] The success of the strategy is suggested by a number of analyses of public opinion survey data that demonstrate that, indeed, those most hurt by the reforms tend either to retreat into apolitical apathy or to vote for the political left.[103]

A number of studies have looked to the legacy of the prior regime or factors related to the way in which it collapsed for explanations for the reemergence of the left in the politics of the countries of the region. A common thesis is that the former communist parties owe their resurgence to the advantages they possess in property, experience, leadership, and organizational strength. Using many of these same resources, they have capitalized on the privatization process and added control of a significant share of the economy to their political strengths.[104] A more nuanced argument accounting for variations in the degree to which the former communist parties have been able to achieve a role in the political life of the country focuses on the prior regime. John T. Ishiyama has been in the forefront of developing the thesis that if the prior regime was more liberal, in the sense that it permitted a limited degree of opposition, the communist party was consequently more capable of adaptation. Growing out of an environment of internal contestation, these parties were less doctrinaire and better able to change to take advantage of the new political realities in the post-communist era.[105] Those parties not able to do so have been far less successful with the electorate, even under conditions of economic hardship.[106]

Particular attention has been given to the adaptive capacity of the Communist Party of Russia (CPRF). The findings here have been inconclusive. One study argues that the CPRF lost the 1996 presidential race because it failed to broaden its appeal to the electorate, a strategy it successfully pursued in the 1995 legislative elections. Instead, the party became doctrinaire and dogmatic in its statements and platform. The result was a resounding defeat.[107] However, a second, more detailed analysis of the CPRF and its factions concludes quite the opposite. During the legislative races, the CPRF successfully distinguished itself from its rivals to its immediate left and right on the political spectrum and mobilized its base of support. As a result it won a large number of seats in both the district races and party list vote. In the presidential race, the CPRF attempted to broaden its base by adopting an explicitly nationalist-populist platform. The strategy succeeded in drawing voters to the party; its final vote tally was larger than the size of its political base. However, the CPRF did not succeed in capturing the middle of politically active Russian society. Unlike former communist parties in east-central Europe that had transformed themselves into Western social-democratic parties, the CPRF remained fundamentally anti-Western and committed to a renewal of the central role of the military-industrial complex in the Russian economy and state.[108]

Scholars generally accept the proposition that popularly elected assemblies do much to legitimate and undergird democracy. In fact, there is no democracy that exists without a legislature. Many of its roles are performed with the party system acting as an intermediary. This includes interfacing with the population, representative functions, and organizing the legislative agenda. Indeed, the general consensus is that a legislature can not long survive without a strong party system.

Most legislative studies have been case studies of particular assemblies or comparative analyses largely consisting of efforts to categorize or define legislatures.[109] There have been very few theoretical efforts. Perhaps the best effort to develop a comprehensive theory of legislatures is the work of Fred W. Riggs, who postulates that the most important function performed by a legislature in a democracy is to hold the executive branch accountable. Since the legislature is inherently less organized than the executive branch, the necessity of a strong party system becomes all the more important, for without one the legislature is virtually incapable of organizing itself. Elected representatives bring the discipline, policy concurrence, and patterns of cooperation provided by their respective parties with them into the assembly. If the party system is incapable of sustaining an organized and cohesive legislature, the assembly becomes susceptible to efforts by the hierarchically structured executive branch to marginalize it or disband it altogether. The former undermines democracy, and the latter spells its end, since the executive branch is the captive of a single faction of the political elite. When the executive branch becomes so powerful that it overwhelms the legislature, that part of the political elite that has captured the executive branch has the institutional power necessary to rule without competition. Hence, strong legislatures, as unwieldy and raucous as they can be, are essential to a democracy. Without them, there is no forum for continued competition between disparate factions of the political elites.[110]

The threat from the executive branch, however, does not come from a single source. Not only must the legislature be able to hold an elected head of government or state accountable to a significant degree, it must also be able to rein in the bureaucracy.[111] In post-communist systems this may be the biggest challenge of all. Indeed, it may well be why scholars of democratic consolidation in post-communist systems have devoted attention to the development of legislatures. Their analyses, like the general literature on legislatures, have largely comprised case studies of the ability of legislatures to organize their work.[112] Among the issues considered have been the emergence of a factional system and the institutionalization of the legislature. In either case, the primary concern has been with determining factors that unite and divide the legislature.

Those looking at the factional system have generally focused on the discipline within party factions. Roll-call analysis is used to determine whether the party system provides the legislature with the degree of policy agreement necessary to form a majority on any issue or set of issues.[113] The effect of the electoral system (proportional representation and single mandate) on party discipline and factional unity has also been considered.[114] Roll-call analysis is further used to determine if the party system permits the legislature to sustain governments in parliamentary and premier-presidential systems,[115] a question related to the rich literature on cabinet durability.[116]

Studies looking at the institutionalization of the legislature have considered a number of dimensions. Olson and Norton present a series of essays on individual legislatures that address the primary factors contributing to the development of the rules by which the legislatures conduct their business.[117] Olson in a later essay presents a cross-national analysis of the difficulties that post-communist countries have encountered in institutionalizing. Among these have been inadequacy of the infrastructure (staff and facilities) to support the new legislative activities, unfamiliarity with multiparty politics, the still evolving nature of legislative rules and committee systems, and a lack of public faith in the new institutions.[118]

Democratic consolidation emphasizes the role of political elites in the transition process. While the public is most certainly involved, it is political elites who actually make the decisions leading toward or away from democracy.[119] It is this focus on political elites that informs the strategic choice approach discussed at the beginning of this chapter. The approach rests on a rational-choice calculus rooted in Dankwart Rustow's maxim that elites will not make the choice for democracy unless the prevailing balance of power is such that no one side can seize all political power without incurring unacceptable costs.[120] Adam Przeworski adds that the elite calculus is further complicated by uncertainties of the actual balance.[121]

Reflecting a behavioralist predisposition, post-communist scholarship has placed greater stress on the commitment of elites to democratic values than their having made the choice solely on the basis of a cost-benefit analysis (rational choice). The field has been more concerned with democrats who are democrats on the basis of normative preference. As a consequence, many scholars of post-communist systems have looked at the value system of the current leadership as an explanatory factor in the trajectory of change in the post-communist era. Using such an approach, Dimitar Mircev contends that the former Yugoslavia remains authoritarian owing to a lack of leadership committed to democratic values.[122] Kullberg, Higley, and Pakulski argue similarly that the lack of progress toward democracy in some parts of eastern Europe and the former Soviet Union owes largely to a lack of elite commitment.[123] Kullberg in an earlier article contends that the elite conflict culminating in the 1993 violent dissolution of the Russian legislature was rooted in irreconcilable ideological conflict between elites. The tendency toward violence was reinforced by an unwillingness to compromise on the part of the Eltsin administration, a government that was following a radical reform policy at odds with the majority of Russia's elites.[124] Despite this, most studies have concluded that elites are more positively oriented toward democracy and the market than is the public.[125]

Scholarship on post-communist Europe has been equally concerned with analyzing the process of elite circulation, the underlying assumption being that elites emerging during the post-Soviet era will be more likely to adapt to the new democratic and market values. Early analyses of the issue found that the process of elite circulation had been less intense in Russia than in east-central Europe. This owed largely to members of the Russian elite having successfully taken advantage of their previous political positions, personal contacts, and entrepreneurial skills to attain the lion's share of the economic wealth of the country.[126] These findings have since been qualified by Rigby, who argues that circulation at the uppermost levels of the elites has been high in Russia,[127] and challenged by Lane and Ross. Analyzing career data and responses to survey questions provided by Soviet and Russian elites, they argue convincingly that there has been a circulation of elites in post-Soviet Russia. Soviet-era elites have generally failed to retain their political positions in the new regime being replaced by newer elites with a commitment to the reform process.[128]

What We Are Not Asking

This chapter has demonstrated that the study of politics in post-communist studies has been dominated by a paradigm, democratic consolidation. The paradigm's pervasiveness is evident in the substantial literature that has emerged in the field since the collapse of communist rule. This is not necessarily bad. For one thing it helps give coherence and direction to the research agenda of a discipline. A dominant paradigm establishes the boundaries of what are considered important and therefore legitimate questions, it gives scholars a common language, and it permits some degree of accumulation of knowledge. However, the focus that a paradigm gives a discipline necessarily means that some questions are ignored. Even issues that the paradigm itself would suggest as important topics for research can go unnoticed or underdeveloped. In the next chapter we consider the distortions that democratic consolidation has introduced to the field of post-communist studies. What issues have we addressed inadequately or failed to address altogether as a result of its paradigmatic control of the discipline's research agenda?

Chapter Three

The Missing Agenda

Paradigms help us to make sense of the world. They provide us with a set of assumptions about reality that predisposes us to ask certain questions. In so doing, they help us to sort out the important from the irrelevant. The downside is that while they help us to focus our efforts, they also necessarily limit our vision. We are blinded to possibilities not suggested by the paradigm. As a consequence, there are questions that go unasked. At the same time, there are issues that the paradigm addresses, but only tangentially. These areas tend to remain underdeveloped. In this chapter we look at these issues and questions.

Careful readers will note that we did not address research in three arenas of a consolidated democracy in the previous chapter: civil society, the rule of law, and a usable state bureaucracy. Post-communist studies has both benefited from and contributed to the further development of democratic consolidation and its research agenda. Nonetheless, these three arenas have yet to be adequately addressed by scholars. We will begin by looking at what research has been undertaken in these areas and then turn to a discussion of issues that have been altogether left out of the research agenda of post-communist studies.

Bringing Society Back In

Scholars of democratic consolidation have tended to focus largely on institutions and the strategic choices of key actors as primary explanatory variables. This is dictated by what many consider to be the paradigm's concern with elite behavior and the institutions over which they contest for control. While the role of the public has been far from completely ignored, correspondingly less attention has been paid to it. This seems strange given that a consolidated democracy requires that both elites and the public become habituated to the rules and norms of democracy to the degree that there is no other accepted game in town. Recently, however, a number of studies of democratic consolidation have sought to bring society back in. Many of these studies have been of post-communist systems. Indeed, post-communist scholars have devoted considerable attention to civil society given the role played by the public in the "revolutions" of 1989. These scholars have pointed to the importance of civil society not only during the collapse of the authoritarian regime but during the consolidation phase as well. Their general position, in the behavioralist tradition, is that democracy is to a considerable extent dependent upon public values and attitudes.[1] Indeed, analyses of the arena of civil society are the most explicitly behavioralist of all scholarship in post-communist studies.

Robert D. Putnam is generally credited with the renewed interest in the role of civil society in democratization. Analyzing the Italian experience with reform of local government, Putnam found that the adoption of new institutions changed the political behavior of political elites and the public. However, he noted that there was a distinct difference between the Italian north and the south in the performance level of these same institutions. He concluded that differences in political attitudes and values based on different historical experiences best explain the variation in institutional performance. Northerners have a better developed sense of civic duty. This in turn provides them with previously existent patterns of cooperative social behavior that have facilitated their ability to adapt to the democratic norms associated with the new institutions of local governance. In essence, the social context within which institutions are planted is of equal importance to the outcome of the democratization project.[2]

Putnam's analysis points to two different aspects of society that have become the focus of attention of scholars of democratic consolidation: the distribution of democratic norms and the development of a civil society. He argues that norms such as trust and cooperation are widely distributed within the population of the Italian north. These norms contribute to a civic consciousness that is reflected in a well-developed web of associational activity autonomous from the state—what has been referred to by others as a civil society.[3] Together they comprise "social capital," a reservoir from which a country can draw in order to facilitate the consolidation of democracy. Both of these elements of social capital have been the subject of scholars studying the contribution of society to the consolidation of democracy in post-communist systems. However, substantially less attention has been devoted to the emergence of civil society.

The Distribution of "Democratic" Values

It is generally conceded that the distribution of values provides the framework of a political culture, although we do not know how and to exactly what effect. Students of democratic consolidation analyzing shifts within systems of social values are in essence studying changes in political culture.[4] The question dividing scholars, however, is whether values and attitudes facilitate the emergence of democracy or democracy causes a change in political culture. In social science terms, what is the direction of the causal arrow? The question is not an unimportant one. If democracy is dependent upon historically conditioned cultural values, then it is not likely to emerge for generations where democratic values are absent. On the other hand, if democracy can effect value change, then these values can in turn act to consolidate democracy by shoring up public support for the new regime. In short, democracy itself can help create a situation in which the public is not willing to countenance any other form of governance.

The question of causality is the very question motivating Putnam's study. His analysis leads to the pessimistic conclusion that democracy is dependent on political values to sustain it. Ronald Inglehart reaches the same conclusion in a cross-national empirical assessment.[5] However, criticizing Inglehart's model as one that tests only for the unidirectional effect of political cultural values on democracy, Muller and Seligson test a bidirectional model. They find strong support for the thesis that causality is in both directions, with the stronger relationship being the effect of democracy on value formation and change.[6]

This debate has found its way into post-communist studies. The essence of the disagreement concerns to what degree political values and norms are amenable to adaptation and change. Are they relatively impermeable over long periods of time, or can they adapt to the demand of new institutional designs and political realities based on a rational-choice calculus?[7] If the former is the case, then we must determine whether the traditional attitudes and behaviors of a given country impede or facilitate democratization and marketization. This is the traditional political cultural argument and the prevailing view among scholars during the Soviet era. Stephen White[8] and Walter Laqueur,[9] for example, are among those pointing to the difficulties posed by traditional Russian values to any reform attempts in the Soviet era. In essence, they argue that democracy is dependent upon the existence of a democratic political culture without which it will have difficulty sustaining itself. Further, the values of the existing political culture (whether democratic or not) are relatively fixed and resistant to rapid change. Some have continued to hold to this position in the post-communist era. Harry Eckstein et al., have concluded that attempts to democratize post-Soviet Russia are likely to suffer from a troubled developmental pattern owing to incongruence between the norms of democracy and the autocratic norms of both society and existing institutions mediating relations between individuals and the state.[10]

Most who adhere to the traditional view that political culture evolves only slowly over time also contend that Russian political culture is nondemocratic. A notable exception is Nicolai N. Petro, who argues that an alternative political culture supportive of democracy has historically existed alongside an autocratic culture in Russia. The more democratic tradition contains elements placing a check on the power of the autocrat and holding him/her accountable. This is apparent among other things in the relations between church and state prior to Peter the Great in which the church constrained the autocrat. Extending the argument to the current regime, Petro views the presidency as strong, but accountable to the public in accordance with this more democratic alternative Russian political culture.[11]

The prevailing view in the post-communist era, however, has tended toward the malleability thesis that the public is not captive to either historical tradition or the norms of the communist era.[12] Russian citizens are capable of adapting to democracy when rational self-interest dictates that they should do so. Among the most forthright advocates of this position is Jeffrey W. Hahn.[13] Using survey data from the town of Yaroslavl, Hahn concludes that Russians are rapidly adapting to the norms demanded by democracy. There is a clear tie in this argument between citizen values and democratic consolidation. The degree to which political reforms open opportunities for the citizenry is the degree to which the public will accept the new political rules and institutions. In essence, the efficacy of the new democratic institutions determines their legitimacy.

If political values can change, are they changing in the post-communist era? Public survey research is the primary tool employed in addressing the issue, in spite of questions concerning whether such data can be meaningfully employed to determine values during times of intense social transformation.[14] Among the norms considered have been political efficacy, political interest, political knowledge, political participation, support for elections, support for human rights, and support for a free press. A number of studies have reached optimistic conclusions.[15] The general consensus is that these values are most widely distributed among the young, those with a higher education, and residents of urban areas. However, a number of observers have noted a lesser degree of commitment to democratic values in Russia and other states of the former Soviet Union.[16] The most common finding is that post-Soviet citizens exhibit low levels of political tolerance.[17] Among the more pessimistic analyses, Nichols contends that there is a lack of trust as well as a lack of social capital in general that is acting to undermine democracy.[18]

Civil Society

Besides analyses of the distribution of values and attitudes among the public, post-communist scholarship has also looked at the existence of civil society, understood as a society marked by the existence of a dense pattern of non-state-sponsored associational activity. Nonetheless, this is one area of scholarship that remains relatively underdeveloped.

Not all theorists of democracy agree that a civil society contributes to democracy. E.E. Schattschneider, for example, argues that interest groups and other similar associations unfairly advantage the well-to-do over the less fortunate by providing them with a vehicle for avoiding democratic majoritarian rules.[19] Joel S. Migdal's concern about a strong civil society extends to the ability of private associational activity to impede the state from establishing effective control over the economy. As a result, the economy is less effectively managed and democracy is undermined.[20] Within post-communist Europe itself there is a debate as to whether civil society is necessary to democracy. Some argue that all that is needed is to open opportunity for individual economic and political activity. They fear that calls for cooperative activity will revive the collectivist and statist mentality of the communist era. Others claim that democracy lacking a collective conscience and communal spirit will be a hollow freedom for the majority.[21]

Among the few analyses of civil society in post-communist Europe, most agree with Robert A. Dahl that a civil society is an important and necessary condition for democracy,[22] but it may not be a sufficient condition.[23] Given the general absence of a civil society in the communist era, associations autonomous from the state are particularly important in the post-communist context. They serve to mediate between the individual and the state.[24] Further, contrary to the view of Schattschneider, some contend that such associations provide voice to those who are otherwise underrepresented.[25] In so doing, they are indispensable to providing a check on the state and undergirding democracy. Hence, the role of the public and particularly that of civil society in democratization occupies an important position in post-communist studies.

The general scholarly consensus is that civil society in post-communist systems remains weak and largely underdeveloped.[26] Indeed, the lack of a strong civil society is one of the greatest impediments to the consolidation of democracy in the region. The most common thesis is that the emergence of a civil society is impeded by the legacy of the communist era. In essence, the communist system was largely successful in suppressing citizen involvement in collective activity outside of state sponsorship. As a consequence, in the post-communist era, society remains weakly organized and dependent upon the state.[27] Others argue that the traditional cultures of the region suppress citizen activity.[28] Reisinger, Miller, and Hesli, however, argue that post-Soviet citizens are highly participatory, but that the organizational means for their doing so are underdeveloped.[29] Finally, there are those who argue that the roots of civil society existed during the communist era, often in the form of protest and dissident movements. These movements have emerged in the post-communist era to form the basis for a rapidly developing civil society.[30]

The underdevelopment of civil society in post-communist Europe is addressed in several analyses of particular organizations and movements. For instance, Baglione and Clark have considered the factors impeding the development of strong labor unions in Russia. They conclude that much of the explanation lies in the lack of worker trust in unions left over from the Soviet era, bureaucratic barriers, and economic constraints.[31] Yanitsky's analysis of the Russian environmental movement concludes that it is in decline owing to the collapse of the energy system and the lack of a coordinated environmental policy among the newly independent states.[32] Focusing on the role of religious institutions in facilitating the emergence of a civil society, Goeckel argues that the continued economic dependence of the Baltic churches on the state significantly reduces their capacity to take part.[33] In a more optimistic assessment, Snajdr looks at the emerging ecological movement in Slovakia and concludes that it is attracting strong leadership and a youthful membership, both of which are assuring it an active role in the country's domestic politics. Nonetheless, the movement is limited by inadequate resources and continued dependency on support from similar movements outside the country.[34]

As we have discussed previously, analyses of post-communist systems have tended to emphasize interaction across the arenas of democratic consolidation. The same is true for analyses of civil society. In particular, scholars have noted a linkage between the development of civil society and nationalism, a linkage that provides the most direct connection with scholarship on issues of stateness. The general thesis is that the continued development of democratic freedoms in post-communist Europe depends upon the emergence of civil society. However, civil society in many states is being impeded by an exclusivist form of nationalism that undermines the freedoms accorded to minorities.[35] Some believe that economic development is the best hope for releasing the grip that divisive nationalism currently has on civil societies throughout the region.[36]

Social Movements

The economic difficulties under which democratization is taking place in post-communist Europe would suggest that a better framework for analyzing the emergence of a participatory citizenry is within the context of the politics of disenfranchisement. This seems all the more appropriate given the underdevelopment of democratic political institutions necessary to process newly emerging social demands. Such a framework is provided by social movement theory. Despite the apparent good fit, however, there have been relatively few efforts to employ the theory to the democratizing countries of post-communist Europe.[37]

This is perhaps accounted for by the fact that the theory was developed to analyze the politics of the dispossessed in Western liberal democracies. As a consequence, there is a predisposition to suppose that such a politics only exists in consolidated democracies. Where the model has been employed, it has helped us to consider the human rights dimension of democracy, a dimension that is often missing owing to the paradigmatic concern of democratic consolidation with elite political institutions and macroeconomics. (One study argues that there is a correlation between the existence of social movements and a political system's respect for human rights.)[38]

The inequalities and disenfranchisement that can attend the reforms associated with democratization can be so great as to call into question the very quality of democracy. Social movements are a response to disenfranchisement. In contrast to interest groups, which are organized in order to make demands at well-defined and often institutionalized points in the political process, social movements mobilize those whose interests are being ignored by the political and economic system. In essence, they provide the means by which protest can be productively channeled and expressed. As this occurs, violence is less likely and citizens begin to experience some sense of political efficacy.[39]

The few analyses of social movements in post-communist Europe have generally concluded that owing to the fact that those left behind by the reforms constitute a majority, civil society, such as it is, is better understood as social movements.[40] Some of these studies have also facilitated a more nuanced consideration of the role in the democratization process of women, who as a group tend to more involved in social movements.[41]

The Rule of Law

Most scholars assume that the role of the judiciary, particularly an independent one, is fundamental to the operation of democracy. Despite this, very little scholarly attention has been paid to the judiciary and its development in post-communist systems. This is no doubt partially accounted for by its having being largely ignored by democratic consolidation in general. Indeed, Linz and Stepan are among the first to identify it as an arena with which scholars need to concern themselves. The oversight remains an important one begging to be redressed.

Those studies that have looked at the issue have been largely concerned with the degree to which the courts have been able to establish themselves as autonomous from the legislative and executive powers. Failing to do so, they are less able to fulfill their role of clarifying the rules of the game in a manner best able to persuade the largest proportion of the political elites that it is in their best interests to abide by the rules. The general view is that the courts have had difficulty in establishing themselves as an independent branch of government, particularly in Russia. Some scholars find the cause of the problem in the legacies of the Soviet and pre-Soviet eras. These legacies encompass both residual institutions and behaviors.

Among the institutional problems noted in the literature are an underfinanced infrastructure, a need for training, the continued intervention and interference of the Ministry of Justice and Procuracy, and the absence of judicial standards.[42] As a consequence, the courts have been reduced in their ability to limit the state and protect citizen rights. Perhaps the single most problematic of the institutions is the Procuracy.[43] Invested with wide-ranging powers, the same body not only prosecutes criminal cases, it supervises the entire judicial process. Further, it exercises supervision over the courts and police. Indeed, its supervisory functions extend to the entire realm of state officialdom to ensure compliance with state policies. Taken together, the Procuracy's functions not only amount to a courtroom bias in favor of the state, they seriously undermine any independent course that the courts may wish to pursue.

Those scholars arguing that the behavioral legacies of the past serve as a major impediment to the emergence of an independent judiciary generally focus on a legal culture rooted in pre-communist era traditions and values. In Russia, in particular, this problem is reflected in the lack of a rule of law tradition encompassing the idea of a limited state.[44] While citizens are understood to be limited by laws in their relations with the state, the notion that the state also is regulated in these relationships is foreign to the legal tradition.

While some scholars have focused on legacies of the past regime to explain the relative lack of autonomy of the judiciary in post-communist political systems, a smaller number have adopted a more explicitly rational-choice approach. Largely cross-national comparisons, their analyses focus on the strategic decisions made by self-interested political elites during the bargaining process over the contours of the constitutional order. Magalhaes, for example, argues that the Communist Party will insist on the creation of a strong, independent judiciary if it calculates that it is likely to lose legislative and executive elections. By doing so, the party, which dominates judicial positions and appointments, insulates the judiciary from the other two branches and makes it harder for judges to be removed.[45] Smithey and Ishiyama have found support for a similar contention in a test of multiple causes.[46]

A Usable State Bureaucracy

A third arena of a consolidated democracy that has been inadequately addressed by post-communist studies is the bureaucracy. The most comprehensive theoretical consideration of the role of the state bureaucracy in the democratization process is that of Adam Przeworski et al.[47] They take pains to point out that in the absence of a usable bureaucracy, the state is unable to implement either economic or political reform. Further, in its absence, the central government is so weakened that fragmentation threatens, a problem related to the "stateness" precondition addressed by Linz and Stepan.[48]

In comparison with the judiciary, a usable state bureaucracy has been the subject of a somewhat greater degree of empirical concern. Most analyses of the bureaucracy in east-central Europe and the former Soviet Union have been conducted by specialists in public administration. As a result, few have been explicitly concerned with contributing to the literature on democratic consolidation, reflecting instead a disciplinary concern with prescribing remedies to the region based on public administration and public policy practice in the West.[49] Nonetheless, many recognize both explicitly and implicitly that the bureaucracy is the chief agent of the democratic and market reforms in the region.[50]

There have been two major lines of questioning in this literature. The first is with the need for training, the general argument being that communist-era administrators are ill prepared for the demands of public administration in a democratic state. Public administrators in a communist state were permitted little room within which to exercise discretion, the idea being that they should faithfully carry out the commands of political officers. A democratic state, on the other hand, requires a separation of functions between the politician and the professional public servant. The former establishes the general contours of public policy programs which the latter, as a technical specialist, then implements with minimal oversight. In the absence of such a model, post-communist politicians frequently interfere in the minutest of details. This is particularly problematic for reformers, who in many cases were members of the communist-era intelligentsia with little to no expertise in the technical matters in which they are now engaging. To correct for these problems, training programs have to focus not only on changing work habits and attitudes but on developing a competent and neutral professional public administration capable of commanding the respect of all political parties.[51]

The second issue in the literature concerns the problem of state corruption. The general thesis is that bureaucratic corruption undermines democracy. While most studies have attempted to detail the extent of the problem and determine its causes,[52] one of the more interesting contributions has looked at the problem comparatively. The authors found that levels of corruption varied across the region and that corruption and efficiency were inversely related.[53]

Issue Areas Outside the Agenda of Democratic Consolidation

Were civil society, the judiciary, and the state bureaucracy the only issue areas not adequately being addressed by post-communist studies, the case for the argument that democratic consolidation has deterred us from addressing important questions would be a very weak one. This is all the more so given that some theorists have at least identified them as constituting important arenas for research. In fact, however, there are quite a few other areas of research that remain relatively underdeveloped. Many of them are closely related to the arena in which most of the research agenda has focused, the institutions of political society. Among these are principal-agent relations and local government.

Principal-Agent Problems

Legislative Committee Systems

What is surprising is how little attention has actually been given to some very important aspects of the legislature. While electoral laws and their effects on the party system have been considered in extraordinary detail, much of the internal organization of parliaments has hardly been considered. This is particularly so for committee systems. The very act of adopting a committee system entails what is known as a principal-agent problem. Such a problem exists when the agent (in this case the committees) has the potential to usurp the authority of the principal (in this case the legislature) that created it.

The problem has been the subject of much research in the United States.[54] This is not surprising given the central role of the U.S. Congress in policy making. Very few legislatures are as active in the drafting of legislation as is the U.S. Congress. The committee system is integral to this. Both houses of Congress have delegated responsibility to their respective committees to write and mark up drafts of legislative proposals in areas under their jurisdiction. More important, no piece of legislation can make it to the floor without first being approved by a committee. While there is disagreement over the degree to which this is actually the case,[55] some argue that it amounts to the committees' exercising a virtual veto over legislation.

Given the power of the committees over the congressional agenda, some scholars have gone so far as to describe them as a system of property rights in which committee membership entitles one to control over policy (legislation) within the jurisdiction of the respective committee.[56] The committees, as the agents of the parent assembly, can control the work of that very assembly. That is even more the case if the committee chairs are relatively independent of the house leadership (a condition that attains when appointments to committees and chairmanships are determined on the basis of seniority). Noting this, some scholars argue that the congressional leadership has in effect abdicated control of policy to the committee chairs.

More recent scholarship, however, argues that such is not the case.[57] Instead of examining a legislative agenda controlled by powerful committee chairs, these studies focus on a committee system in the service of the majority political party. Reform of the committee system in the 1970s scrapped the seniority system and gave party leaders greater control over committee appointments. Since then the congressional leadership has been able to reassert control and use the committees as an efficient means to achieve the legislative agenda of the majority party.

There is yet another position in the literature on committees, according to which they serve as forums in which legislators specializing in certain policy matters can fully discuss the implications of proposed legislation with functional experts from government, business, and society at large. These discussions can do much to unearth the potential costs and benefits of a given proposal. Consequently, the committees serve an invaluable informational role.[58]

It is tempting to simply dismiss the importance of committee systems by noting that European parliaments in general play far less a role in legislation than their American counterpart (focusing instead on cabinet making and breaking). However, the fact that they exist in every democratizing legislative assembly commends them to us as a potential focus of research. Further, research on the legislative committee systems in postcommunist Europe can contribute to the debate on the roles of committee systems that has emerged in the analysis of U.S. congressional committees. Thus far, however, there has been only one effort to do so, and that was conducted in the highly problematic case of the Russian Duma.[59]

Executive-Legislative Relations

Principal-agent problems are equally evident in relations between the executive and legislative branches. With the exception of the office of the prime minister—and if provided for in the constitution, the president—most executive agencies are creations of the legislature. Hence, they, like the committee system, are agents of the assembly. The challenge to the principal, the legislature, is how to control these agents when they work for the executive. This is a particularly important issue, since abdication on the part of the assembly can severely undermine democracy by surrendering too much power to the executive. Scholars have noted that this is the essential problem of presidential and president-parliamentary systems.[60]

Legislatures do not create agencies and empower them to carry out specific functions with the intent to surrender control over these functions. They do so in order to achieve certain policy outcomes. Hence, the agencies and programs are created in the interest of the legislature. However, there will always be conflict between the bureaucratic agency and the assembly, as the former will behave opportunistically to pursue its own interests, some of which may be contradictory to the intent of the legislature. The ability of the agency to do so is increased by its functional specialization and monopoly of information. (The latter is referred to as a problem of asymmetric information.) Asymmetric information in particular permits the bureaucratic entity to engage in corruption, shirk its responsibilities, or substitute its own goals for those of the legislature. The latter of course undermines the normative principle of democracy as it is the legislature, not the government bureaucracy, that is elected to represent the popular will.

Legislatures are not powerless; they can undertake certain measures to overcome these principal-agent problems. Among them are monitoring, the creation of institutionalized mechanisms to overcome the asymmetric information problem, the installation of "fire alarms," and limiting the discretion of agencies.[61] Monitoring generally involves legislative oversight. It is most often expressed when an assembly engages in interpellation or censure of an agency. It is the least effective set of measures, as it detects violations of legislative intent but does little to preclude them from occurring (short of the threat of censure itself). The other three sets of measures focus on stopping bureaucratic violations before they occur. Administrative law can be used to force an agency to be more open in its operations. Such laws typically include a proviso that bureaucratic regulations must go through a period of public scrutiny before they are implemented. Other stipulations, such as a requirement to maintain a filing system sufficient to permit the agency to respond to public inquiries on its activities, have a similar effect by making the agency's activities more transparent. Among other things, "fire alarms" mandate that representatives of specified social organizations be represented in the decision process of an agency as well as in the creation of special administrative courts for hearing citizen complaints on agency activities. Finally, assemblies may limit the discretion of bureaucrats by requiring them to submit detailed reports on proposals prior to implementation, reducing their budgets, or requiring legislative approval of certain types of activities.

Since analysis of the effectiveness of these solutions has been confined to the U.S. political system, studies of democratizing systems in post-communist Europe could contribute much to understanding which of these measures are most likely to be employed and under what conditions in political systems in general. Indeed, any theories developed on the basis of the experience of only one political system remain highly suspect.

Local Government

Local governments are often the creation of the legislature. As such, they, like committee systems and bureaucratic agencies of the government, represent a principal-agent problem, although this problem is often left to the government or chief executive to resolve. For this reason, what little attention has been paid them by theorists of democratic consolidation has tended to view them as problematic. For example, Przeworski argues that they can provide a base of support for separatist elites to challenge the central government and threaten fragmentation of the state. In this sense they contribute to a stateness problem.[62] Even theories of local government themselves have raised serious questions as to how, if at all, they contribute to democracy. Early theorists argued that local governments were dominated by elites that effectively excluded the voices of the majority of citizens.[63] Pluralists challenged the elitist view in the 1960s, contending that local policy emerges out of the give and take between citizen groups, which engage in a complex game of coalition building on a wide array of issue dimensions.[64] Belonging to any number of such groups, citizens are assured political voice in local politics.

Subsequent theories for the most part favor the elitist perspective. Logan and Molotch, for example, focus on the influence of local capital.

They argue that local politics is dominated by a coalition of local business interests, the core of which comprises those who own commercial property. Possessing a nonmobile asset, these rentiers seek to increase local land values in order to increase their potential profits. If land values increase, they are able to charge more for the use of their assets. Closely allied with them are other groups that also will profit from increasing land values: bankers, construction companies, real estate firms, newspapers, universities, and politicians who benefit from higher tax revenues. Together they comprise a "growth machine." To increase land values, the growth machine diverts local resources to entice businesses to locate in the area, creating a demand for commercial property. While politicians representing the poor, minorities, and other groups disadvantaged by these policies may be elected to office, they are likely to be dissuaded from redirecting the flow of local resources away from economic development programs by the realization that such efforts could reduce the tax revenues available to them and their constituencies. Should they nonetheless attempt to do so, the growth machine is able to muster the economic, political, social, and informational resources necessary to throw the offending party out of office in subsequent elections.[65]

Urban regime theory is another perspective arguing for the dominance of global capital in determining policy outcomes at the local level. Urban regime theorists note the existence of a dual base of power. While economic power is in the hands of private business interests, political power is held by elected officials. They are distinct from each other, yet neither is independent of the other. Business is subject to local policy, but policy may result in the loss of jobs, since capital in the global economy is mobile. That is, businesses can merely relocate elsewhere in response to local policies they find overly constraining. However, business communities comprise competing interests. This competition permits political officeholders to engage in bargaining that gives them greater room to meet the demands of their constituencies than might otherwise be expected.[66]

Given this rather negative view of the role of local government in democracy, it is not surprising that scholars focusing on democratic consolidation have generally avoided addressing this level of governance. What work has been done has looked at federalism. The work on federalism has focused on Russia. It reflects Przeworski's concern that greater regional (or local) autonomy may lead to integration problems.[67] Further, much of it has shown little concern for theory, which is not surprising given the negative conclusion that most theory draws on the contribution of local government to democratization.[68]

Institutional Development

While democratic consolidation clearly focuses on institutional development, the relations between some of these institutions have not been addressed. Particularly interesting is that although significant attention has been given to the problem of executive-legislative relations, little has been devoted to how the legislature might be strengthened in the relationship short of simply changing the constitutional arrangement between the two. Riggs has argued that strong party systems are essential to providing legislatures with the cohesion necessary to balance the executive branch and the bureaucracy serving it. In particular, party systems must avoid too much fragmentation and polarization so that a clear governing majority can emerge. It is equally important that parties are sufficiently institutionalized that their leadership is capable of organizing a corpus of deputies around a program of legislation. If the legislature can not do this, the executive branch, at the urging and with the support of the public administration, will most likely usurp the legislative prerogative in order to assure that the government can function.[69] The argument is a compelling one, providing theoretical coherency to party systems, the legislature, the executive, and the bureaucracy. Nevertheless, there has been no sustained effort to consider these links. Further, Riggs's theory sheds light on issues of cabinet formation and durability.[70] Here again there is much room for research in post-communist countries.

What Is To Be Done?

Our discussion to this point has only begun to explore the topics that democratic consolidation has not permitted scholars to adequately explore. Indeed, the complexity of the political world is such that the list of issues yet to be investigated is virtually infinite. In that sense it is really quite unfair to criticize paradigms. As I have argued from the beginning, one of the primary purposes of paradigms is to give focus to our research. Lacking focus, a discipline's scholars will dissipate their efforts in a fruitless attempt to "discover everything knowable." While this may be a noble attempt, it is futile. The point of this chapter is therefore not to provide a list of all the issues that post-communist scholarship has failed to address. That would be an impossible task. What I have attempted to do instead is to make the case that many important issues have not been addressed, among them those that should be included in democratic consolidation's agenda.

While the agenda established by democratic consolidation is an important issue, there is, however, an even more important concern that scholars should have with the paradigm. A research agenda is appropriate to a set of countries to the degree that the paradigm itself is appropriate. Democratic consolidation suffers from a predisposition to view all political systems as forever transitioning to democracy. Seeing neither reversals nor consolidation itself, scholars therefore apply the paradigm's approaches to an overly broad set of political systems. In the next chapter, I consider this problem and propose an explicitly rational-choice theoretical framework to resolve it.

Chapter Four

Reformulating Democratic Consolidation

Given that each of the issue areas addressed in the previous chapter has a self-evident connection with democracy, it seems strange that scholars have paid so little attention to them. The reason for the apparent paradox lies in a lack of theory, particularly for the second stage, democratic consolidation. The lack of theory, however, creates a problem demanding a resolution. We really do not know how or when a political system has become a consolidated democracy. As a consequence, we may well be employing a paradigm establishing a research agenda that is not at all appropriate in some cases. This is most certainly so when the country has either ceased democratization because it has reverted to authoritarianism or it has achieved a stable democratic political system.

This chapter proposes a theory of democratic consolidation intended to resolve this problem. Theories and paradigms are not the same thing. Paradigms are higher order worldviews comprising broad sets of overarching and often diffuse groupings of assumptions about how we understand a universe of phenomena. In essence, they define the limits of a discipline, including the questions we ask and the approaches and theories we employ to resolve them. It is in this sense that democratic consolidation is a paradigm. Theories, on the other hand, are tightly argued and conceptually coherent constructs permitting us to deduce testable hypotheses about the causes of particular phenomena.

While both communist and post-communist studies have been greatly influenced by paradigms, neither has shown much concern for theory. Soviet studies, in particular, was isolated from most theoretical scholarship in the social sciences, a situation that scholars such as Frederic J. Fleron[1] and Alexander J. Motyl[2] called upon social scientists to rectify. Conditioned by a tradition of an atheoretical approach to the subject matter, post-communist studies has shown the same penchant to ignore theory.[3] This is unfortunate; theory is important. It is the medium through which we are able to compare cases by juxtaposing what we have discovered elsewhere, as represented in the theoretical constructs that are informed by that knowledge, with the "facts" in the particular case be-

60 BEYOND POST-COMMUNIST STUDIES

fore us. Absent this process we must rediscover the wheel each time we engage in research. Further, we can not engage in the exchange of ideas and information that permits any degree of accumulation of knowledge. And most important, we can not truly know the answer to the question "why?"

Transition Theory

Scholars of democratization have posited the existence of two phases in the transition from an authoritarian state to a stable democratic system. The first phase, mislabeled the transition to democracy, involves the breakdown of the authoritarian regime and the instauration of an unstable set of democratic institutions. In the second phase, democratic consolidation, these institutions stabilize. All salient political forces become so habituated to democratic rules and norms that none contemplates efforts outside of them.

Theorists have succeeded in developing a fairly cohesive framework defining the first stage. At the forefront in the development of this framework were the studies sponsored by the Woodrow Wilson Center that adopted a minimalist definition of democracy. Arguing from Joseph Schumpeter's empirical observation that democracies are essentially defined by elections,[4] they maintained that democracies are distinguished by fair and open elite contestation for political office, the outcomes of which are decided by the public in accordance with broadly inclusive rules of participation.[5] Consequently, the popular election of a legislature in multiparty competitive races was taken to mark the end of the first phase.

The process of the breakdown of the authoritarian regime is focused on the decisions taken by political elites. While the focus on elites is much maligned by those arguing that the people play an important role in overturning dictatorships, it is defensible on the grounds that elites occupy strategic positions at key junctures identified in the democratization process by the Woodrow Wilson scholars. They posited that the process begins with an authoritarian regime facing a crisis. Uncertainty over how best to deal with the crisis leads to a fragmentation of a hithertofore relatively homogenous ruling elite. This in turn may result in an opening for the possible introduction of liberal reforms, intended by less conservative elements within the ruling elite to resolve the initial crisis. If introduced, these reforms may give rise to a resurgent society providing a potential base of support for counter-elites. The ensuing contest between regime hard-liners, reformers, and newly emerging counter-elites sets the stage for a series of negotiated pacts between these competing elites that may ultimately end in a compromise solution— the decision to permit a contested popular election to a national legislature (and perhaps executive). Russell Bova first employed this general framework in post-communist studies in his analysis of the implosion of the Soviet Union.[6]

Troubled by what they perceived to be definitions that largely ignore the human rights protections that democracies afford citizens, some subsequent studies adopted more cumbersome definitions of democracy. (Among the more popular alternative definitions of democracy is that of Dahl, who includes freedoms of speech, association, and the press along with open contestation and participation.)[7] The impetus to move to a largely normatively focused definition of democracy was given particular force by Larry Diamond's argument that minimalist (electoral) democracies are far less durable (and therefore less likely to become consolidated) than substantive democracies, which incorporate broad sets of personal freedoms and human rights.[8] In a similar vein, Samuel Huntington argued that in order to survive, democracies must adopt Western values, not just procedures.[9]

The problem with all of these definitions however is not whether they correctly identify the set of human rights that would assure the most stable form of democracy. Indeed, the fact that much of this debate revolves around normative issues suggests that such a set may not be empirically verifiable (a point made by Schumpeter in his original formulation). The real problem is that the definitions have to do with attitudes, values, and behaviors. As a consequence, it is difficult at best to identify specific stages in the process of the breakdown of the authoritarian regime with the adoption of a particular value. Further, there is no way to argue in a theoretically coherent manner why any one value would be adopted at any given point in the process. Indeed, why would authoritarian elites become democrats? Failing to resolve these issues, the first stage (the transition to democracy) remains a theoretically diffuse argument permitting the discussion of any number of pacts at any number of points for any number of reasons.

Adam Przeworski resolves this problem by introducing an altogether different concept of democracy. In so doing, he is able to distill thinking on the transition to democracy into a more elegant and theoretically coherent framework.[10] In Przeworski's reformulation, democracy is a system of governance in which the rules by which political decisions are taken are certain, however, adherence to these rules assures uncertainty of policy outcomes.[11] Certainty of rules requires the rule of law, while uncertainty of outcome requires opening the political process up to as many political voices as possible.

Przeworski's conceptualization of democracy rejects a behavioral notion based on values and attitudes and instead clearly focuses on institutions and rules. This in turn permits him to adopt an explicitly rational-choice perspective as a means for ordering the stages in the transition to democracy, explaining why choices are made at critical junctures. Identifying the key points at which strategic actors engage in critical decisions, he is able to predict under what conditions regime hard-liners will likely attempt a countercoup, why and under what conditions reformers will form an alliance with newly emergent moderate leaders (leading that part of society now mobilized against the authoritarian regime), and why these same reformers will not choose to form a coalition with hard-liners to repress the mobilized society.

The rational calculus of strategic actors is critical to Przeworski's[12] analysis at each juncture in the process of the breakdown of the authoritarian regime (the transition to democracy stage). In order for a strategic actor to take a given action, he must first have reason to believe that a particular decision will result in some personal gain. If there is no gain in it, there is no reason to take a given action. Second, the strategic actor must calculate that she has a better than even chance of success. This is similar to the concept of the calculus of an intra-elite balance of force introduced by Dankwart Rustow in his early essay on the democratization process.[13] Merely being a member of the ruling elite carries with it significant rewards. While the chance for gain serves as a substantial enticement to action, the rewards of one's current situation serve as an impediment, since failure carries with it the potential to lose something (perhaps everything). Hence, both the potential for personal gain and victory must significantly outweigh the potential for defeat and the personal loss that would result.

We should note that the introduction of a rational-actor calculus not only strengthens the focus on elite actions during the transition to democracy, it provides a strong rationale for their actions. Instead of an awkward inability to explain changes in attitudes and values, we are focused squarely on an effort for personal gain. The emphasis on the manifest self-interest of political elites stays away from the behavioral problem of trying to explain why authoritarian elites adopt democratic values. In the rational-choice perspective, they do so because it is in their interest to do so, not because of some conversion to democracy as a preeminent value. The former is explicable; the latter is not.

Beginning with the crisis facing the authoritarian regime, Przeworksi[14] argues that no decision to implement liberal reform of the system will be undertaken unless those favoring reform are in a clear majority within the ruling elites. In the face of such a majority, conservatives opposed to the reforms will most certainly "go along to get along" and not endanger their positions. The introduction of the reforms gives an opening to society. The easiest decision is to accept the new deal offered by the regime. However, if some element of society (or within the ruling elite) views the reforms as an opportunity for greater personal gain or a sign of a weakening regime, then a resurgent civil society demanding more than the regime has offered is the likely result. These self-interested counter-elites will use the reforms to mobilize society by appealing to a general sense that the current regime is so repressive that any degree of risk is acceptable in order to achieve even the slightest gains.

If events take this direction, then the position of the reformers within the ruling elites weakens vis-à-vis the conservatives, and an attempt to violently repress the social upsurge (and end the entire process) is possible. Indeed, the emergence of a counter-elite threatens the interests of conservatives and reformers alike. However, reformers are dissuaded from closing ranks with the conservatives if they calculate that they will ultimately be purged for their part in contributing to the problem in the first place.

Should the process continue, counter-elites leading a mobilized society will be locked in a three-way confrontation with reformers and conservatives. The ideal situation for any of the three would be to rule without the other two. In such a case, they would not need to share power. That is precisely what they will attempt to do should they reason that the balance of forces is such that they can destroy the other two with an acceptable likelihood of success and without sustaining unacceptable damage to their own interests in the process. Should any side in the contest succeed, then democracy is not possible, as there is no incentive for the victorious elite (counter-elite) to hold elections to decide who will rule. They will decide the issue among themselves. A miscalculation, of course, leads to the same outcome. Or it could lead to a stalemate.

In fact, it is only when a stalemate is reached—whether it be the result of rational calculation or a miscalculated attempt at force—that democracy is possible. Under conditions of a rough balance of power between two or more groups of would-be ruling elites, all sides are compelled to engage in negotiations to secure as much of their interests as possible. Further, recognizing a roughly equal balance of power and wishing to deny total victory to each other, they will agree to periodic elections for political office. When a new legislature has been installed in accordance with the negotiated pacts (which have found their way into a constitution) following the first of these elections, the first phase (the transition to democracy) has come to a conclusion.

Toward a Theory of Consolidation

In comparison to the theoretical coherence achieved for the first stage of democratic consolidation (the breakdown of authoritarian rule or transition to democracy), the conceptual frameworks and approaches for analyzing the second stage, the consolidation phase, remain considerably less coherent. This is partially accounted for by the continued fuzziness of its key concept, a consolidated democracy. There is substantial agreement on the definition of a consolidated democracy as a political situation in which democracy has become the only game in town.[15] In essence, democratic procedures and norms have become so deeply internalized in social, institutional, and psychological life that no significant political groups seriously consider pursuing their goals outside of these procedures. As a consequence, elected governments are no longer dominated by the problem of how to avoid democratic breakdown.[16]

There are some serious problems with this definition, not the least of which is that scholars are divided as to whether a consolidated democracy refers to the ideal end-state itself or the process of achieving this end-state. Even among those who argue that it is best understood as a process, there is considerable confusion over just what constitutes the process. In an insightful essay, Andreas Schedler identifies at least five different processes addressed by democratic consolidation. The first two are concerned with regime survival: avoiding democratic breakdown (going from electoral or liberal democracy to authoritarianism), and preventing democratic erosion (going from liberal to electoral democracy). The remaining three focus on advancing the democratization project:

completing democracy (going from electoral to liberal democracy), deepening democracy (going from electoral or liberal democracy to advanced democracy), and organizing democracy (strengthening liberal democracy).[17] Many of these concepts are equally vague. While we are able to distinguish electoral democracy from liberal democracy—the former involving no more than the adoption of democratic procedures such as elections, the latter requiring the broad-scale implementation of rights associated with democracy—the definition of advanced democracy remains illusive.

Obviously, if we can not identify a consolidated democracy in a coherent manner, we can not meaningfully posit an end to the process of democratization itself. Faced with such a situation, scholars naturally treat the countries of the region as if they were all still undergoing democratization, since they have no way of judging completion of the project. Paradoxically, what we are faced with is a bias toward viewing these systems as unchangeable. They can never be democratic; they are forever immature and unstable. Just as Soviet studies was incapable of forecasting the collapse of the Soviet Union because none of the reigning paradigms admitted of any possibility of instability, post-communist studies can not see a qualitative change in the democracies of east-central Europe (in this case achieving stability).

Conceptual confusion in turn produces theoretical incoherence. As the reader will recall, Linz and Stepan have argued for the existence of five arenas in a consolidated democracy. They further argue that these arenas are interdependent and equally important to the democratization project. In making the case for interdependency, they attempt to outline some of the links between the five arenas. However, these attempts are largely ad hoc, focusing on particular links and relationships between the arenas. No theoretical linkage emerges as a result, leaving Linz and Stepan open to the charge that they have defined a model for a static, ideal end-state (a consolidated democracy). Hence, the arenas would appear to be of little utility to post-communist studies, as the discipline is concerned with a set of states, none of which has achieved democratic consolidation.

The way out of the morass is to build a theory that permits scholars to meaningfully consider an end to the process without sacrificing consideration of stagnation or reversals. Only such a theory can adequately address the entire set of states that are included in post-communist Europe. The best way to achieve this is to recast the consolidation phase within an explicitly rational-choice framework in much the same manner as Przeworski recast theoretical work for the first phase. Just as Przeworski has developed an institutional definition for democracy in order to permit the development of a more coherent theory for the first phase, so an institutional definition for a consolidated democracy is required to permit progress in theorizing about the second phase. This will permit us to develop a rational-choice argument that will clarify the logical relationships between Linz and Stepan's five arenas. It is to that task that I now turn.

A Theory of Democratic Consolidation

We will begin by reconsidering the definition of a consolidated democracy. The currently fashionable definition, a political system in which democracy is the only game in town, is a behavioral one. It focuses on the changing values of political elites and the public. When both hold to democracy as a value in and of itself, then a democratic system is held to be stable. While such a definition has a normative appeal, as most behaviorally rooted definitions do, it defies theorizing. How and why does loyalty to democracy develop? Why would ruling elites in authoritarian systems suddenly adopt a democratic ethos? How much time does it take to do so? What are the theoretical concepts that give these ideas elegance and coherence? Once a value is established, how does it erode? Can it erode? These are all troubling questions that invite answers that are unfortunately ad hoc and incoherent.

Just as important, the definition is confused with one of the arenas of a consolidated democracy, the rule of law. Indeed, the rule of law is more than the set of institutions that assure that the procedures are properly interpreted and followed (the judicial and legal systems). The arena includes the acceptance of democratic norms. This is precisely what the phrase the only game in town means.

I contend that Przeworski provides us with a more theoretically useful definition. The reader will recall that in this reformulation, democracy is understood as a political system marked by certainty of rules and uncertainty of outcomes. In order for decision-making rules and institutions to constitute the basis of a democracy, they must be certain in their application (that is, some other set of rules may not substitute for them). Further, their application must result in uncertainty of outcomes (that is, no institution or set of political actors may preordain the outcome).[18] A stable democracy, then, is one in which all salient political parties adhere to these rules. However, contrary to the currently dominant view, they do not do so because they are habituated to democratic values in a normative sense. They do so because they calculate that they can do no better under any other set of rules. That is, manifestly self-interested political actors view the costs of attempting to break the rules as too high in comparison to the gain to be had by continuing to play by the rules. In essence, democracy is not the only game in town because no one can think of any other set of rules or norms that they would prefer. It is the only game in town because it is the *best* game in town for all salient political players. With this definition of a consolidated democracy we can now begin to build a theory of democratic consolidation. Our theory will start where phase one ends, with the instauration of a legislature elected on the basis of a new constitution negotiated among competing elites.

Phase one is marked by a process of elite fragmentation. For the democratization process to continue on to phase two, democratic consolidation, there must be at a minimum two groups of political elites of relatively equal strength. If there is only one elite group or one that dominates all the others, democracy is not possible. In such a case, the newly elected legislature is nothing more than a façade for a new authoritarian regime. Therefore, a theory of democratic consolidation must begin with the existence of a divided elite as a necessary precondition.

Assuming that there are at least two groups of contesting elites of roughly equal strength, the basis for a democracy is present. As our previous theoretical discussion of phase one indicates, it is often the case that there are three such groups: those opposed to the initial reforms carried out by the ruling party (conservatives), the reformers, and the counter-elites who emerged at the head of a resurgent civil society. A divided and competitive elite, however, is not sufficient to ensure the consolidation of democracy. To understand why, we must import a rational-actor perspective into our theory.

A competitive elite produces the basis for an electoral contest. However, each side in the contest is still calculating whether it can muster the necessary force to achieve a total victory and thereby end the need for democratic institutions (elections, legislatures, and the like), the very purpose of which is to institutionalize the elite competition. In essence, all salient political actors continue to maneuver for opportunities to impose a new set of rules that permit greater certainty of outcomes in their favor. They are willing to adhere to the democratic rules only as long as they calculate there is a higher payoff from doing so than from defecting (attempting to seize power by whatever means available). As long as the potential still exists that a significant number of political actors may yet calculate the possibility of greater personal gain outside the rules, the newly emergent democracy remains unstable.

The challenge of the second phase, democratic consolidation, is to create an essential equilibrium in which no salient political force can calculate with any acceptable degree of certainty that it can gain more by defecting from the negotiated constitution than continuing with the rules that it establishes. As long as the equilibrium is maintained, the democratic institutions and rules remain stable. This, of course, means that democracy itself can be disrupted, a theoretically (albeit not normatively) appealing possibility, as it permits us to consider democracies much more dynamically than do explanations relying on changing social values. Democracy and authoritarian regimes become poles on a continuum along which political systems can move based on changes in the equilibrium of the decision-making rules.

The best means for achieving an equilibrium favoring democratic rules is to increase the uncertainty of outcomes that the constitutional rules create. This can be done in either of two ways. The most obvious and direct means is to weaken the position of each of the contending parties so that no one of them perceives it might be able to overturn the democratic rules (that is, impose a new set of rules intended to serve its interests). This almost always entails increasing the number of salient political forces. The result is to complicate the rational calculations that political elites must make and thereby to raise the risk involved with breaking the rules. The easiest and most certain calculations can be obtained when there are only two salient political forces. Having only each other to contend with, they can judge the balance of forces with the least amount of error. The possibility of error increases dramatically with an increase in the number of players, while the likelihood that any one side can muster enough force to defeat the others decreases. Second, an increase in the number of institutions involved in the decision-making rules has the effect of increasing uncertainty of outcomes as well. The greater number of institutions that the rules require be involved in a political outcome, the less likely that those occupying any one of them can predetermine that outcome. In essence, the capacity of each to dominate the decision-making process is reduced.

Weakening and Increasing Competing Forces

The first means for increasing uncertainty focuses on reducing the likelihood that any political force might engage in efforts to overthrow a democratic regime. It requires that politically salient forces be both weakened and increased in number. This is a serious problem at the beginning of democratic consolidation. Whether the transition to democracy ends with two or three contesting groups of elites, each will have a base of support that it will attempt to use to increase its gains. The remnants of the former ruling party (conservatives or reformers, or perhaps both) are most likely to find their base of support within the state bureaucracy. The counter-elites will of course find theirs within civil society. In order for democracy to survive and stabilize (consolidate), both bases of support must be broken up. That is, the base of support for both must be weakened. Should the bureaucracy continue in support of any faction of the old regime, it could ultimately use its position to muster the state's resources to suppress civil society. On the other hand, a mass society mobilized by a single political force could be used to smash the state. As long as both remain intact, there is a rough balance of power. (If there had not been such a balance in the first place, no negotiated agreement establishing the initial deal resulting in the legislative elections would have been possible.) However, it is not a stable one, since each side believes that it may well have a base from which it could potentially seize full control of the political system.

Two sets of reforms are essential to change this situation. The first that is often undertaken by most post-communist regimes is economic reform. This involves mass privatization of state-owned assets, which in turn will help to break up society by introducing social differentiation. This in turn will lay the basis for a class system and a more differentiated party system. Privatization would appear, however, to run the risk of weakening the political forces behind the counter-elites without in any way reducing those supporting the former ruling elites. Hence, we might expect that economic reform would inevitably result in the reversal of democracy, as the former ruling elites backed by the bureaucracy will consolidate their position in the system in the face of a fragmenting and weakening opposition. This is only partially true, since it ignores the fact that privatization divests the bureaucracy of the basis of a substantial portion of its political resources. Nonetheless, the threat clearly exists, particularly if the bureaucracy is not reformed. This is not likely to happen concurrently with privatization if for no other reason than that the bureaucracy is needed to ensure that the privatization process occurs in a managed fashion. Herein lies the threat that they will use this control to seize the former state assets (or move them to those whom they favor).

There are two safeguards against such an abuse of power. The first is related to the choice of executive-legislative relations made in the constitutional deal struck at the end of phase one. In parliamentary and premier-presidential systems,[19] the government (comprising the cabinet, or the heads of the various ministries) is directly subject to the legislature, from which it derives its right to govern. Most often the government is formed from a coalition of parties assuring broad representation of interests in the oversight of the bureaucracy. Even the influence of the legislative minority is felt vis-à-vis the threat of a no-confidence motion, the exercise of censure, and legislative control of the budget. Bureaucracies managing the process of privatization in parliamentary and premier-parliamentary systems are therefore less likely to be able to abuse their powers. On the other hand, the government in presidential and president-parliamentary systems is shielded from the legislature working under the supervision of the president. If the president and the bureaucracy support the interests of one group of the elites, that group and the bureaucracy are both likely to gain substantially from privatization. They will be empowered by the process to overwhelm their opponents. Hence, the choice of executive-legislative relations is crucial. Indeed, it essentially serves as a second precondition (along with a divided elite) for democratic consolidation to take place. However, both are necessary, but not sufficient conditions.

The second safeguard against bureaucratic abuse is the degree to which global capital is permitted to engage in the privatization process. While many political forces in a democratizing state are concerned by the potentially overwhelming influence of global capital, it can have a highly beneficial effect by providing strong financial backing to newly emergent classes and social groups. This in turn can strengthen them in their political competition with former ruling elites and their bureaucratic supporters. Indeed, it is unlikely that there is a substantial degree of capital in the country that is not in the hands of the former ruling elites or the bureaucracy. Hence, at the very time that the solidarity of society is being weakened by social differentiation introduced by privatization, global capital can markedly increase the strength of one or more of its elements to undergird it in further competition with the former ruling elites. It is instructive that those countries that have opened their borders more widely to global capital have made greater progress in democratizing (Poland, Hungary, and the Czech Republic, for example) than those that have not been able to entice such investment or have closed their doors to it altogether (Ukraine and Russia, for example).

The second reform that is necessary to break up the base of support of the elites emerging from the transition to democracy is that of the public administration. As we mentioned in the foregoing paragraphs, reform of the bureaucracy is not likely to be undertaken early. But it must be undertaken at some point in the process to ensure the success of democratization. The primary challenge here is to introduce a professional bureaucracy, one that is employed on the basis of its competence and protected from political purges. This involves retraining of the bureaucracy, a probable mass hiring of oppositional elements to bring better ideological balance, and the introduction of new control methods. The latter would appear to be the most dangerous, as it entails granting the bureaucracy greater discretion in administrative matters and removing elected politicians from management of day-to-day operations. However, such a reform also has the effect of severing the bureaucracy from its former political masters. This in turn weakens both by creating the conditions for a greater differentiation of interests between the two.

Increasing Institutional Involvement

The second means for increasing the uncertainty of political outcomes and inducing a democratic equilibrium is to increase the number of salient institutions involved in decision making. This in turn provides an incentive to all parties to adhere to the democratic rules by increasing the probability of positive gain. The precondition of a parliamentary or premier-parliamentary system plays an important role here. Given the government's dependence on the legislature, which by its very nature is fractious, there is necessarily a considerable increase in the number of players involved in the decision-making process. In presidential and president-parliamentary systems, the legislature's role is greatly reduced. Further, the president is the captive of a single elite interest. Hence, his direct control of the government prejudices the system in favor of this interest and in so doing decreases the uncertainty of political outcomes.

There are of course reforms that can be undertaken that complicate the political process by adding actors. The two most important are judicial reform and local government reform. The order in which these reforms are undertaken is not that important. What is important is that they are begun in both arenas. During the communist era, the judiciary operated under the close supervision of the ministry of justice and the office of the procurator. The former provided resources and guidance while the latter served as a means for assuring that decisions of the courts accorded with the dictates of the Communist Party. One of the fundamental requirements of judicial reform therefore is undertaking the steps to create an independent judiciary. At a minimum this means that the courts will enter the political game as interpreters of the law. More important, they will decide whether government action was undertaken in accordance with the intent of the legislature. Further complicating the political process, the courts may also be given the right of judicial review. (In other words the courts not only judge whether the law was properly applied but they have the power to decide if the law itself was proper. Was it constitutional?) In most systems, this power is invested in a separate court (often titled the Constitutional Court).

To be truly independent in the execution of these powers, the courts must be detached from the supervision of government ministries and agencies. This is not always an easy process, as these entities do not wish to surrender the resources that accrue to them owing to their control of the courts. This in turn suggests that the courts must have an independent budget. Further, judicial independence requires the establishment of professional associations capable of establishing ethical norms and imposing meaningful sanctions on judges who violate them. Absent such norms and sanctions, judges who are accustomed to working for party bosses will all too easily slip into past behavioral patterns, particularly if some monetary gain can be had for doing so.

Reform of local government can have the same effect as judicial reform by adding to the number of actors in the political process. This not only serves to increase the uncertainty of outcomes, it also adds to the number of positions that individuals may seek to occupy and thereby creates a positive incentive for political elites to continue with the democratic rules of the game. As with judicial reform, the primary concern of the reforms here must be to create autonomous units of local governance. Lacking meaningful autonomy, local governments become mere field offices of the central ministries (state bureaucracy). To the degree this is the case, the incentive to seek these positions is reduced.

REFORMULATING DEMOCRATIC CONSOLIDATION   73

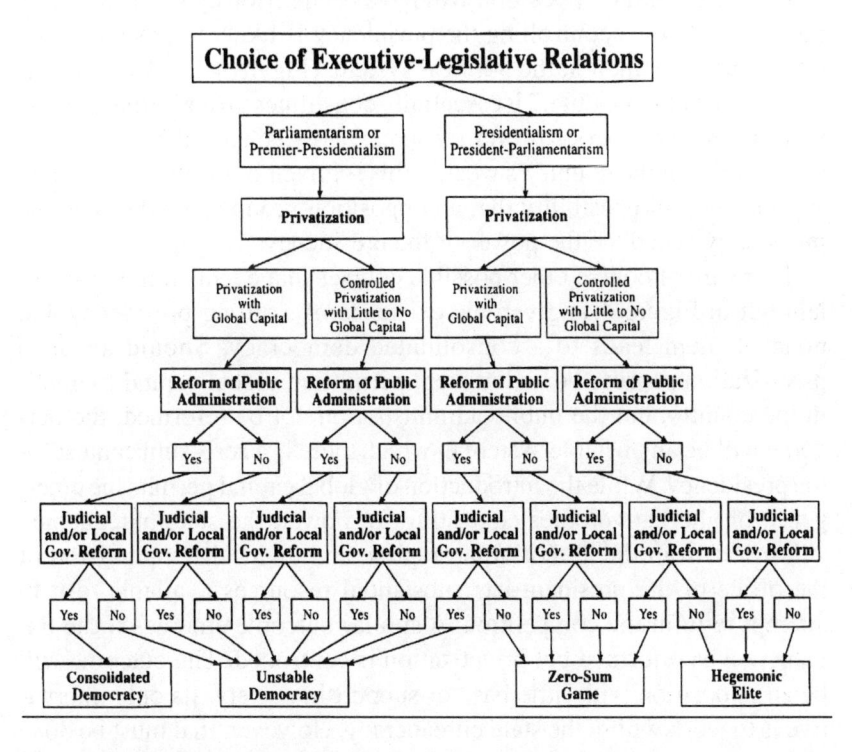

Figure 4.1 **The Process of Democratic Consolidation**

```
                    ┌─────────────────────────────────────────┐
                    │ Choice of Executive-Legislative Relations │
                    └─────────────────────────────────────────┘
                         /                                \
              Parliamentarism or                  Presidentialism or
              Premier-Presidentialism          President-Parliamentarism
                      │                                     │
                 Privatization                        Privatization
                   /      \                             /       \
          Privatization  Controlled              Privatization  Controlled
             with       Privatization                with       Privatization
         Global Capital with Little to No       Global Capital  with Little to No
                        Global Capital                          Global Capital
              │            │                         │              │
         Reform of    Reform of              Reform of        Reform of
          Public       Public                 Public           Public
       Administration Administration     Administration   Administration
           / \          / \                   / \              / \
         Yes  No      Yes  No               Yes  No          Yes  No
         /    \       /    \                /    \           /    \
     Judicial Judicial Judicial Judicial Judicial Judicial Judicial Judicial
     and/or   and/or   and/or   and/or   and/or   and/or   and/or   and/or
     Local    Local    Local    Local    Local    Local    Local    Local
     Gov.     Gov.     Gov.     Gov.     Gov.     Gov.     Gov.     Gov.
     Reform   Reform   Reform   Reform   Reform   Reform   Reform   Reform
     /  \    /  \    /  \    /  \     /  \    /  \     /  \    /  \
   Yes No  Yes No  Yes No  Yes No   Yes No  Yes No   Yes No  Yes No

   Consolidated   Unstable              Zero-Sum         Hegemonic
    Democracy    Democracy                Game            Elite
```

Further Explicating the Theory

Figure 4.1 visually outlines the theory of democratic consolidation developed in the previous paragraphs. The basic precondition is that phase one, the transition to democracy, has ended with a fragmented and competitive elite. However, for democratic consolidation to occur, the constitutional decision has to have been made to adopt a parliamentary or premier-presidential system. Any other system will create such a strong presidency that political elites will be enticed to use the position to ensure their interests against those of all others. The resulting zero-sum game will negate any possibility of an equilibrium being achieved. The most likely scenario will be that the president will refuse to reform the bureaucracy and use it instead to carefully manage the privatization process to ensure that it is effected in a way calculated to most benefit the elite group of which he is a part. At the same time, the process will leave most of society impoverished and more dependent upon the state bureaucracy than before. Under such conditions, democracy is not possible. Any potential opposition will have been seriously weakened, and the group of elites controlling the presidency is likely to emerge as the undisputed hegemon in the political system. (Figure 4.1 labels this outcome a "hegemonic elite." It essentially constitutes an authoritarian system.) Using its superior power resources, now enhanced by control of the majority of the country's wealth, this segment of the elites will deny any meaningful possibility that an opposition group can either win the presidency or reduce the power of the presidency.

There are of course other possible courses that events might take (as laid out in Figure 4.1) given the existence of a strong presidency, but none of them leads to a consolidated democracy. Should an open privatization process be undertaken, permitting global capital to invest in the country, but the public administration not be reformed, the outcome will be an unstable system in which there is a zero-sum contest for the presidency. While the introduction of global capital permits the emergence of alternative elites contesting for power, the state bureaucracy still intact from the authoritarian regime and under the supervision of the office of the president has substantial resources available to it to attempt to limit the competition. A similar outcome emerges if the bureaucracy is reformed but privatization is controlled. The outcome will be an opposition with little base of support in society. Its only alternative is to work within the state bureaucracy. However, that must be done under the supervision of the president.

The best outcome in the event that a presidential or president-parliamentary system is chosen is if broad-scale privatization and reform of the public administration are both undertaken. An unstable democracy will emerge in which civil society has given emergence to a number of counter-elites. Further, the president's own party has been weakened by the reforms of the state bureaucracy. The result is likely to be a struggle to control the presidency. However, a zero-sum game can be avoided if the president finds himself forced to reduce his powers over time.

The outcomes are considerably more optimistic if either a parliamentary or premier-presidential system has been adopted. The choice of either removes the threat of a zero-sum game in a contest for control over a powerful presidency. For democracy to have a chance of consolidating, privatization and reform of the public administration must be undertaken. These reforms break up the base of support provided to the two or three contesting elite groups that emerge from the transition to democracy. Not only does this weaken each of the contesting parties, it also lays the basis for a more highly fragmented elite in which the calculations involved in political struggle are necessarily more complicated by the larger numbers of contestants. Should these reforms not be undertaken, the system remains unstable, as the potential exists that one side may well calculate that it has more to gain by attempting to defect from the democratic pact.

While privatization and reform of the public administration are necessary, they are not sufficient for achieving a consolidated democracy. For the process to ultimately achieve a stable equilibrium, the number of institutions engaged in the political process must be increased. The fact that there is no powerful presidency in the system has already contributed much to this. However, the addition of an independent judiciary and a set of autonomous local governments will further add to the number of institutions. Should they not be added, the system remains unstable, since power calculations revolve around a relatively limited number of institutions.

Implications

The reader will note that our theory has nothing to say about stateness as a precondition for democratic consolidation. The logic of the theory argues instead that a stateness problem indicates the existence of a political elite that has calculated that it has sufficient strength to eschew compromise. It has been able to mobilize a sufficient portion of the population (in this case based on ethnic or national identity) to give it a reasonable chance to achieve independent statehood. The mobilizing elites would have access to uncontested power in the new state. The chance of their accomplishing this goal is thought to be less than the risk of failure and the ensuing loss of whatever positions they would have been assured had they not sued for their own state. Uncontested power of course brings with it a very high payoff. Therefore the higher the chances of success, or the lower the assured gain from not defecting, the higher the likelihood that the mobilizing elites will sue for independent statehood.

Przeworski has argued elsewhere that granting autonomy to local governments can provide an incentive for the emergence of a stateness problem. In his view, autonomous local governments can provide separatist-minded elites with a base of support.[20] This could well be the case if local government reforms are enacted too early in the democratization process. If however, as I have argued, these reforms are undertaken after privatization and reform of the public administration, they then provide a base of support for merely one more actor in a system. A local elite bent on secession would find it far more difficult to calculate the potential of victory in such circumstances. Further, it is far more likely that society itself, even at the local level, would be far less monolithic following a broad-scale privatization and therefore less susceptible to being mobilized in sufficient numbers for such purposes. Finally, the reform of the public administration would also reduce the incentive (the calculated benefit) to defect. Such a reform would not only provide all elites with an opportunity to obtain a base of support within the government, it would in turn deny any one element of the elites the ability to use the state bureaucracy to deny others the potential to achieve its interests.

In addition to placing the stateness problem in a different context and introducing local government as an important element of democratic consolidation, the theory establishes a logical link between Linz and Stepan's otherwise ad hoc arenas. The first of these arenas, economic society, concerns the rules and institutions that govern the market.[21] In our theory, privatization not only creates the basis for economic society, it breaks up the relatively monolithic society that had backed the counter-elites in the struggle against the former regime. This permits the emergence of divergent interests and gives impetus to a greater number of players to engage in the political process. As the number of players increases, the uncertainty of political outcomes increases.

It is the creation of economic society that gives birth to the second arena, civil society. Civil society comprises the set of private associational activities autonomous from the state within which citizens may choose to participate. They are alternative channels for articulating or even providing for the interests of the general population. They further serve as an intermediary between the state and the private citizen and in so doing reduce the likelihood of state encroachment on the rights of citizens. Participation in the process by citizen groups increases the number of political actors and contributes to uncertainty of outcome.

The remaining three arenas define the institutions of the state. These are the institutions over which the elites contest. Political society provides them with access to policy control, a competent and effective state bureaucracy affords them the ability to actually implement policy,[22] and the rule of law (the judiciary) permits them to enforce it.

Political society includes elections, the party system, and legislative-executive relations. The institutionalization of elections marks the end of the transition to democracy. They will not continue for long if elites have no incentive to continue with them. Therefore, elections are largely the consequence of democracy, not its cause. So too with party systems. Parties are the only vehicle available to elites contesting elections whereby they might mobilize public support. Therefore, they are a natural response in any number of political systems, to include consolidated democracies, unstable democracies, zero-sum struggles over the presidency, and those marked by the presence of a hegemonic elite. However, they, like elections, will not last long if there is no reason for the continuation of electoral contests. It is not parties that create these contests. It is the institutionalization of conditions sustaining a highly divided and competitive elite. As long as this condition continues, parties will continue.

In our theory, the most important element of political society is legislative-executive relations. What is crucial is the design of legislative and executive control over the state bureaucracy (a fourth arena). Systems marked by a strong presidency with direct supervisory powers over the ministries reduce the uncertainty of political outcomes. They further introduce a zero-sum contest for control of the executive. Just as problematic in our theory, however, is an unreformed state bureaucracy. Such a public administration substantially exacerbates the problem of a presidential or premier-presidential system.

Finally, the rule of law is the arena comprising the institutions by which the policy and laws emerging from the institutions of political society are adjudicated and enforced.[23] The judiciary and its associated legal institutions collectively serve to clarify the rules and procedures of both the market[24] and the political system. They perform this role by providing the institutional means to adjudicate differences between political elites as well as a framework within which those same elites can be assured of their own and the opposition's adherence to the established rules and procedures. In essence, they serve as the mechanism for assuring the certainty of the constitution and laws. Further, their involvement increases the uncertainty of outcomes.

Applying the Theory

I have made the claim that the theory developed in this chapter can be applied to draw distinctions between the countries of post-communist

Europe. We are now in a position to demonstrate this. I will do so by comparing how the theory evaluates the progress toward democratic consolidation in two very disparate cases, Russia and Lithuania. In the case of the former, the theory argues that the political system has regressed toward an authoritarian state marked by the hegemony of one elite group. Lithuania, on the other hand, has successfully achieved consolidation. However, as is the case for all consolidated democracies, the equilibrium is nothing more. As with all equilibria, it can be disrupted.

Russia

The collapse of Soviet rule left Russia with an only weakly divided elite. The former ruling elites were terribly weakened as a consequence of the collapse, while the counter-elites, behind whom stood that part of society that had been mobilized, appeared to dominate the presidency, the government, and the legislature. However, within a short period the new ruling elites divided along institutional lines. The Soviet-era constitution provided for an ambiguous relationship between the legislature and executive branch. Ultimate authority over the government was even less clear. This soon became the main political contest over which the new elites divided: Those in the legislature pressing for a parliamentary system, and those in the executive branch led by Boris Yeltsin arguing for a president-parliamentary system.

Yeltsin and his allies quickly won the support of the mobilized public and worked feverishly to assure the support of the bureaucracy. By mid-1993, it was clear they held the upper hand. A public referendum in the spring of that year decided four issues by overwhelming margins in favor of Yeltsin. Further, the government was increasingly siding with the president. Unable to get the legislature to surrender to his demands in a constitutional convention over the summer, Yeltsin forcibly disbanded the assembly in October. A new constitution establishing a president-parliamentary system was established in a December referendum.

Global capital had not participated in what little privatization had been accomplished to this point due to a lack of interest as much as anything else. However, in the large-scale privatization of the country's wealth in the years following the installation of the new political system, foreign capital was explicitly excluded. At the same time, no effort was undertaken to reform the public administration. Together with the president and his administration, the government bureaucracy manipulated the privatization to personal advantage. The wealthy were essentially licensed by the state in exchange for bribes and payoffs. Worse, public assets were sold for a song, "hollowing out the state" and leaving the mass of the population impoverished.

Not surprisingly, Russian civil society remains underdeveloped. In two successive presidential elections (the first in 1996, the second in 2000) political forces behind the incumbent president have successfully used the resources of the state to mobilize Russia's masses. Hence, we can not speak meaningfully of the existence of a competitively divided elite in Russia. As the theory argues, there is no basis for such an elite. The presidency has removed virtually all uncertainty of outcomes in the political system. It is capable of predetermining most political decisions with relatively minimal input from other institutions, to include the legislature and judiciary. (An effort to reform the latter was undertaken following the collapse of the Soviet Union when the Constitutional Court was created. Efforts were also made to create an independent judiciary. However, since the 1993 disbanding of the legislature, the Constitutional Court has been reined in and government supervision of the court system strengthened.)

Nonetheless, some balance to the Yeltsin-led elites in the central government was provided by regionally based elites who managed to use the opportunity provided by local government reforms and the chaos created by the legislative-executive struggle of 1992–1993 to carve out substantial autonomy. Since this occurred in the absence of opportunities provided by open privatization or reform of the public administration, some of these regional elites sued for independence. This was most notably the case in Chechnya. To avoid similar outcomes in other regions, the Yeltsin administration engaged in extra-constitutional deals. At the time of the writing of this book, President Vladimir Putin was moving to eliminate these deals and end the limitations placed on the presidency by the regional governors.

Lithuania

Like Russia, Lithuania found itself independent following the collapse of the Soviet Union in late 1991. Further, both had already engaged in a prolonged transition to democracy during which a counter-elite had emerged to the former ruling elites in the Communist Party. Hence, both had achieved the basic precondition for the beginning of democratic consolidation. However, their paths diverge from this point. While Russia's trajectory has been toward the institutionalization of a hegemonic elite, democracy has consolidated in Lithuania.

Lithuania, like Russia, found itself in a constitutional crisis by 1992. In Lithuania the crisis resulted in a gridlocked legislature. However, unlike Russia, Lithuania made the choice for the introduction of a much weaker president. The counter-elites who had led *Sajudis*, the broad-based popular front, wanted a strong presidency, while the former ruling elites, having reorganized into a social-democratic party (the Democratic Labor Party), supported a parliamentary system. The compromise that was achieved institutionalized a premier-presidential system. The Lithuanian compromise reflected the roughly equal balance of strength between the two elite factions. Unlike Russia, where the Yeltsin faction dominated both civil society and the bureaucracy, in Lithuania, *Sajudis* was already beginning to fragment and the bureaucracy had experienced a significant degree of personnel turnover.

The impetus for some of the weakening of *Sajudis* was related to privatization of agriculture and small business that had occurred by 1992. The sale of land in particular led to the creation of rich and poor farmers, the latter eschewing *Sajudis* and throwing their support behind the former ruling elites. The pace of social differentiation was increased with the privatization of major enterprises from 1993 to 1999. It was given even greater impetus when global capital participated in the auction of some of the country's most lucrative industries. The national telephone and communications company was sold to a Swedish-Finnish consortium, while a major share in the oil industry was purchased by an American firm.

The emerging class system that resulted from privatization was increasingly reflected in the party system. Unlike Russia, where parties have remained relatively weak with no clear class basis, Lithuanian political parties have developed far stronger identities with social groups. The political left has appealed to the working class, peasants, national minorities, and owners of large industries. The political right has its base of support among large farmers, small businessmen, and pensioners. As privatization and social differentiation have continued over the course of the ten years since the collapse of the Soviet Union and the consequent restoration of Lithuanian independence, the number of competitive political parties has increased. This reflects both a weakening of particular groupings of political elites as well as the increase in the number of competitive groupings. The result has been that, increasingly, no one element of the elites has been able to muster enough political resources to calculate that it could deny others the right to contest for power.

In the 1992 elections to the *Seimas*, the national legislature established by the constitution of that same year, the Democratic Labor Party won just short of an absolute majority. A few months later the party's candidate was elected to the newly established presidency. These electoral victories for the political left gave rise to some concern that paramilitary organizations supporting right-wing parties might attempt a coup. The threat quickly passed, however, when all political parties condemned any such efforts. In fact, the political right reasoned that it lacked sufficient public support for a coup. The left for its part was not able to govern without a coalition. Further, the coalition was reduced to less than a majority within two years.

The political right won a stunning victory in the legislative elections of 1996. Nonetheless, as was the case for the left-wing victory of 1992, a two-party coalition was required to form a majority government. Further, the left retained a strong presence, while the center emerged as a significant force in the new legislature. The emergence of the center became even more pronounced with the election of a nonparty moderate to the presidency in 1998.

The 2000 legislative elections provided the greatest evidence of the degree to which the political elite has fragmented. For the first time neither the right-wing remnant of *Sajudis* nor the former ruling elites (now the Democratic Labor Party) were in the governing coalition. The majority coalition comprised four centrist parties spanning the political spectrum from just left of center to just right of center. At the same time, both the left and right had a strong presence in the assembly.

Since 1992, a number of important reforms have been undertaken. The most important were those of the public administration, local government, and the judiciary. The reform of the public administration introduced a civil service system and mandatory training requirements. The civil service system divided positions into two categories. The first comprised those to which political appointments could be made; the second was reserved for career specialists. The introduction of the latter category did much to ensure that personnel changes made under right-wing rule were not overturned. The introduction of training requirements furthered the process of creating a more ideologically diverse and professional civil service. This in turn has weakened the institutionalized base of support in the government for the former ruling elites of the Democratic Labor Party.

Reform of local government introduced competitive elections to cities and regions. The newly elected local governments quickly created a local politics. While local campaigns in the first elections largely reflected national campaign issues, subsequent elections have increasingly been differentiated from national elections. Indeed, local party organization and the voter recognition and appeal of local candidates is a more important determinant of victory in these races than are national trends. This has been reflected in a willingness of local party organizations to challenge the national parties. It is also evident in the efforts of mayors to lobby the central government for resources and laws. All of this suggests that alternative routes to power have been opened up to political elites.

Reform of the judiciary has revolved around establishing the courts as an independent branch of government. While uneven progress has been made, the general trajectory of change has been encouraging. A code of ethics has been introduced, and there has been a substantial turnover in judges. At the same time, the supervisory role of the Ministry of Justice over the courts has been weakened. Most important, the Constitutional Court has assumed a proactive role in the political system in extending human rights. It has also not been afraid to challenge both the president and the legislature.

The result of the reforms of local government and the judiciary has been to further institutionalize uncertainty of political outcome. This has interacted with the fragmentation and consequent weakening of individual elements of the political elite to create an extremely complicated calculation of the costs and benefits of defecting from or playing by the constitutional rules. In effect, there is far greater certainty that the benefits of playing by the rules are greater than are the costs of not doing so. In fact, no segment of the elite has the necessary resources to attempt to rule alone. Further, the introduction of alternative paths to power at the local level, in the public administration, and in the judiciary gives them every incentive not to attempt to do so. Hence, an equilibrium has been reached, and we can speak of democracy as having been consolidated. This does not mean that the equilibrium will be retained indefinitely. However, a major shock will be required to disrupt the current situation.

That being the case, continuing to study a country such as Lithuania from the perspective of the democratic consolidation paradigm makes no sense, unless of course we wish to do historical analyses of how the process occurred. Most political scientists, however, are far more interested in studying the current system. To do so, we will have to engage in research within the boundaries of more appropriate paradigms. Otherwise, we will be forced to treat the countries of post-communist Europe as if they were different cases of essentially the same phenomenon. This is a mistake, as these countries are not similar. However, the solution is not to treat each uniquely. The best approach would seem to be to disaggregate the states of the region into those not democratizing, those still in the throes of democratic transition, and those that are consolidated. The first group should be addressed using tools borrowed from communist and authoritarian studies or in some cases analytical tools used with effect in analyzing similar processes in the third world. The second group should continue to be under the focus of students of democratic consolidation. The third group of states is that on which I will focus in the remaining chapters of this book. We should be asking a different set of questions in these states. Further, we should be asking how these states contribute to our knowledge of processes in other functioning democracies.

In the next chapter I discuss one option, rational choice. While I most certainly would not contend that it is the paradigm of choice for even a majority of political scientists, it is hard to argue that it does not exercise extraordinary influence over the discipline's most prestigious journals, graduate programs, hiring and promotion decisions at its premier universities, and major granting agencies. As such, it offers scholars of post-communist studies an ideal path for aligning the field more closely with political science.

Chapter Five

Imagining Post-Consolidation Studies

Democratic consolidation is no longer an appropriate paradigm for directing research efforts in the set of consolidated democracies of east-central Europe. These states have entered the post-consolidation era. Scholars studying them should be posing similar questions to those in Western, consolidated democracies. We should also be considering how the consolidated democracies of east-central Europe contribute to our knowledge of processes in other functioning democracies. Further, the tools that we use to analyze and the questions we ask should be those used for Western-style liberal democracies. This will permit us to consider how these states contribute to the development of theory. In short, a new paradigm is needed. In this and the following chapter, I demonstrate how rational choice might suggest itself as one possibility.

Rational-choice scholars have focused primarily on the development of deductive theory. They have devoted comparatively less attention to testing the hypotheses derived from their theories in country-specific settings. Most scholars of communist and post-communist studies are uncomfortable with formal theory. However, they excel in testing hypotheses in specific countries of interest to them. Thus, it would seem that opportunities for collaboration (even if only a tacit form of collaboration) are ripe. Until now this was not possible, as rational-choice theories address problems of consolidated democracies. However, given the fact that at least some of the states of post-communist Europe are arguably stable democratic political systems, the door is open to such collaboration.

Fundamentals of Rational Choice

Rational-choice theories begin with the assumption of individual preference. That is, individuals prefer some political outcomes to others. This fundamentally distinguishes rational-choice theories from behav-

Figure 5.1 **Preferred Defense Budget for a Hypothetical Lithuanian Voter**

1.0%	1.5% v*	2.0%

ioral and cultural approaches. The latter focus on group preferences that are premised on historically conditioned sets of norms, attitudes, and behaviors. Rational-choice scholars argue that it is not groups that have preferences, but rather individuals. Further, when individuals take action collectively (that is, as members of groups), the outcome of the action is often not what was intended. Instead, it reflects the interaction of the members' attempts to achieve their personal preferences. We will discuss why this is so in the next chapter, but for now it is important that we understand the attention given to the individual and her choices and preferences by rational-choice theories.

If individuals have preferences, then they prefer some outcomes to others. Hence, all preferences can be ordered from most to least preferred. (One can also be indifferent to a set of outcomes. In this case, the choices involved are treated as a tie.) To illustrate this, let us suppose that Figure 5.1 depicts the preferences of a hypothetical Lithuanian citizen concerning the proportion of the national GDP that should be devoted to the defense budget. She knows that NATO has established 2.0 percent as a target for candidate members. She also knows that the country has had difficulty achieving this goal in the current economic crisis. Indeed, like many of her friends, she is deeply disturbed by the state's inability to provide sufficient funding for education as well as persistent reports of abuse and waste in the "fat" defense budget. At the same time, however, she does not want to seriously endanger the country's security policy. After all, Russia is not very far away! So, she prefers a defense budget consuming a proportion of the GDP equivalent to that at position v*. Given this preference, she can rank order all the alternatives presented her. In Figure 5.1, she would prefer 1.5% to 2.0%, but she would also prefer 2.0% to 1.0%. In both cases the choice she prefers is that closest to her own at v*. She is also indifferent to choices given her that are equidistant from her ideal point. Hence, if v* is 1.6%, then she doesn't care whether the final choice is 1.5% or 1.7%. (They are both 0.1% removed from her ideal point.)

Spatial Analysis

Given these very simple assumptions, we can begin to analyze politics in a democratic society. In essence, the ("spatial") distance of an individual's preference from a menu of alternatives provided by a set of democratic institutions gives us a means for resolving the likely outcome. I will demonstrate the concept by continuing the discussion of our notional Lithuanian citizen. In a direct democracy (or by referendum), she would vote for v^*. However, in the overwhelming majority of cases, she can not vote directly for the policy she wants. Instead, she must vote for a party that most closely adheres to her own policy convictions. In other words, she chooses from among a menu of choices offered her by the political parties in the system.

Figure 5.2 depicts the policy choices on the defense budget offered her by Lithuania's political parties. The parties of the political left—the Social-Democratic Party (SD) and the Democratic Labor Party (DL)—propose devoting percentages close to 1.0 percent of the GDP to defense. This is not surprising, as these two parties are ambivalent about entry into NATO. They argue that Russia is not a security threat and that NATO membership could do further harm to the already depressed economy by disrupting access to the eastern markets (Belarus and Russia). Three parties—from left to right, the New Union (Social Liberals) (NU[SL]), the Center Union (CU), and the Liberal Union (LU)—are clustered around the 1.5 percent mark. They contend that Lithuania must join NATO in order to avoid being left out of the European security architecture and thereby consigned to a gray zone of uncertainty. However, the country must do so in a manner calculated not to harm its long-term economic interests. Those interests demand greater investment in human infrastructure, to include health, education, and an information-technology society. Midway between the parties of the left and center is the Peasants' Party (PP), a party whose members are more focused on gaining access to markets for agricultural goods than they are on security issues. In particular, they wish to maintain eastern agricultural markets in grains while developing western markets for sugar beets and vegetables. On the political right, supporting the 2.0 percent expenditure level, are the two parties most worried about aggressive Russian intentions, the Christian Democratic Party (CD) and the Homeland Union (Conservatives of Lithuania) (HU[CL]). The latter comprises the right-wing remnants of the former *Sajudis* movement that successfully led

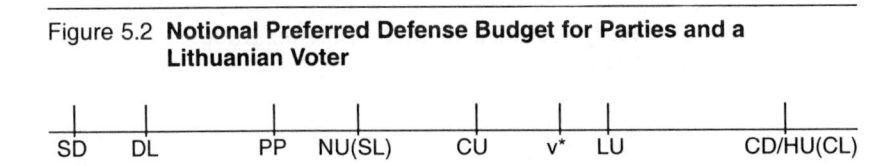

Figure 5.2 **Notional Preferred Defense Budget for Parties and a Lithuanian Voter**

```
|     |      |      |        |     |    |           |
SD    DL     PP   NU(SL)    CU    v*   LU         CD/HU(CL)
```

the country in its drive for independence, which they fear losing. For them, economics is not unimportant, but they are concerned that the country is overly dependent on Russia. This gives Russia leverage in the relationship that it can use to undermine Lithuanian independence. Thus, they support moving West as rapidly as possible. Their strategy involves rapid accession to NATO and the radical de-linking of the country's economy from the East.

Our fictional citizen mulls over her choices on the party-list vote in the October 2000 legislative elections. Given that she has decided that her ideal position is at v*, her party preference ranking in descending order is: LU, CU, NU(SL), CD or HU(CL) (she is indifferent in a choice between the latter two), PP, DL, and SD. These are the parties whose positions are spatially closest to that of her own. Since she gets only one selection on the party-list vote, she will vote for LU, the party closest to her. If she does not, she has violated a second primary assumption of rational-choice theories. That is, individuals make choices based on their preference ranking. Of course, in many instances choices are only indirectly related to preferred policy outcomes. In reality, it is the policy that our notional voter desires. She expects that a vote for LU will result in a defense budget closest to her own ideal. However, he can never be sure. Nonetheless, she makes this vote, despite the uncertainties, given her calculation that it is most likely to achieve her policy preference.

The Median Voter Theorem

We have thus far developed the two fundamental assumptions of all rational-choice theories. First, individuals have preferences for political outcomes that can be ordered. Second, they make choices calculated to achieve the outcome that is closest to their highest order preference. With these fundamentals we can employ spatial analysis to estimate political choices by individuals. The addition of a related concept, the

Figure 5.3 **Notional Party Preferences on the Defense Budget in the *Seimas***

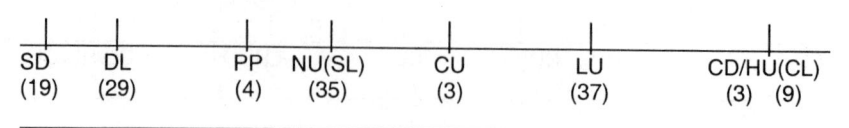

SD	DL	PP	NU(SL)	CU	LU	CD/HU(CL)
(19)	(29)	(4)	(35)	(3)	(37)	(3) (9)

median voter theorem, permits us to extend spatial analysis to consider political outcomes both within and between democratic institutions.

Let us assume that an election has been held and that the parties that we have been discussing so far occupy the number of seats in the national legislature (the *Seimas*) indicated in parentheses below each party in Figure 5.3. Also included in the party's deputy total are deputies who have joined the party faction or are likely to vote with the party on most issues. There are 141 seats in the *Seimas*. The major parties, all of which are included in Figure 5.3, together with their closest political allies, hold 139 seats. For reasons that I will make clear a little later, we need not concern ourselves with the remaining 2 deputies, both of whom are leaders of minor parties that have no political allies in the parliament.

Suppose that a vote is to be taken on the defense budget. (The parties have been placed as before at their position on the issue.) What will be the result? To begin with, while theoretically an infinite number of proposals could be presented to the *Seimas*, this will not happen in this case because Lithuanian parties are relatively disciplined. That is, their members generally adhere to the party position on an issue. Therefore, once the party has decided in its own internal caucus on a position, there is not likely to be a maverick deputy who will propose an alternative to that of the party on the *Seimas* floor. Hence, given that there are eight parties (with their allies), there will be eight discrete proposals. Those proposals are the positions occupied by the parties as indicated in Figure 5.3.

Assuming that each party knows all eight proposals and that the winning proposal will be the proposal that receives a simple majority of votes, which proposal will emerge victorious? The answer is that it will be the proposal supported by the median legislator (voter) in the *Seimas*. (This is the median voter theorem, which was first discovered by Duncan Black.)[1] The reason is straightforward and based on the fundamental assumptions of rational-choice theory, which we previously outlined. Each legislator will prefer that policy outcome that is closest to that of his own party. He will rank order all other preferences based on their distance from this ideal. It is clear that a position at either of the polar extremes can not win unless the party making this proposal has an absolute majority in the legislature. That is because every other party will vote for the proposal immediately adjacent to that of the party at the extreme, since it is closer to their own preferred policy (ideal point). Following this logic, the reader can work through the options to deduce that a central position held by the median voter is the only choice that can defeat all other alternatives. It is preferred by a majority to all other policy proposals.

In our example, that position is occupied by the New Union (Social Democrats) (NU[SL]). In a 141–seat legislature, the median legislator is the 71st deputy. If you begin from the left of the diagram and add the number of legislators in each party until a total of 71 or more is achieved, you will stop at the NS(SL) position. The deputy total here is 87 (19 + 29 + 4 + 35 = 87). If you begin from the right and add going to the left, once again you will stop at the NS(SL) position, the total being 87 (9 + 3 + 37 + 3 + 35 = 87). The Lithuanian *Seimas* will therefore vote to spend less than 1.5 percent of the GDP on defense.

Why can we exclude the two deputies with no allies in the *Seimas?* First, because as it turns out their votes do not matter, as they do not change the location of the median voter. No matter where we place these two deputies, the median voter remains at the NU(SL) position. Further, these two deputies will vote against any proposal. Since they have no legislative allies, they know they can not win on any issue. Consequently, they do not even engage in the process of forming legislative proposals, being effectively excluded from it. In essence, they are relegated to a nonconstructive role.

Legislative Roll-Call Vote Analysis

The foregoing is an example of how spatial analysis can be used to predict voting outcomes in legislatures. If we have the positions of the major legislative factions relative to one another and the number of deputies in each faction, we can not only explain legislative outcomes, we can predict them. Figure 5.4, which depicts the positions of Lithuanian political parties on economic development issues, is an example of how that can be done. The parties are displayed in ascending order from left to right based on the stated predisposition of their candidates in the 1996

90 BEYOND POST-COMMUNIST STUDIES

Figure 5.4 Spatial Illustration of Party Preferences on Economic Issues

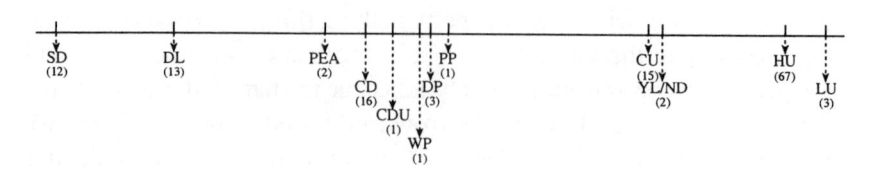

```
  ↓         ↓          ↓          ↓             ↓          ↓
  SD        DL         PEA        PP            CU         HU
 (12)      (13)        (2)       ↓(1)          (15)↓      (67)    ↓
                                 CD    ↓DP     YL/ND              LU
                                (16) ↓ (3)      (2)               (3)
                                 CDU
                                 (1) ↓
                                     WP
                                     (1)
```

CD—Christian Democratic Union
CDU—Christian Democratic Union
CU—Center Union
DL—Democratic Labor Party
DP—Democratic Party
HU—Homeland Union (Conservatives of Lithuania)
LU—Liberal Union
PEA—Polish Electoral Action
PP—Peasants Party
SD—Social-Democratic Party
WP—Women's Party
YL/ND—"Young Lithuania" and National Democratic Party

legislative contest favoring market responses to economic growth. (That is, the parties are placed in spatial position to each other.) The parties whose candidates least favored market approaches were the Social-Democratic Party (SD) and the Democratic Labor Party (DL). The Liberal Union (LU), Homeland Union (HU), Center Union (CU), Young Lithuania (YL), and the National Democratic Party (ND) most favored market solutions. More centrist in their economic orientation were the Christian Democratic Party (CD), the Christian Democratic Union (CDU), the Peasants' Party (PP), the Women's Party (WP), Polish Electoral Action (PEA), and the Democratic Party (DP). The number of deputies in the unicameral *Seimas* from each of these parties is shown in parentheses under the initials of the party. The parties depicted at Figure 5.4 account for 136 of the deputies in the legislature. An additional three were independents, who seldom voted. When they did, they either abstained or voted against a proposed bill. Two seats were vacant, as successive elections failed to achieve the 40 percent turnout required to validate an election result according to Lithuanian law.

Table 5.1

Seimas Roll-Call Vote Outcomes on Economic Bills, 1997

		Vote Outcome		
Date of Vote	Issue	For	Against	Abstain/Absent
25 Feb 1997	Funding for Butinga Oil Terminal	59	43	37
27 Mar 1997	Privatization of Two State Banks	47	32	60
3 Apr 1997	Enterprise Law	58	39	42
3 Apr 1997	State Assets to Be Privatized after 2000	60	35	44
17 June 1997	Enterprise Bankruptcy Law	60	25	54
2 July 1997	Further Funding for Butinga Oil Terminal	65	26	48

Source: Chancellor of the *Seimas* of the Republic of Lithuania.

Unless a bill involves a change to the Lithuanian Constitution, a simple majority of those voting is sufficient, assuming of course that there is a quorum present. (A quorum requires one-half of the 139 deputies, or 70 deputies.) This means that passage requires the votes of 35 deputies. However, certainty that the bill will pass can only be assured if party factions supporting the bill can muster 70 votes. Hence the position of the median voter (*Seimas* legislator) on any bill is decisive. In the case of the 1996 *Seimas* depicted at Figure 5.4, the median voter (calculated in either direction) is a member of the Homeland Union (Conservatives of Lithuania) (HU). Hence, we can predict that any bill related to economic growth or development that is supported by the Homeland Union will be passed by the *Seimas*.

There was some doubt expressed immediately following the 1996 legislative elections that the Conservatives would be able to pass their economic agenda. This was particularly the case because the party fell short of an absolute majority. Its actual operating strength was further reduced when several of its members took positions in the government. (Lithuanian law permits members of the government to retain their seats in the parliament; however, in practical terms they can only take the time to vote on the most urgent of bills.) Even more important, observers pointed to the policy differences on economic issues between the Conservatives and their coalition partners, the Christian Democratic Party (CD). (The reader can see the policy distance between the two in Figure 5.4.) Despite these concerns, the Homeland Union was able to pass its entire economic package. Table 5.1 lists the major economic bills considered by the *Seimas* during its first session in 1997. In keeping with our prediction in the previous paragraph, all easily mustered the necessary plurality.

Legislative Committee Systems

The foregoing example of spatial analysis focused quite a bit on rules such as quorums, plurality vote requirements, and the like. Legislatures conduct their business by rules. Indeed, all institutions do so. The rules constrain the behavior of participants. If politicians wish to emerge victorious in policy disputes, then short of resorting to armed force (which in democratic systems is tantamount to defecting from the democratic agreement), they must use the rules to advantage. One of the most understudied set of rules in post-communist states concerns those regulating committee systems in legislatures. Committees invested with a gatekeeping role (exercising a veto over legislation within its jurisdiction) have important implications for legislative outcomes. Spatial analysis can be used to demonstrate this.

We begin with the spatial diagrams at Figure 5.5. Suppose that the legislature is operating under a closed rule. That is, no bill submitted to the floor by a committee can be amended. Let us further suppose that the median voter in the assembly has a preference on a given bill denoted by "C" in diagram (1). The median legislator in the committee having jurisdiction over the issue with which the bill deals, however, has preference "c*." The current policy, which any new legislation is intended to modify, is denoted as "SQ" (status quo). Given these conditions, the committee will not report the bill ("open the gate") that it favors to the floor of the parent chamber, as doing so will only result in its being defeated. The legislative majority will prefer the status quo (which is closer to the majority's position than the committee bill). On the other hand, if the positions of the respective preferences (and status quo bill) are those shown in either (2) or (3), the committee will report its bill (c*) to the parent chamber. In both cases, a legislative majority will support c* because it is closer to the preference of the median voter in the assembly than the status quo.

While the U.S. Congress often operates under a closed rule, very few committee systems in Europe do. The exception is when the government is constitutionally empowered to submit a bill to the legislature with the proviso that it can not be amended. In such an instance, the

Figure 5.5 **Spatial Comparisons of a Status Quo Bill (SQ) with the Policy Preferences of a Committee (c*) and the Parent Legislature (C)**

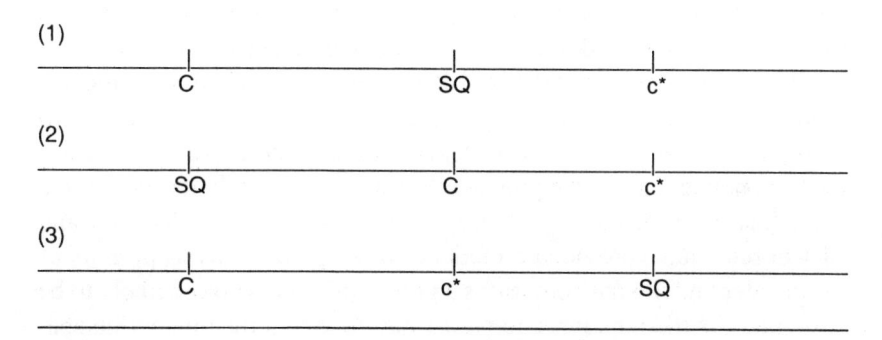

(1)
```
———————|————————————|————————————|———————
        C            SQ           c*
```

(2)
```
———————|————————————|————————————|———————
       SQ            C            c*
```

(3)
```
———————|————————————|————————————|———————
        C            c*           SQ
```

government can be treated like a committee and one can judge the policy outcome in much the same fashion as in the foregoing analysis. More often, however, European parliaments operate under an open rule or some modification thereof. An open rule simply means that once a committee reports a bill to the parent assembly, any number of amendments or alternative bills can be offered. However, the committee still acts as the gatekeeper. If the committee does not report a bill, no bill can be offered and the status quo bill remains in force.

The open rule still gives the committee substantial power over legislation. To see this, let us once again consider the three possibilities in Figure 5.5. Given the situation depicted in diagram (1), the committee will not report the bill to the floor. Were it to do so, the chamber would ultimately settle on a policy at position "C." Since "C" is further from the committee's preferred policy "c*" than is the status quo bill "SQ," the committee will keep the gate closed and settle for the status quo. By the same logic, the committee will report the bill given situation (2). So far, the committee would do the same thing whether the rule is open or closed. The only difference is that in the case of (2) it will gain outcome "C" instead of "c*." However, if the situation is that defined by (3), the committee under an open rule will not report a bill. That is because the resulting bill "C" is further from its preferred position than is the status quo. (The reader will recall that under the closed rule, the committee would report the bill, because it would obtain its preferred bill "c*.")

Relations with a President

Premier-presidential systems have a split executive. The head of government, the prime minister, must have the confidence of parliament to rule. On the other hand, the head of state, the president, is elected to a fixed term by popular vote. The role in premier-presidential systems is more than ceremonial. Most presidents in such systems exercise two prerogatives: the power to veto legislation and the power of appointment. In neither case is the president's power absolute. In the case of the veto, for instance, the legislature can vote to over-ride. Kiewiet and McCubbins[2] have provided a model of how spatial analysis permits us to consider under what conditions a president's veto is more likely to be sustained. As their analysis demonstrates, to model the interaction spatially we must understand the rules of the game that apply in the relationship between the president and the assembly.

Presidential Vetoes

In the Lithuanian political system, legislation passed by the *Seimas* requires a simple majority of a quorum (no fewer than 35 deputies). If the president vetoes legislation, the *Seimas* can only over-ride the veto by an absolute majority of the deputies (71 votes). If the assembly fails to over-ride the presidential veto, then the status quo situation remains in force. Figure 5.6 depicts four different circumstances. In the first (1), the legislature presents the president with a bill (L) that is closer to his preference (P) than the status quo situation (SQ). In this case, the president will sign the bill. The policy positions reflected here also demonstrate that the mere existence of a substantial policy distance between the president and the legislature does not always necessarily result in conflict. The president will also sign the bill under the circumstances depicted by diagram (2). Despite the fact that the bill calls for a radical change in policy, the outcome will nonetheless be closer to the president's preferred position. What both of these otherwise quite different situations have in common is that the bill preferred (and passed) by the legislature reduces the policy distance between that of the president's preference and the policy in place. In fact, the president will sign any bill the legislature presents that effectively does this. However, if the legislative bill increases the policy distance, the president will exercise the veto. This means that the president can use the veto to try to move policy closer to his ideal preference.

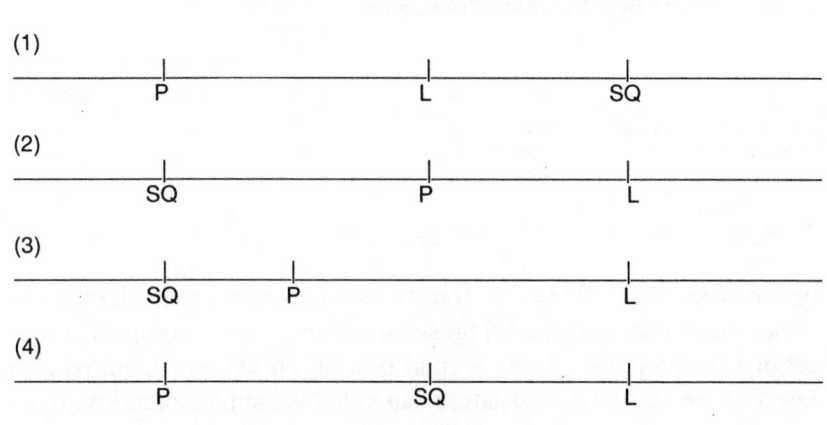

Figure 5.6 **Spatial Comparisons of the Status Quo (SQ) with the Policy Preferences of the *Seimas* (L) and the President (P)**

(1)
```
―――――|―――――――――|―――――――|―――――
      P           L         SQ
```

(2)
```
―――――|―――――――――|―――――――|―――――
     SQ           P         L
```

(3)
```
―――――|―――|―――――――――――――――|―――――
     SQ   P                 L
```

(4)
```
―――――|―――――――――|―――――――|―――――
      P          SQ        L
```

Despite this, the Lithuanian presidential veto is not as powerful a tool as it might seem. While a mere plurality vote suffices to pass legislation, the logic of the median voter theorem dictates that legislation reflect the preference of the median legislator to be assured of passage. If it does not, then a determined opposition can muster the votes necessary to defeat it. The practical implication of this is that any piece of legislation making its way to the president can at least theoretically be passed by a legislative majority over a presidential veto.

Nonetheless, presidential vetoes have been sustained. Indeed, the effort to over-ride the presidential veto is a politically costly one that can potentially undermine the legislature's support (and consequently that of the government) with the public. However, if the political stakes surrounding a particular policy are high enough, a determined legislature will over-ride a presidential veto. Such is likely to be the case when the policy distance between the president and legislature is greater. Under such circumstances, the probability increases that the assembly will over-ride a presidential veto. Hence, the veto in situation (3) at Figure 5.6 is more likely to be sustained than that in situation (4).

The *Seimas* is also more likely to over-ride a presidential veto when there is a condition of sustained conflict between the two institutions. In effect, political conflict between the president and legislature over a period of time magnifies the perception of the policy distance between the two. Table 5.2 lists the number of vetoes exercised by Lithuania's

Table 5.2

Use of the Veto by Lithuanian Presidents

President	Time Period	Veto	Proposed Amendments Number	Adopted
Algirdas Brazauskas	1993–1996	22	83	68
Algirdas Brazauskas	1996–1998	9	22	2
Valdas Adamkus	1998–2000	9	19	18

Source: Chancellory of the President of the Republic of Lithuania.

two presidents over three time frames. What is instructive is the success of proposed amendments. All presidential vetoes are accompanied by a set of such proposals. In its second hearing on the bill (required as a result of the veto), the legislature can vote by a simple plurality to accept the president's proposals. If it refuses them, it then must pass the initial bill by an absolute majority. Using legislative acceptance of proposed amendments attending a veto, President Brazauskas, during his first years in office, and President Adamkus were quite successful in their use of the veto. Both were able to use it to move legislation closer to their preference. President Brazauskas was not at all successful during the latter part of his term, a period in which he was faced with a hostile legislative majority.

Presidential Appointments

The second power of presidents in premier-presidential systems is that of appointment. Similar to the veto, appointments can create the potential for conflict with the legislature. Presidential appointments require the confirmation of the assembly. A simple plurality usually suffices. As we argued previously, the practical implication of this requirement is that the preference of the median legislator will determine the fate of the appointment. The game is much the same as that depicted for the veto in Figure 5.6, except in this case the players have switched roles. The president has initiated the process with a proposal that the assembly must decide whether to essentially veto. If it does so, the status quo continues. That is, the current official remains in place (or a deputy) until a subsequent candidate is nominated and confirmed.

The legislature wants a presidential nomination (P) as close as, or closer than, the current appointee (SQ) to its preferred position (L). This condition is met by diagrams (2) and (3). In these cases, the presidential nominee will be confirmed. Situations (1) and (4), however, signal the likelihood of a troubled confirmation process. The further removed the candidate is from both the legislature and the current appointee, the less likely it is that he will be confirmed. While Lithuanian presidents have generally avoided confrontations with the *Seimas* over appointments, a very serious one occurred in early 1999. President Adamkus appointed Kestutis Lapinskas as state controller, replacing an appointee who was closely associated with the legislative leadership. The state controller is responsible for monitoring the government's financial activities. The president had expressed concerns about the lack of transparency in those activities, which had resulted in an inability to properly account for large sums of money involved in energy sales to neighboring Belarus. To rectify the problem, he nominated Lapinskas, a highly experienced financial expert from a party not in the governing coalition. The nomination created an uproar in both the government and the *Seimas*. When his nomination was rejected, the president nominated Lapinskas yet a second time to no avail.

The Courts as Political Players

While we do not often think of them as such, courts are political players as well. This is particularly so when they are constitutionally entrusted with the power of judicial review. In post-communist systems this power is given to a special constitutional court. The court reviews legislation and the acts of government to determine if they violate constitutional norms and standards. In most systems, a case must be referred to the constitutional court. That is, the court can not simply hear a case on its own initiative. In practice, the distinction is not a very great one, since there are a significant number of actors who have the right to refer a case to the court.

Spatial analysis can be used to analyze the constitutional court's exercise of its prerogatives. By treating the court in this fashion, we are assuming that it, like any other political actor, has policy preferences that it wishes to have implemented.[3] Decisions of the court itself can be determined using the median voter theorem, assuming of course one has the policy positions of the justices on a given issue. (This information is normally constitutionally or statutorily prohibited from being made public in order to protect the image of the court as a neutral ref-

98 BEYOND POST-COMMUNIST STUDIES

Figure 5.7 **Spatial Comparisons of the Policy Preferences of the *Seimas* (L), the President (P), and the Constitutional Court (CC)**

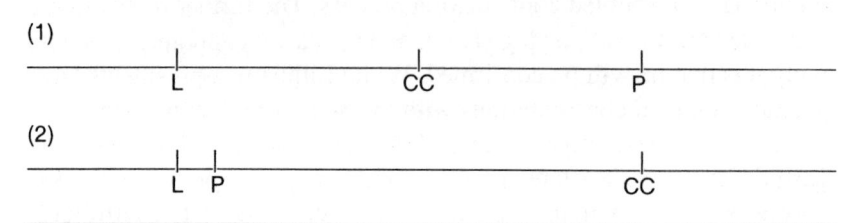

(1)
```
        |                    |              |
        L                   CC              P
```

(2)
```
        | |                                 |
        L P                                 CC
```

eree in the political process.) The court's decision will be the policy preference of the median justice.[4]

Figure 5.7 depicts two political situations in which the Lithuanian Constitutional Court has found itself. Diagram (1) occurred with the inauguration of President Adamkus in early 1998. The new president wanted the power to appoint the prime minister. The constitution was unclear on whether he had the authority to do so. It is not certain if Adamkus intended on nominating a prime minister other than the sitting head of government, but he referred the case to the Constitutional Court, arguing that a president upon assuming office has the constitutional prerogative to nominate anyone whom he wishes to the position (P). The legislature wanted to keep the existing government in place (L) and argued that the constitution does not give the president the right to nominate the head of a new government. The Constitutional Court (CC) staked out a middle position between the two and ruled that the sitting government had to submit its resignation upon a new president's taking the oath of office; however, the president was constitutionally obligated to nominate the current prime minister. The division between the two branches gave the Constitutional Court the opportunity to take a middle position between them.

In fact any substantial degree of policy disagreement between the president and the *Seimas* permits the Constitutional Court to resolve the outcome between the two. Rational-choice theories argue that it will take a position moving policy closest to that of its own preference. However, it can not successfully render a decision that would move the policy outside a range established by the other two institutions. Such a situation is depicted in diagram (2) in Figure 5.7. This situation occurred in 1999–2000. The country was in the throes of a major economic recession. With the intent of sharing the costs of budget cuts as well as demonstrating to the public that state institutions would suffer from the economic woes along with the rest of the country, the *Seimas*, at the urging of the government, passed an act reducing the salaries of judges (L). The effort had the support of the president, although he was willing to accept a somewhat lower decrease (P). Judges affected by the decreases referred the matter to the Constitutional Court, arguing that the salary cuts threatened to undermine the autonomy of the courts as well the financial independence of judges (creating the potential for bribery and corruption). The Constitutional Court issued a nonbinding opinion calling for the reinstatement of the higher levels of remuneration. The government responded that it would not do so, and that it would ignore any court decisions requiring it to do so. This is a situation the Constitutional Court can not win. If it rules against the legislature and requires the reinstatement of judges' salaries to their previous levels, the *Seimas* can change the constitution with a three-fifths vote of the assembly (85 deputies). Since the president is in essential agreement with the legislature on the issue, he will not veto the amendment. Therefore, any attempt to render such a decision will have the likely effect of demonstrating the court's relative weakness vis-à-vis the other branches and undermining its legitimacy.

Analysis of the Party System

Spatial analysis can also be applied to the analysis of party systems to permit us to consider the dynamic of change. We will demonstrate this by looking at what happened to the Center Union in the fall 2000 legislative elections in Lithuania. The overall election results came as no great surprise. However, on the basis of the local elections held in spring of the same year, most observers had expected the Center Union would do substantially better.[5] The Center Union placed fourth in both the number of local deputies with 10.6 percent and mayors with 13.3 percent of the total. But in the elections to the *Seimas* the party won only two mandates (1.4 percent of the total). Spatial analysis demonstrates that the party's efforts to reposition itself in the political spectrum in the face of a shifting electorate ended in an electoral disaster in the elections to the *Seimas*.

Anthony Downs first argued that political parties, in search of electoral victory, position themselves on issues in such a way as to best maximize their electoral strength.[6] Figure 5.8 demonstrates the basic argument. We will let the x-axis represent the continuum of positions on

Figure 5.8 **A Notional Party System**

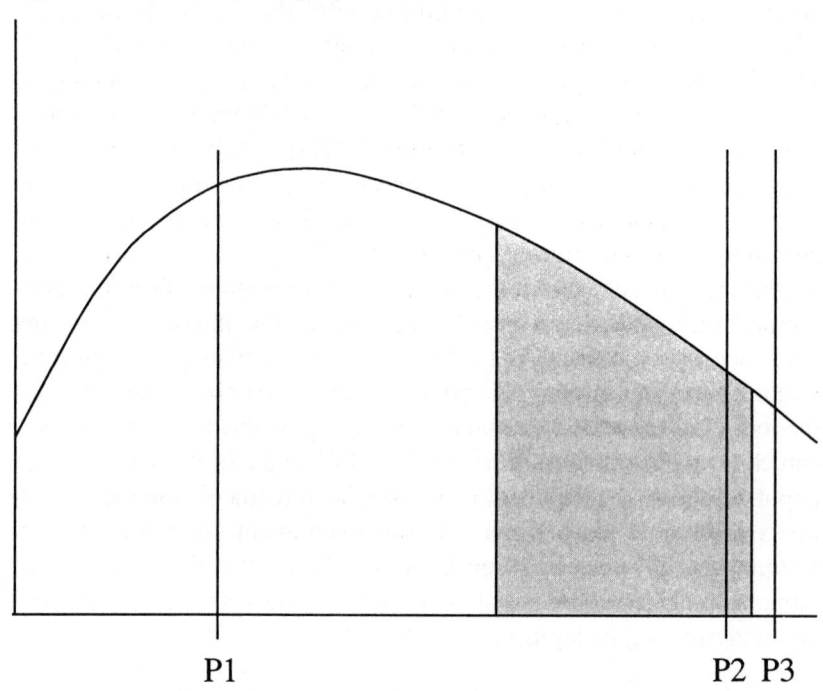

[Figure: A curve over a horizontal axis with three marked positions P1, P2, and P3. P1 is left of center, P2 and P3 are on the right. A shaded region extends from midway between P1 and P2 to midway between P2 and P3.]

          P1   P2 P3

the left–right political spectrum (or the continuum of positions regarding any political issue). If the y-axis is a scale from 1 to 100 percent, the curve represents the distribution of voters across the left–right political spectrum. If we draw two lines, one perpendicular to the y-axis and a second perpendicular to the x-axis, the point at which the first intersects the y-axis is the proportion of the population that identifies itself at the point of the left–right political spectrum at which the second line intersects the x-axis. Let points P1, P2, and P3 represent the positions on the left–right spectrum occupied by each of three political parties. Since voters are rational, they will vote for the party closest to their own position. The hatched area therefore indicates the proportion of the electorate that will vote for party P2. Party P2 will receive all of the votes from its own ideal position to the position midway between it and party P3 to its right and party P1 on its left. Party P3, on the other hand, gets all the votes to its right, since there is no party with which it need concern itself in that direction. However, its electoral potential is limited to its left by the positioning of party P2.

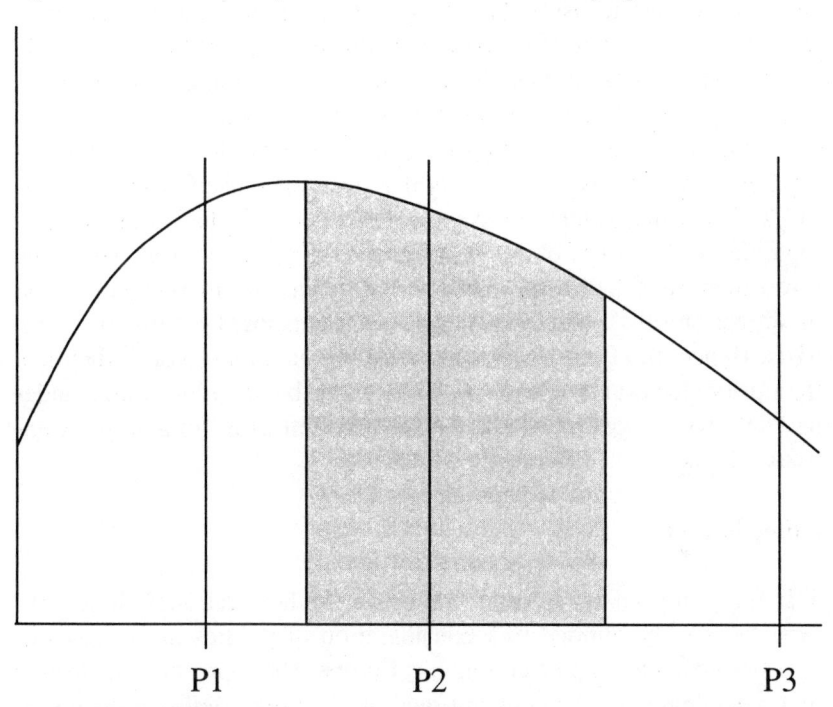

Figure 5.9 **Effect of Party Shifts on the Notional Party System**

P1   P2   P3

To gain a greater proportion of the vote, party P2's best strategy is to reposition itself to the left. Figure 5.9 demonstrates that, in so doing, it increases the total area under the curve (and hence the total percentage of the population that will vote for the party) on both its right and left. In fact, its optimal strategy is to locate itself just to the right of party P1. By so doing, it positions itself to gain the vote of the largest mass of voters. However, in following such a strategy, party P2 incurs two serious risks. First, the farther left it moves, the larger the area it opens up to another party to enter. In fact, the farther left it moves, the more likely this is to happen because the area it vacates becomes increasingly appealing for others to occupy. Second, as Downs takes care to point out, the farther the distance that a party moves, the less voters will trust it. After all, it has left behind a very large number of voters in order to attempt to appeal to a set of voters in which it has hitherto shown little or no interest. In short, voters expect a certain degree of programmatic consistency from political parties. Those that violate this principle are likely to incur the voters' wrath.

This is, in fact, what happened to the Center Union. Hoping to take advantage of public dissatisfaction with the economy, the party began to reposition itself in late 1999. As part of this effort it left the government and formally declared itself in opposition to the ruling Conservative-Christian Democratic coalition. However, the party moved too far from its previous electoral base. Further, it had moved quite close to the Social Liberals, a relatively new party that positioned itself just to the right of P1. Given that voters in this part of the electorate had come to view the Centrists as a party of the right (indeed the party had been part of the government and had been instrumental in passing marketization and privatization bills), they were not at all predisposed to trust the Centrists. Hence, the Centrists not only did not gain these votes, they lost their prior electoral base to a new party, the Liberal Union, which under new leadership positioned itself just to the left of P3 to gain the Centrists' voters.

Rules Matter

The foregoing analyses have demonstrated how rational-choice approaches can be applied to a consideration of politics in the consolidated democracies of post-communist Europe. The approaches all depend to a great degree on the constitutional or legal rules defining the political process. Changing these rules often has the effect of changing the political outcome. This, in fact, is the basis of research focusing on electoral laws.[7] The effect of different electoral rules can be illustrated by a change to the electoral law made just prior to the fall 2000 *Seimas* elections.

In the same way as the 450-member lower house of the Russian Federal Assembly (the *State Duma*), the 141 deputies to the unicameral *Seimas* are elected on the basis of two separate and distinct electoral laws. Seventy seats in the *Seimas* are determined on the basis of a party list vote in which voters cast their ballot for a political party. Seats are then allotted in a manner roughly proportional to the vote that each party receives in the nationwide vote. The seats are filled by the parties from a list of party loyalists in the order in which they appear on the list. (This method of awarding seats is referred to as proportional representation.) The allotment is only roughly proportional, as a party must receive 5 percent of the total votes cast in order to be awarded any seats. Depending on the percentage of the electorate that votes for parties not

Table 5.3

Comparison of Election Results Based on Plurality and Majority Rules in the *Seimas* Single-Mandate District Races, 2000

Political Party	Party-List Seats	Plurality Rule District Seats	Total Seats	Majority Rule District Seats	Total Seats
Liberal Union	16	18	34	17	33
New Union (Social Liberals)	18	11	29	23	41
Center Union	0	2	2	4	4
Democratic Labor Party	12	14	26	9	21
Social-Democratic Party	12	7	19	4	16
Homeland Union (Conservatives)	8	1	9	0	8
Christian Democratic Party	0	2	2	1	1
Peasants Party	0	4	4	5	5
Others	4	12	16	8	12
Total	70	71	141	71	141

achieving this threshold, the victorious parties are likely to be awarded proportionally more seats than the actual percent of the vote they receive.

The remaining 71 seats are elected in plurality, single-mandate races. The country is divided into 71 districts of roughly equal population. One *Seimas* deputy is elected from each district. The law determining the winner in these districts was changed in summer 2000. According to the previous electoral law, the winner was that individual who received an absolute majority (more than 50 percent) of the votes cast. (Lithuanian law requires that 40 percent of the registered voters participate for the election to be declared valid.) If no candidate achieved a majority in the first round, a second round pitted the two top vote-getters. This is referred to as a majority, single-mandate district system.

In the summer of 2000, a new law changed the single-mandate district races from majority to plurality contests, the winner being that candidate receiving the most votes in the first round. (No majority is required.) Table 5.3 juxtaposes the election results based on plurality rules with those based on majority rules in the single-mandate districts. The two parties most affected by the rule change were the Social Liberals and the Democratic Labor Party. The Social Liberals would have won significantly more seats and the Democratic Labor Party fewer seats under the previous majority rules. Rules matter!

Principal-Agent Problems

Committee Systems

Our previous discussion of committees demonstrated that they are important in determining legislative outcomes, but so are the rules determining their relationship to the parent assembly. Committees are particularly powerful if they exercise the authority of a gatekeeper. They decide whether any bill will even be considered. This introduces the potential for what is known as a principal-agent problem. Principal-agent problems emerge when an institution created to perform a specific function (the agent, in this case the committees) by a parent institution (the principal, in this case the legislature) shirks its responsibilities, engages in activities not authorized by the parent institution, or usurps the role of the parent institution. We discussed these problems earlier in chapter three.

It is not always the case that committees are invested by the parent legislature with a gatekeeping role. Indeed, it is easy to understand why parliamentary leaders would be loath to surrender such powers to committee chairs. However, if they could institutionalize procedures to deal with the possibility of a maverick committee, they might well have the incentive to do just that. After all, strong committees with veto power over legislation properly controlled by the assembly leader could become a very useful weapon in ensuring that the opposition is not able to seize the legislative initiative.

This is precisely the purpose that the institutional design of committee-assembly relations serves in the Lithuanian *Seimas*, where the procedures in place argue that the legislative leadership has delegated responsibilities to committees without abdicating control of policy. Hence, the principal-agent problem created by the introduction of a committee system is overcome.

Any *Seimas* deputy may submit a bill for consideration. However, the bill must first go through the committee system. The *Sueiga* (Assembly of Spokespersons) is responsible for assigning draft bills to a committee. The *Sueiga* is dominated by the majority coalition and comprises the chair, the chancellor (the chief administrator, who is a deputy elected to the position), the three deputy chairs (two from the majority and one from the opposition), and representatives from each faction, the exact number of which are based on the size of the faction. From 1996 to 1997, fifteen members were from the parties of the ruling coalition and seven were from the remaining parties. If a committee votes in favor of a legislative proposal, the *Sueiga* schedules it for a hearing and vote on the *Seimas* floor. If the committee votes against it, the *Sueiga* will not schedule a vote on the bill.

These procedural rules permit the chair (the majority coalition leader) to use the *Sueiga* to control the flow of legislation. As long as committees vote in the way that the leadership desires, only that legislation that the majority coalition supports can make it to an assembly vote. Hence, appointments to committees (particularly to the position of chair) are important. Of course, there is still the danger that chairs might use their positions to attempt to establish an alternative base of power. To guard against this, the *Seimas* leadership has a number of tools. The *Sueiga* has the option of sending the bill for consideration to another committee. It may also schedule the bill for a *Seimas* vote despite the committee decision. Further, if an absolute majority of the *Seimas* votes to discharge the bill from the committee or the *Sueiga*, the bill must come to a vote in the assembly. Taken together, these procedures deny the committees an absolute veto over legislation. Further, given the majority's control of both the *Sueiga* and *Seimas*, they provide the chair of the *Seimas* with the means to keep committees in line.

Legislative Oversight

Legislatures face principal-agent problems with bureaucratic agencies of the executive branch as well. Having created and funded these agencies, the legislature is faced with the challenge of assuring that they do not pursue their own independent interests. The problem is depicted in the diagrams in Figure 5.10. In diagram (1), the policy preference between the legislature (the ideal point of the median legislature indicated by "L") and an administrative agency "B" are quite similar. In diagram (2), they are conflicting. Diagram (2) represents a situation in which an agency would have an incentive to attempt to use its control over information (asymmetrical information advantage) in order deceive the legislature concerning its activities, shirk the responsibilities given it by the legislature, or pursue its own agenda in opposition to that of the assembly. The legislative response is to tighten controls on the agency.

Under what situations are the conditions in diagram (2) likely to

Figure 5.10 **Spatial Comparisons of the Ideal Points of a Bureaucratic Agency (B) and the Median Voter in the Legislature (L)**

(1)

```
        |   |
        L   B
```

(2)

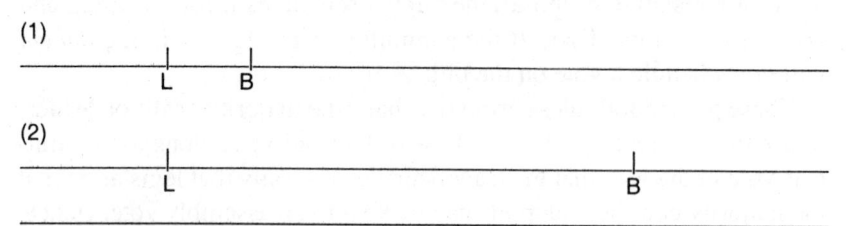

```
        |                              |
        L                              B
```

emerge in post-communist European systems? There are two possibilities.[8] The first concerns the nature of the government's legislative support. A government backed by a single party in the legislature (whether a majority or minority) is one in which all ministerial positions (portfolios) are held by members of the party. In such conditions there is not likely to be any serious conflict with the ministries. Hence, the ministries will be given a considerable degree of freedom of movement. If, however, the government is backed by a legislative coalition, the portfolios will likely be divided between the members of the coalition. This will lead in turn to a greater likelihood of a policy disagreement between each ministry and the coalition partners not allotted the ministry. In this case, the legislature is more likely to rein in the ministries.

A second circumstance under which legislatures are more likely to exercise tighter control over the ministries is low cabinet durability. When there is a relatively frequent degree of turnover of the cabinet heads resulting from fairly frequent changes of government, the career bureaucrats will have an incentive to attempt to gain greater independence. The legislative response is to tighten controls on the government.

It is this latter condition that pertains to Lithuania. Public administrators in the central ministries are given very little power of discretion. Almost all decisions must be approved by a political appointee at the highest level of the agency. This represents a significant burden for the politicians. Indeed, the burden is so heavy that it precludes them from engaging in strategic planning, a very serious shortcoming noted by most observers of Lithuanian government.[9] Nonetheless, it is a burden that party leaders insist on shouldering, given low cabinet durability. (From 1992 to 2000 Lithuania had seven governments.)

Implications

This chapter has most certainly not exhausted the possibilities for studying the newly consolidated democracies of what was communist Europe. (For example, we did not consider the game that results in bicameral legislatures.) Indeed, one could not hope to do so. My aim was far less ambitious: to demonstrate the potential agenda offered by rational-choice theories. The approaches considered in this chapter, however, are united by more than a common theoretical thread. Collectively, they are all part of what has come to be known in the literature as the new institutionalism. The new institutionalism focuses on the sets of constitutional and legal rules under which political institutions operate. Its research agenda is bounded by the analysis of these rules in order to explain the range of probable political outcomes that emerge from the game that they define. While there have been a number of studies of post-communist systems that have used new institutionalist approaches, they have generally done so within the confines of democratic consolidation. I have endeavored in this chapter to demonstrate that a more explicitly rational-choice framework offers greater coherence to their employment.

In the next chapter, I will further elaborate on the potential research agenda that rational-choice theories offer for studying stable democracies of post-communist Europe. The approaches considered will focus on the potential for chaos in political systems. Institutions play a fundamental role in reducing the problem of chaos. Without them, political decisions would not be possible and humans would be unable to govern their affairs.

Chapter Six

Further Extending the Post-Consolidation Agenda

The institutions discussed in the previous chapter function to reduce the number of policy options. In most cases they leave political actors with only two choices. For instance, a committee system operating under a closed rule gives the parent legislature a choice of either the committee's proposal or the status quo. Similarly, exercise of the veto or the presidential power of appointment leaves the assembly with a choice between the presidential or legislative preference. When there are only two choices between which political actors may select, a majority will clearly emerge around one. In this chapter we consider rational-choice approaches for studying political situations in which there are more than two options and no majority forms around any one of them. As in the previous chapter, institutions remain fundamental to these rational-choice approaches.

The Majority Cycling Problem

Rational-choice theories start with the assumption of individual preferences that can be rank ordered. The rank orderings of individual preferences are transitive. This characteristic can be best demonstrated with the following example. Let us suppose that a voter's party preference in the party list vote in the fall 2000 elections to the Lithuanian *Seimas* was Liberal Union (LU), Center Union (CU), and Social Liberals (SL) in that order. In other words, he preferred the Liberal Union to the Center Union and the Center Union to the Social Liberals. Mathematically we can express his preferences as follows.

$$LU > CU \qquad [1]$$
$$CU > SL \qquad [2]$$

Given this preference ordering, then it logically follows from the principle of transitivity that this person prefers the Liberal Union to the

Social Liberals (equation [3]). We would conclude that he is irrational if he preferred SL to LU.

$$LU > SL \quad [3]$$

Elections are determined on the basis of more than one voter's preferences. We expect that each voter will have transitive preference orderings. Table 6.1 shows the preferences for three such voters. The reader can check for himself that each preference ordering is indeed transitive. What is interesting, however, is the collective preference ordering of the group. Collectively, as Table 6.2 depicts, they prefer the Liberal Union to the Center Union (equation [1] above), the Center Union to the Social Liberals (equation [2]), but, paradoxically, the Social Liberals to the Liberal Union (the opposite inequality to that in equation [3]). The transitive preference orderings of the individuals in the group result in an intransitive collective preference ordering!

Were the election to be decided on the basis of the most preferred party among these three individuals, no decision could be reached, for the simple reason that there is no one party most preferred by the group. In fact, the voting would go on endlessly. At the end of each paired contest, someone could call for a follow-on contest with the winner, which would most certainly end with the defeat of that winner. Looking at the results of the group preference listed at the bottom of Table 6.2, the reader can see that should the Liberal Union be declared the winner, all one need do is call for a contest with the Social Liberals. Following the victory of the Social Liberals, the loser could call for a contest with the Center Union. And so it would go on endlessly. This is what is known as a majority cycling problem.

The problem exists when a large number of individuals with a wide range of preferences must decide collectively on a single outcome. The solution to the problem, discovered by Kenneth Arrow, is a "dictator" with the power to artificially impose an end to the decision process. The dictator would most certainly use his power to ensure certainty of outcomes, a violation of one of the conditions of democracy. However, the dictator need not be a person. Rules and institutions have the same effect of resolving the majority cycling problem. This is precisely what the institutions do that we considered in the previous chapter. When the number of options is reduced to two, no majority cycling problem is possible, because in a choice between two options, a majority will al-

Table 6.1

Party Preference Orderings for Three Notional Lithuanian Voters, 2000 *Seimas* Elections

	Voter		
	1	2	3
1st preference	Liberal Union	Center Union	Social Liberals
2nd preference	Center Union	Social Liberals	Liberal Union
3rd preference	Social Liberals	Liberal Union	Center Union

Table 6.2

Winners in Head-to-Head Pairings of Parties in Table 6.1

Liberal Union vs. Center Union	=	Liberal Union
Center Union vs. Social Liberals	=	Center Union
Liberal Union vs. Social Liberals	=	Social Liberals

Group preferences:
    Liberal Union > Center Union
    Center Union > Social Liberals
    Liberal Union < Social Liberals

ways favor one. As a consequence, a winner can be declared. In effect, the rules help us to avoid a majority cycling problem, by imposing an artificial end on an otherwise chaotic and endless process. This insight permits us to analyze a large number of institutions to determine how they work to reduce the number of policy options and thereby bring order to what would otherwise be chaos.

Legislative Agenda

One institution that is particularly fruitful for such analysis is the legislature. Given the large number of deputies, each with their own separate sets of preferences on issues, an assembly is particularly susceptible to the majority cycling problem. Even in the presence of strong party discipline, the problem could manifest itself if there are more than two parties. Take, for example, the party preferences for a privatization plan in Table 6.3. Three parties—"Left," "Right," and "Center"—with respective voting strengths of 55, 37, and 49 (displayed in parentheses below the party name in Table 6.3) have the preference orderings indicated for three plans (A, B, and C). No one plan has a clear majority. If

Table 6.3

Party Preferences on Three Privatization Plans (A, B, and C)

	Party (Deputy Strength)		
	Left (55)	Center (37)	Right (49)
1st preference	Plan A	Plan B	Plan C
2nd preference	Plan B	Plan C	Plan A
3rd preference	Plan C	Plan A	Plan B

Table 6.4

Winners in Head-to-Head Pairings of Privatization Plans in Table 6.3

Plan A vs. Plan B	=	Plan A
Plan B vs. Plan C	=	Plan B
Plan A vs. Plan C	=	Plan C

Assembly preferences:
Plan A > Plan B
Plan B > Plan C
Plan A < Plan C

it did, that plan would be selected in every contest. In the fictional situation before us, however, no plan can emerge victorious in the absence of a set of rules forcing an artificial end to the process. (See Table 6.4 for the outcomes.) In a contest between plans A and B, A will win; however, the "Center" party (for whom plan B is the most preferred outcome) can call for a contest between A and C. It will do so because plan A is its least preferred outcome, while plan C is its second most preferred outcome. The "Right" party, which achieves its second most preferred outcome in the victory of plan A over plan B, will gladly support the "Center" party in defeating plan A with its most preferred plan, plan C. And so it will continue.

In cases such as the one before us, the question is how do different legislatures "manufacture" a majority when one does not exist in order to bring closure? Rational-choice theories inform us that we are most likely to find the answer in the rules they choose. These same theories tell us that the choice of rules influences the outcome. As William Riker has demonstrated, different rules will result in different outcomes.[1] That being the case, then we should expect that political officeholders will try to use control of the rules to their advantage.

One place for us to look are the rules governing the committee system. A rich literature points to committees as instrumental in avoiding a majority cycling problem.[2] Indeed, committees often operate to reduce the number of choices available to assemblies. Under closed rules, they can reduce the options to two. Were it not for committees, legislatures might well be so inundated by proposals and amendments that no choice could command a majority vote. At the same time, however, legislative leaders can use the gatekeeping power of the committees to manipulate the legislative agenda to assure policy outcomes they support by denying the ability of opposing legislation even to make it to a floor vote. Another rule set that we might study is that having to do with agenda control.

As we discussed in the previous chapter, by his party's dominance in the *Sueiga*, the chair of the Lithuanian *Seimas* effectively controls when and how bills will be heard. The power to control the order in which proposals are heard can be decisive in determining the outcome. This can be easily demonstrated in the notional debate on a privatization plan that we developed above (Table 6.3). Suppose that the chair of the *Seimas* supports plan B, the plan with the least support among the chamber's deputies. He could easily secure passage of the plan by arranging the following agenda: In the first round, plan A would be pitted against plan C. The victor, plan C, would then be paired against plan B, a contest in which plan B would emerge the victor (all other proposals having been vanquished).

In order for the chair to engage in this kind of manipulation, however, there must be a potential majority cycling problem, which might not exist even if there are more than two options available to the legislature. An additional requirement is that preferences on the issues underlying the proposals can not be arranged in some logical order to which all the deputies agree. In the example of the legislative contest over three privatization plans, there is no such logical preference ordering. But what if the three plans could be arranged on the basis of the degree to which the economy would be privatized? Suppose plan A (since it is supported by the "Left" party) retains most of the national wealth in the hands of the state, while plan C (supported by the "Right" party) permits privatization of virtually all state assets and plan B (the moderate plan supported by the "Center" party) represents a middle solution. Assuming that all deputies see these plans as representing these positions on this dimension, then the preference ordering

Table 6.5

Party Preferences on Three Privatization Plans (A, B, and C), Changing "Right" Party Preferences

	Party (Deputy Strength)		
	Left (55)	Center (37)	Right (49)
1st preference	Plan A	Plan B	Plan C
2nd preference	Plan B	Plan C	Plan B
3rd preference	Plan C	Plan A	Plan A

Table 6.6

Winners in Head-to-Head Pairings of Privatization Plans in Table 6.5

Plan A vs. Plan B	=	Plan B
Plan B vs. Plan C	=	Plan B
Plan A vs. Plan C	=	Plan C

Assembly preferences:
  Plan B > Plan C
  Plan C > Plan A
  Plan B > Plan A

for the "Right" party in Table 6.3 is not logical. (That for the "Center" party may or may not be correct depending on the relative support for plan C versus plan A.) Rearranging the "Right" party preferences, we have those shown in Table 6.5. The outcomes are shown in Table 6.6 and mathematically expressed as:

$$\text{Plan B} > \text{Plan C} \quad [4]$$
$$\text{Plan C} > \text{Plan A} \quad [5]$$
$$\text{Plan B} > \text{Plan A} \quad [6]$$

The intransitivity is gone and no majority cycling problem exists. In this case, the legislature will adopt plan B, no matter what the order in which the plans are proposed, since plan B will defeat every proposal offered against it. The reader can see for himself that the same is true even if the preferences for the "Center" party are changed to Plan B > Plan A > Plan C.

Budgets relating to a single issue generally do not result in a majority cycling problem, because money provides an easy means by which to

Figure 6.1 Notional Spatial Illustration of Party Preferences on the Defense Budget

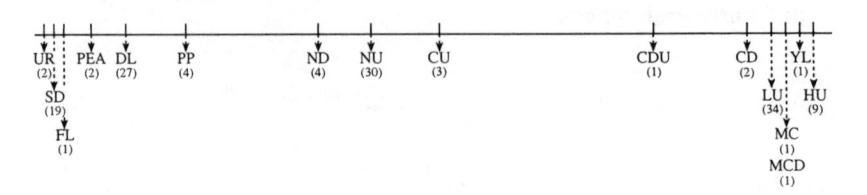

```
┼┼┼   ┼     ┼       ┼   ┼   ┼           ┼       ┼ ┼┼┼
UR   PEA  DL       PP      ND  NU  CU          CDU      CD   YL
(2)  (2)  (27)     (4)     (4) (30) (3)         (1)     (2)  (1)
SD                                                      LU   HU
(19)                                                    (34) (9)
FL                                                      MC
(1)                                                     (1)
                                                        MCD
                                                        (1)
```

CD—Christian Democratic Union
CDU—Christian Democratic Union
CU—Center Union
DL—Democratic Labor Party
FL—Freedom League
HU—Homeland Union (Conservatives of Lithuania)
LU—Liberal Union
MC—Moderate Conservatives Union
MCD—Modern Christian Democratic Union
ND—New Democratic Party
NU—New Union (Social Liberals)
PEA—Polish Electoral Action
PP—Peasants Party
SD—Social-Democratic Party
UR—Union of Russians
YL—"Young Lithuania"

order preferences. All agree on what amount of currency is closer to or further from one's personal spending preferences. This can be demonstrated in the matter of Lithuanian spending on defense. Suppose a bill is proposed to reduce the defense budget to 1.5% of the GDP, the current defense authorization being 2%. Let us further suppose that the chair of the *Seimas* supports a continuation of the 2.0% level. The notional positions of the political parties on the issue are at Figure 6.1 (their voting strengths are indicated in parentheses). The Social-Democratic Party (SD) supports a 1.0% spending level, the Homeland Union (HU) supports the current 2.0% level, and the median party, the New Union (Social Liberals) (NU), supports the proposed 1.5% level. The remaining parties are arrayed in relation to these three parties.

In our notional situation, the 1.5% spending level will win in a fair and open contest against both the status quo 2.0% level and any alternative offered by the parties on the left (closer to 1.0%). In fact, any proposal made by the Social Liberals will emerge the winner by the logic of the median voter theorem, which we developed in the previous chapter. The floor vote would proceed as follows: The 1.5% funding level would be offered; the "left" would then offer a counterproposal of 1.0%. By the rules of the legislature, a vote must first be taken on the counterproposal versus the proposal, the victor in that contest going on to be paired against the status quo. In the contest between the counterproposal (1.0%) and the proposal (1.5%), the "center" and "right" will vote for the proposal. The 1.5% proposed level is closer to the "right's" preferred level of 2.0% than is the counterproposal of 1.0%. The vote will be 82 to 59 in favor of the proposed 1.5% defense authorization level. In the follow-on contest between the proposal (1.5%) and the status quo (2.0%), the "center" and "left" will vote for the proposal (1.5% is closer to the "left's" preferred funding level of 1.0% than is 2.0%). The vote will be 89 to 52. Hence, the new defense expenditure will be 1.5% of the GDP.

While the foregoing suggests that a legislative leader is powerless if the issue is not susceptible to the majority cycling problem, such is not the case. The chair of the *Seimas*, for example, can use the amendment procedure to induce a legislative outcome he wants.

One likely scenario is for the chair to have his political allies propose an amendment to the 1.5% defense spending proposal adding privatization of the national rail system to the list of state enterprises to be auctioned in 2001. Both the "center" and "right" support this proposal; the "left" is opposed. Using his powers to determine the agenda, the chair can then arrange the following voting order.

The 1.0% counter proposal versus the 1.5% proposal [1]
If the 1.5% proposal wins, the amendment to the 1.5% proposal [2]
The winner against the status quo 2.0% level [3]

In round [1], the 1.5% proposal will pass, with the votes of the "center" and "right," 82 to 59. In round [2], the amendment will pass, with the votes of the "center" and "right," 82 to 59. But in round [3], the status quo will defeat the amended 1.5% defense budget, with the votes of the "right" and "left," 104 to 37. The "right" will vote for its preferred higher budget level of 2.0%, while the "left" will vote against privatization of the national railroad. While it might be objected that the "right" would be tempted to vote for the amended 1.5% budget in round [3] in order to support the privatization, it need not do so. Since the "center" and the "right" support such action, it will likely come up as a separate bill.

Knowing the relative strengths of each of the positions on the issue, the chair in our example has successfully manipulated the agenda to get the desired outcome. However, the ability to do so was the consequence of legislators voting in accordance with their true preferences—this is called sincere voting. Certainly, the "center" and "left," both of which prefer the 1.5% defense budget level to the 2.0% level, know what the chair is attempting to do. Could they not act to reverse the effect of agenda manipulation? Let us say that in round [2] the "center," recognizing what is in effect a "killer amendment," votes the amendment down. Then the round [3] vote would pit the 2.0% status quo against an unamended 1.5% proposed defense budget, with the latter (the funding level preferred to all others by a majority) emerging victorious. In this example of sophisticated voting (versus sincere voting) a set of legislators has voted against their interests at one point in the process in order to achieve their most preferred outcome.

It is not always necessary for a legislative leader to fabricate killer amendments, as many legislative proposals induce majority cycling problems on their own (in which case the chair need merely engage in agenda setting). They do so because they are two-dimensional in nature. What the *Seimas* chair did in effect by introducing the killer amendment in our example above is to introduce a second dimension to the legislative proposal. As it turns out, the likelihood of a majority cycling problem is quite high when an issue for which there are more than two options comprises two or more dimensions. This is, in fact, the situation for most budget bills. A typical budget bill decides spending on the entire range of government spending. As long as spending items are not linked by a single underlying rationale (say, for example, accession to the European Union), then budgets are almost by definition multidimensional.

Take, for instance, the 1997 Lithuanian budget, devoting resources to 1) economic and financial efforts to create a market economy and 2) defense. The positions and deputy strength of the major parties in the political system on these two issues are shown spatially in Figure 6.2. Under these conditions, there is sure to be a majority cycling problem, in which case legislative leaders may be able to use the powers of the committee system and agenda setting in many cases to induce outcomes they want.[3]

Rational-choice theorists have developed their arguments concerning legislative agenda issues in a largely deductive fashion.[4] What evalu-

Figure 6.2 **Spatial Representaion of Lithuanian Political Parties on Economic (X-axis) and Defense Spending (Y-axis), 1997 Budget**

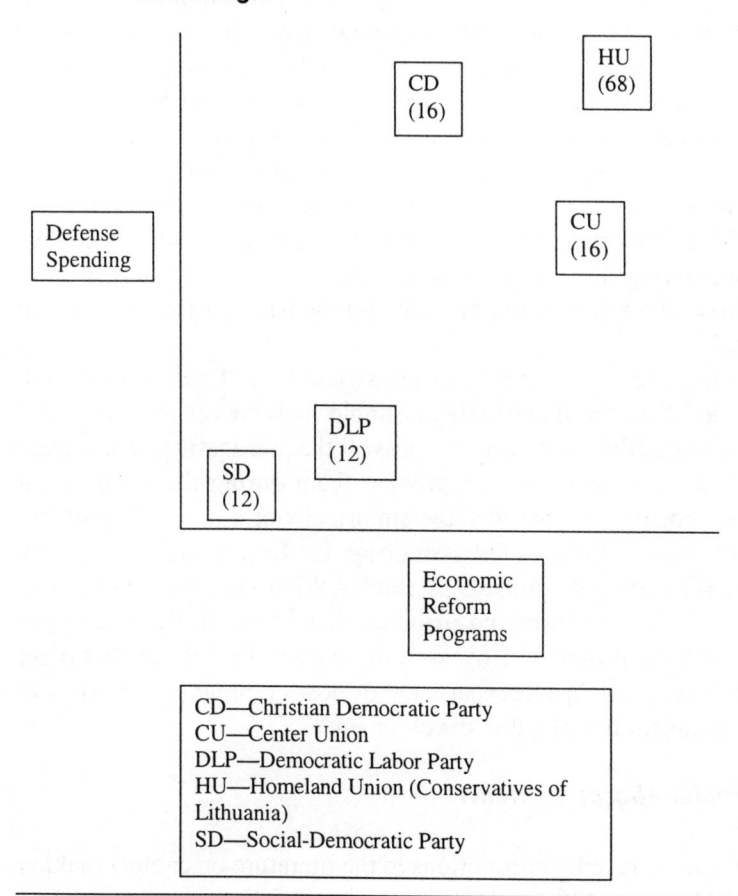

```
                          CD              HU
                         (16)            (68)

    Defense                              CU
    Spending                            (16)



                    DLP
                   (12)
              SD
             (12)
                          Economic
                          Reform
                          Programs
```

CD—Christian Democratic Party
CU—Center Union
DLP—Democratic Labor Party
HU—Homeland Union (Conservatives of Lithuania)
SD—Social-Democratic Party

ations of their hypotheses that have been undertaken have been almost entirely in the United States. There is much room here for scholars of consolidated democracies in post-communist Europe to contribute to our knowledge on these issues. Among the questions raised are to what extent is agenda manipulation undertaken in post-communist legislatures? What role do committees play in these efforts? Do parties or committees play a more important role in agenda setting? Are deputies sincere or sophisticated voters? To what extent is legislative leadership able to induce outcomes by agenda control?

Cabinet Formation

One area involving the majority cycling problem in a multidimensional setting in which there has been substantial research is cabinet formation. However, relatively few studies of the process have been conducted in post-communist political systems.[5] The problem can be visualized similarly to that displayed in Figure 6.2. Political parties hold different preferences on policy on a number of dimensions, all of which are salient insofar as they inform what policies they wish a government to pursue. More important, there is nothing to suggest that there need be a single underlying dimension uniting these policy preferences. Hence, parties may take any position in the two-dimensional space depicted at Figure 6.2.

All of this argues that governments should be difficult to form and, once formed, they should be highly unstable. This is even more the case, given that legislative leaders do not possess the prerogatives that agenda control and committee systems provide them during the government formation process. Despite this, the empirical world is replete with examples of stable cabinets. The issue begs for further investigation by scholars. Why are governments so stable? What processes and procedures permit them to form and maintain themselves in the face of the majority cycling problem? How well do existent models answer these questions? How might the experience of post-communist government formation inform their further development?

The Portfolio Allocation Model

One of the most recent contributions to the literature on cabinet making is Michael Laver and Kenneth A. Shepsle's portfolio allocation model.[6] In contrast to previous literature, the portfolio allocation model postulates that governing coalitions do not form based solely on the size principle[7] or some general policy agreement.[8] Instead, cabinets in multiparty systems form on the basis of multidimensional agreements on a particular ministerial allotment alternative preferred by a majority to all others. It may well be a minority cabinet that all parties prefer to any other.[9] Indeed, Laver and Shepsle provide a particularly clear rationale for the formation of minority governments.

Their model begins with the assumption that political parties are ultimately concerned with enacting policy.[10] Even if their primary motivation is merely to achieve office, political parties must pay attention to policy or pay the electoral consequences of failing to deliver on their promises. Hence, all parties to a coalition are concerned with the policies that a government pursues. Since each party is associated with particular policies relevant to each of the ministries in a government, the decision to allocate a portfolio to a party is in essence the decision to abide by the policy preferences of that party on the policy dimensions managed by the given ministry. Once the coalition is formed, the policy line of the government is established. The policies pursued by a government are essentially determined by the allocation of cabinet positions (ministerial portfolios) to specific political parties entering a governing coalition.

Hence, the set of available cabinets is constrained. The available policy choices do not cover the entire range of options. They are limited to those offered by the potential partners to a coalition. Coalitions can not freely take any position in the policy space for a particular issue. They have available to them only the number of policy positions represented by the parties to a potential coalition. Since there is therefore only a "finite number of potential governments"[11] the likelihood of a majority cycling problem is reduced to the extent that there exists some set of equilibrium cabinets among the potential governments.

Laver and Shepsle argue that the cabinet-making process will result in the selection of one of the equilibrium cabinets. The set of equilibrium cabinets comprises those governments that are preferred by the majority to all others. In a vote against any alternative, an equilibrium cabinet will win. The portfolio allocation model predicts that the government that will form will be included in the set of equilibrium cabinets. In the absence of such a set of cabinets, the model can make no prediction as to what cabinet is likely to be selected by the legislature. However, in most situations, there is more than one such cabinet. Therefore, once the existence of a set of equilibrium cabinets is determined, the question is which of them is likely to result from the cabinet-making process.

Laver and Shepsle begin by considering whether the status quo cabinet is in the set of equilibrium cabinets. Those cabinets able to muster a majority against the status quo cabinet are in its win set. If the status quo win set is empty, the status quo cabinet remains as the government, irrespective of the existence of other equilibrium cabinets (with one exception, which we shall discuss shortly).[12] If the status quo cabinet win set is not empty, it is likely to be replaced. However, if is to be replaced, it can only be replaced by an equilibrium cabinet in its win set.

The set of equilibrium cabinets may comprise minority, surplus majority, and minimum-winning governments. A minority cabinet is one in which the number of deputies in the legislature from parties holding ministerial positions (portfolios) constitutes less than a majority of the legislature. The portfolio allocation model predicts that this will occur when there are strong parties. Strong parties may be very strong or merely strong. A very strong party is one whose ideal point (a cabinet in which it holds all portfolios) has an empty win set and is at the generalized median. The generalized median cabinet is that cabinet located at the median position on each salient dimension (the dimension by dimension median). When such a cabinet exists, it will in every case become the next cabinet. This is true even when the status quo cabinet has an empty win set. Hence, it follows that when a very strong party exists, all portfolios are awarded to a single party. In such cases, a minority government is the result.

In the absence of a very strong party, a merely strong party may exist. A merely strong party is any party that participates in every cabinet in the win set of its ideal point. Such a party is strong, since it can veto any cabinet in its win set by refusing to participate in it. This sets up a contest between the merely strong party, which would prefer to control all cabinet positions, and the remaining parties in the legislature. Merely strong parties do not always win such standoffs. Their ability to do so is dependent on the party's strengths and weaknesses at the time. Hence, merely strong parties in contrast to very strong parties do not necessarily always get their preferred outcome (that is, their ideal point, in which they hold all cabinet positions). Whether a minority cabinet emerges from the government-making process depends on the ability of the merely strong party to win standoffs.[13] If there is a very strong party, it will rule as a minority government, while a merely strong party can potentially rule as a minority government.

Surplus majority governments are those in which the removal of any party (or set of parties) from the government would still result in the remaining parties to the coalition retaining a legislative majority. The portfolio allocation model predicts that this may occur if there are more than two salient political dimensions along which political parties are divided. In most political systems, however, two political issues (defense and economic policy) dominate the cabinet-making process. In the absence of a strong party, these two-dimensional systems will produce either a minority or a minimum-winning coalition at the generalized median. (The minimum-winning coalition is one in which the removal of any party from the government would deny it a legislative majority.)

Explaining Lithuanian Cabinet Formation, 2000–2001

Rational-choice models such as that of Laver and Shepsle lend themselves to application and testing in post-communist political systems. How well do such models predict outcomes in these systems? What theoretical shortcoming might the experience with cabinet formation in post-communist Europe point to or help to resolve? It is clearly beyond the purview of this book to give a definitive answer to these questions, but a short consideration of the 2000 Lithuanian cabinet formation outcome will help to make the case that post-communist studies in the post-consolidation era may well have much to contribute.

I will use WINSET, a computer program developed by Laver and Shepsle, to assist in analyzing the 2000 Lithuanian cabinet-making process within the parameters of the portfolio allocation model. In order to determine the existence of strong parties and to calculate win sets for both the status quo cabinet and that at the generalized median, WINSET requires information on the number of deputies who are members of each party in the legislature, the number of politically salient issues, and the relative position of each party on these issues. Given that the factions determined the voting outcome of the legislature, I use membership in a party's legislative faction in the 2000 *Seimas*. The overwhelming majority of the deputies ran as members of political parties in the 2000 elections. Those who did not all joined a party faction at the first session of the newly elected *Seimas*. (For instance, one independent joined the party faction of the Center Union, increasing its membership to three. It should be further noted that the same deputy had been a member of the Center Union, but chose to run as an independent during the campaign.) The strength of each party faction in the 2000 Lithuanian *Seimas* along with the set of legislative coalitions that could elect a government (the decisive structure) are listed in Table 6.7. (The reader should note that while these coalitions are necessary to electing a government, not every party in a coalition need hold a ministerial portfolio in the government.)

The Democratic Labor Party (27 deputies) and the Social-Democratic

Table 6.7

The Decisive Structure of the 2000 *Seimas*

Party	Seats
Social Democratic Coalition	46
Liberal Union	34
New Union (Social Liberals)	30
Homeland Union (Conservatives)	9
Peasants' Party	4
New Democratic Party	4
Center Union (LCU)	3
Christian Democratic Party (LCDP)	2
Polish Electoral Action	2
Union of Russians	2
Modern Christian Democrats	1
Moderate Conservatives	1
Christian Democratic Union	1
"Young Lithuania"	1
Freedom League	1
Total	141

Winning legislative coalitions:	Seats
Social Democratic Coalition + Liberal Union	80
Social Democratic Coalition + New Union	76
Social Democratic Coalition + Homeland Union + Peasants' Party + New Democratic Party + Center Union + Christian Democratic Party + Polish Electoral Action + Union of Russians	72
Social Democratic Coalition + Homeland Union + Peasants' Party + New Democratic Party + Center Union + Christian Democratic Party + Polish Electoral Action + Modern Christian Democrats	71
Social Democratic Coalition + Homeland Union + Peasants' Party + New Democratic Party + Center Union + Christian Democratic Party + Polish Electoral Action + Christian Democratic Union	71
Social Democratic Coalition + Homeland Union + Peasants' Party + New Democratic Party + Center Union + Christian Democratic Party + Union of Russians + Modern Christian Democrats	71
Social Democratic Coalition + Homeland Union + Peasants' Party + New Democratic Party + Center Union +Christian Democratic Party + Union of Russians + Christian Democratic Union	71
Social Democratic Coalition + Homeland Union + Peasants' Party + New Democratic Party + Center Union + Polish Electoral Action + Union of Russians + Modern Christian Democrats	71
Social Democratic Coalition + Homeland Union + Peasants' Party + New Democratic Party + Center Union + Polish Electoral Action + Union of Russians + Christian Democratic Union	71
Social Democratic Coalition + Homeland Union + Peasants' Party + New Democratic Party +Christian Democratic Party + Polish Electoral Action + Union of Russians + Modern Christian Democrats + Christian Democratic Union	71
Liberal Union + New Union + Homeland Union	73
Liberal Union + New Union + Peasants' Party + New Democratic Party	72
Liberal Union + New Union + Peasants' Party + Center Union	71

Liberal Union + New Union + New Democratic Party + Center Union	71
Liberal Union + New Union + Peasants' Party + Christian Democratic Party + Polish Electoral Action	72
Liberal Union + New Union + Peasants' Party + Christian Democratic Party + Union of Russians	72
Liberal Union + New Union + Peasants' Party + Polish Electoral Action + Union of Russians	72
Liberal Union + New Union + Peasants' Party + Christian Democratic Party + Modern Christian Democrats	71
Liberal Union + New Union + Peasants' Party + Christian Democratic Party + Christian Democratic Union	71
Liberal Union + New Union + Peasants' Party + Polish Electoral Action + Modern Christian Democrats	71
Liberal Union + New Union + Peasants' Party + Polish Electoral Action + Christian Democratic Union	71
Liberal Union + New Union + Peasants' Party + Union of Russians + Modern Christian Democrats	71
Liberal Union + New Union + Peasants' Party + Union of Russians + Christian Democratic Union	71
Liberal Union + New Union + New Democratic Party + Christian Democratic Party + Polish Electoral Action	72
Liberal Union + New Union + New Democratic Party + Christian Democratic Party + Union of Russians	72
Liberal Union + New Union + New Democratic Party + Polish Electoral Action + Union of Russians	72
Liberal Union + New Union + New Democratic Party + Christian Democratic Party +Modern Christian Democrats	71
Liberal Union + New Union + New Democratic Party + Christian Democratic Party + Christian Democratic Union	71
Liberal Union + New Union + New Democratic Party + Polish Electoral Action + Modern Christian Democrats	71
Liberal Union + New Union + New Democratic Party + Polish Electoral Action + Christian Democratic Union	71
Liberal Union + New Union + New Democratic Party + Union of Russians + Modern Christian Democrats	71
Liberal Union + New Union + New Democratic Party + Union of Russians + Christian Democratic Union	71
Liberal Union + New Union + Center Union + Christian Democratic Party + Polish Electoral Action	71
Liberal Union + New Union + Center Union + Christian Democratic Party + Union of Russians	71
Liberal Union + New Union + Center Union + Polish Electoral Action + Union of Russians	71
Liberal Union + New Union + Center Union + Christian Democratic Party + Modern Christian Democrats + Christian Democratic Union	71
Liberal Union + New Union + Center Union + Polish Electoral Action + Modern Christian Democrats + Christian Democratic Union	71
Liberal Union + New Union + Center Union + Union of Russians + Modern Christian Democrats + Christian Democratic Union	71
Liberal Union + New Union + Christian Democratic Party + Polish Electoral Action + Union of Russians + Modern Christian Democrats	71
Liberal Union + New Union + Christian Democratic Party + Polish Electoral Action + Union of Russians + Christian Democratic Union	71

Party (19 deputies) are treated as a single party, the Social Democratic Coalition. This is justified by the extraordinary level of cooperation between the two, which were pledged to work together in a coalition government. The agreement was reflected in their presenting a single list of candidates in both the district races and the party list vote. (Indeed, by year's end, the two had merged into a single party.)

Of the one hundred forty-one deputies elected to the 2000 *Seimas*, twenty-two were elected as members of eleven small parties (those with four or fewer deputies in the new *Seimas*). Of these parties, five had one deputy each, three had two deputies, one had three, and two had four. Several of these parties, particularly those with only one deputy, had no intention of entering the government, having declared themselves neutral or in opposition to any government. As such, they represented a vote against any government. These parties included the Freedom League (one deputy), "Young Lithuania" (one deputy), and the Moderate Conservatives (one deputy). Therefore, following Laver and Shepsle, I have excluded these parties from the set of potential legislative coalitions listed at the bottom of Table 6.7. Members of the remaining small parties were active in the government formation process. This was particularly the case for the Center Union (three deputies), the Peasants' Party (four deputies), the New Democratic Party (four deputies), and the Polish Electoral Action (two deputies). They are included in the calculation of potential winning legislative coalitions at Table 6.7.

Laver and Shepsle argue that any cabinet that forms must be elected by one of the legislative coalitions listed at the bottom of Table 6.7. However, this does not mean there need be a one-for-one correlation between the parties voting for a government and the actual parties taking ministerial positions in that government. The government may well comprise a surplus majority government. As discussed previously, the portfolio allocation model predicts that this may occur if there are more than two salient political dimensions along which political parties are divided. For our purposes, I will assume that the same two salient political dimensions that Laver and Shepsle argue dominate the cabinet-making process in the majority of political systems (defense and economic policy) dominated the Lithuanian political system in 2000. This seems a reasonable assumption given the centrality of two issues during the campaign: the continued economic recession and NATO entry.

Figure 6.3 estimates the relative positions of Lithuania's political parties on the issue of the means for resolving the continuing economic

Figure 6.3 **Estimated Party Positions on Economic Development Model, 2000**

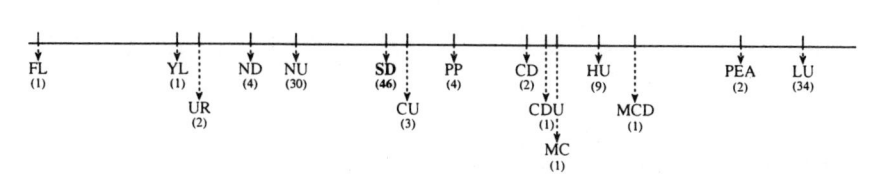

```
┬───┬─┬─┬─┬─┬─┬─┬─┬─┬┬┬─┬───┬───┬
↓   ↓ ↓ ↓ ↓ ↓ ↓↓↓ ↓   ↓   ↓
FL  YL ND NU SD PP CD HU  PEA LU
(1) (1) (4)(30)(46)(4)(2) (9) (2)(34)
    ↓      ↓     ↓    ↓
    UR     CU    CDU  MCD
    (2)    (3)   (1)  (1)
                 ↓
                 MC
                 (1)
```

CD—Christian Democratic Party
CDU—Christian Democratic Union
CU—Center Union
FL—Freedom League
HU—Homeland Union (Conservatives of Lithuania)
LU—Liberal Union
MC—Moderate Conservatives Union
MCD—Modern Christian Democratic Union
ND—New Democracy Party
NU—New Union (Social Liberals)
PEA—Polish Electoral Action
PP—Peasants Party
SD—Social-Democratic Coalition
UR—Union of Russians
YL—"Young Lithuania"

crisis. These estimates are based on an analysis of the respective party platforms. Those parties farther to the right on the diagram favor market solutions while those farther to the left favor state intervention. Figure 6.4 depicts the estimated positions of the political parties on the issue of NATO entry. Those farther to the right favor immediate entry, while those to the left are opposed to NATO entry. Each figure also indicates the number of deputies each party successfully elected to the 2000 *Seimas*. The party with the median legislator on both questions is bold highlighted.

Since there are only two salient political dimensions, the portfolio allocation model does not predict a surplus majority coalition to emerge from the 2000 elections to the *Seimas*. That leaves the possibility of either a minority or minimum-winning coalition, but which one? Using the data in Table 6.7 and Figures 6.3 and 6.4, the WINSET program indicates that there are 215 cabinets majority preferred to the previous (status quo) cabinet. The status quo cabinet comprised the Homeland

126 BEYOND POST-COMMUNIST STUDIES

Figure 6.4 **Estimated Party Positions on Defense Policy, 2000**

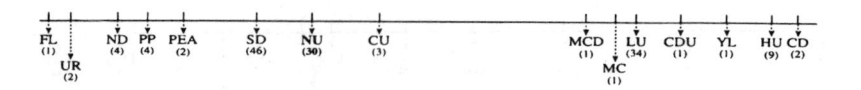

```
FL    ND  PP  PEA   SD   NU   CU              MCD   LU   CDU  YL   HU CD
(1)   (4) (4) (2)   (46) (30) (3)             (1)   (34) (1)  (1)  (9) (2)
UR                                                  MC
(2)                                                 (1)
```

CD—Christian Democratic Party
CDU—Christian Democratic Union
CU—Center Union
FL—Freedom League
HU—Homeland Union (Conservatives of Lithuania)
LU—Liberal Union
MC—Moderate Conservatives Union
MCD—Modern Christian Democratic Union
ND—New Democracy Party
NU—New Union (Social Liberals)
PEA—Polish Electoral Action
PP—Peasants Party
SD—Social-Democratic Coalition
UR—Union of Russians
YL—"Young Lithuania"

Union (Conservatives), which held the Ministries of Finance and Economics (with jurisdiction over the economic dimension), and the Christian Democratic Party, which held the Ministries of Foreign Affairs and Defense (with jurisdiction over foreign policy). The Conservative-Christian Democratic government had been backed by a minimum-winning coalition in the previous *Seimas*. Not surprising, given the losses suffered by these two parties in the 2000 *Seimas* elections, WINSET finds that the status quo cabinet is not an equilibrium cabinet.

The portfolio allocation model argues that one of the 215 cabinets in the former government's win set will become the next government, if it possesses an empty win set. The cabinet-making process is biased in favor of any cabinet with an empty win set at the generalized median. If that cabinet is the ideal point of one political party, that party is a strong party. WINSET indicates there are no strong parties in the 2000 *Seimas*. However, there is a coalition cabinet at the generalized median with an empty win set. This cabinet awards the Ministry of Finance to the Social Democratic Coalition and the Ministry of Foreign Affairs to the New

Union (Social Liberals). The decisive structure in Table 6.7 indicates that this cabinet is supported by a minimum-winning coalition and is itself a minimum-winning cabinet. The portfolio allocation model predicts that this is the cabinet that would emerge from the 2000 Lithuanian legislative elections.

The cabinet that ultimately emerged from the cabinet-making process was in fact the Social Democratic-New Union government. However, it did not form until a cabinet awarding the Ministry of Finance to the Liberal Union and the Ministry of Foreign Affairs to the New Union (Social Liberals) had collapsed following a short six months in office. WINSET predicts that this would be the case, as there are 150 cabinets preferred by a legislative majority—to this cabinet, the Social Democratic-New Union government, among them. Nonetheless, the initial emergence of the Liberal Union-New Union (Social Liberals), cabinet presents an interesting anomaly of the type that is helpful in refining theoretical models.

Lithuanian parliaments have presented other interesting anomalies as well, the most important of which focus attention on a particular shortcoming of the portfolio allocation model. While the model is particularly strong at predicting minority and minimum-winning cabinets, it is relatively poorly developed concerning surplus majority cabinets. Indeed, it is not at all certain why surplus majority cabinets could not form when there are only two salient political dimensions. Lithuania experienced three such cabinets from 1996 to 1999.

Chapter Seven

Some Further Theoretical Considerations

(with Jan Weiss)

I have argued in this book that the research agenda of politics in post-communist Europe has been informed by democratic consolidation. I do not contend that specific theories related to either the transition to democracy or democratic consolidation have dominated the field. Rather, my point is that the various arenas and approaches associated with the general contours of the paradigm have determined the limits of the discipline's concerns. Even those who have found the theories of little utility have followed the research agenda established by the paradigm. This has provided the study of post-communist politics with a substantial degree of focus. At the same time, many equally important issues have been largely ignored. The more serious problem, however, is that scholars have tended to assume that democratization as a process is a virtually endless one. This is accounted for by the paradigmatic shortcomings of democratic consolidation, which starting from the very definition of a consolidated democracy provides us with no theoretically coherent means for judging the end of the process.

The primary purpose of this book has been to put forward a solution to this problem and to make the point that a significant subset of the post-communist states of east-central Europe are now consolidated democracies. Analyses of these states must go beyond post-communist studies. I have endeavored to illustrate how the new institutionalism rooted in rational-choice assumptions might serve as a useful paradigm for doing so. It is not my contention that rational-choice approaches are the only option. I merely note that given the paradigm's dominance in political science, it suggests itself as arguably the best platform for giving structure to post-consolidation studies in such a way as to permit the highest likelihood of advances both substantively and theoretically. Substantively, the literature on Western democracies provides a substantial reservoir of hypotheses and observations for corroboration in post-communist cases. Theoretically, the post-communist states offer an interesting test bed for rational-choice theories. Indeed, the region is likely to provide a rich source of anomalies (of the type noted at the end of the previous chapter), which can provide the gist for theoretically salient case studies. For those who wish to pursue this possibility further, I have included a brief subject bibliography of rational literature at the end of this chapter.

Some may be concerned that I am insisting on participation in the development of theory or formal modeling. I am not. I understand that many of us lack the sophisticated mathematical skills as well as the interest to do so. In any event, it is not necessary. Empirical studies of theoretical propositions and hypotheses will do quite well. To those who suggest that even this is too much, I can only respond that the addition of such efforts can only serve to further enrich our discipline. In any event, I am not arguing that we need a single paradigm. It strikes me as odd that anyone would contend that we should therefore exclude any *one* paradigm.

Having said that, however, I am not sure why we should not endeavor to engage in formal modeling when and where we can. It is to that issue I wish to return in this final chapter. The theory outlined in chapter four sets up a "game" between contestants in which each side engages in calculations of payoff and probability of victory. Democracy is consolidated when the likelihood of the calculation of success from nondemocratic means is judged to be small by all players in the game. In essence, a consolidated democracy is an equilibrium in which all contestants for political power view the potential gains from continuing to play by the democratic rules as at least equal to if not greater than the potential gains of defecting from those rules. Such equilibria can be modeled mathematically. The purpose of doing so is generally to derive conclusions from the model that otherwise might not be intuitively obvious. I propose to engage in the exercise for another equally valid reason: to further clarify the theoretical linkages made in chapter four. I promise the reader that no more than the simplest algebra will be sufficient to accomplish the task.

Toward a Formal Model of an Unconsolidated Democracy

In the simplest form of an unconsolidated democracy, there are only two sets of contestants. In the earliest stages of democratization in the immediate aftermath of the collapse of the communist regime, the system is likely to be either presidentialism or president-parliamentarism.

Such systems grant to the winner of the presidential contest control of the bureaucracy and with it control of the economic and political reform process. This in turn assures the victor control of political outcomes. Hence, these systems essentially generate a zero-sum, winner-take-all game for control of the executive. The payoff from playing according to democratic rules (C) (cooperating) in such cases can be expressed for each contestant as the product of the probability of success (p) (achieving political office) times one (a one hundred percent gain in a zero-sum, winner-take-all contest) as shown in equations [1] and [2].

$$C_1 = p_1(1) \qquad [1]$$
$$C_2 = p_2(1) \qquad [2]$$

Equation [1] is the likelihood of the payoff of cooperation (C_1) to the first of the two competing elites. It is calculated as the probability of success (p_1) times one (a one hundred percent gain in the zero-sum effort). Equation [2] is the likelihood of the payoff from cooperation (C_2) to the other side. When there are only two players (sets of competing elites) involved, the probability of the electoral success of one of the parties is the difference between one and the probability of the electoral success of the other party. Therefore, the above equations can be rewritten.

$$C_1 = p_1 \qquad [3]$$
$$C_2 = 1 - p_1 \qquad [4]$$

Similarly, the gain from defecting from the democratic rules of the game (D) is a zero-sum, winner-take-all game. If successful, the defecting party has gained control of all political power. Hence, the potential gain is calculated in proportion to the probability of success. This can be modeled as follows.

$$D_1 = q_1(1) \qquad [5]$$
$$D_2 = q_2(1) \qquad [6]$$

Equation [5] is the likelihood of the payoff of defection (D_1) to the first of the two competing elites. It is calculated as the probability of success (q_1) times one (a one hundred percent gain in the zero-sum effort). Equation [6] is the likelihood of the payoff from defection (D_2) to the other side. Unlike an electoral contest, however, the probability of the successful defection of one party is not directly related to the probability of the success of the other.

The total cost-benefit calculation (T) to each side is the difference between the gain from continuing to cooperate and the payoff of defecting as modeled in equations [7] and [8].

$$T_1 = C_1 - D_1 = p_1 - q_1 \quad [7]$$
$$T_2 = C_2 - D_2 = (1 - p_1) - q_2 \quad [8]$$

If and only if the cost-benefit calculation (T) is greater than or equal to zero (that is the benefit of cooperation is greater than or equal to the benefit of defection) will the given party choose to continue to cooperate. (Otherwise its best strategy is to seek to overturn the democratic rules in a bid to gain complete political control.) To determine the conditions under which this attains, we need to do some simple algebra. Based on equations [7] and [8], it follows that

$$p_1 > q_1 \quad [9]$$

and

$$1 - p_1 > q_2 \quad [10]$$

By substitution,

$$1 - q_1 > q_2 \quad [11]$$

and

$$1 > q_1 + q_2 \quad [12]$$

Hence, the conditions under which a democratic regime is stable are: 1) the probability for successful defection for either side does not exceed the probability of success under continued cooperation, and 2) the sum of the probability of successful defection of both parties is not greater than or equal to one. Together, these two conditions mean that as the probability increases that any one side in an elite contest will win the presidency, the likelihood that the other side will attempt to overthrow the democratic regime increases. This poses a significant challenge to the stability of a democratic regime when the regime is presidential or president-parliamentary.

This problem can be demonstrated by looking more carefully at the payoff function (C). In presidential and president-parliamentary sys-

Figure 7.1 A Graphic Display of the Relationship between the Payoff (c) and the Proportion of the Vote (x*) for Any Contestant in a Presidential, President-Parliamentary, or Majoritarian Party Parliamentary System

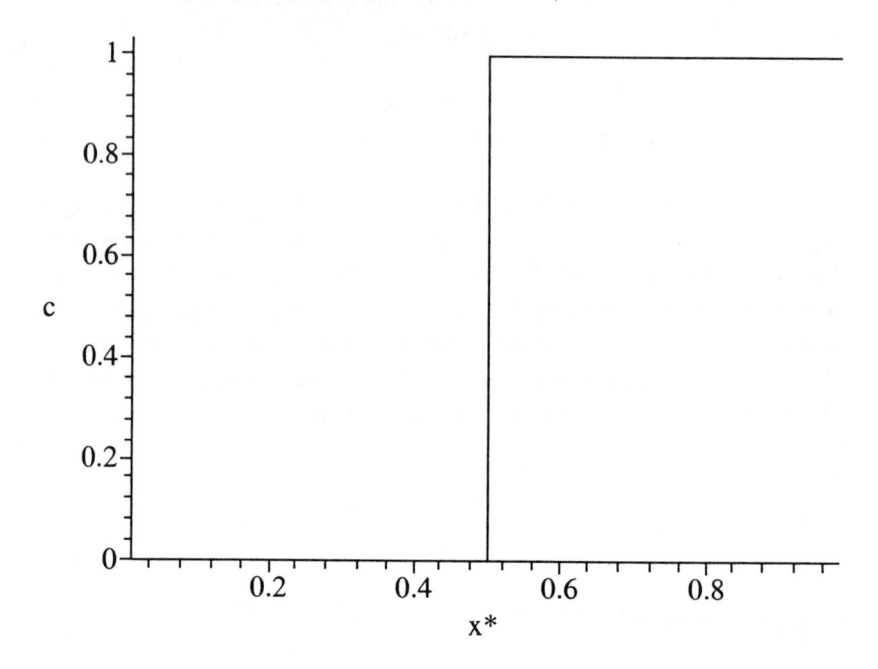

tems, this function is related to the proportion of the vote (x*). The party receiving the majority vote wins the presidency. As it turns out, the same is true for parliamentary systems that have a two-party or majoritarian party system. Elections in such parliamentary systems always result in a single party winning a majority in the parliament. Hence, presidential, president-parliamentary, and majoritarian parliamentary systems create a zero-sum, winner-take-all contest for the executive. The payoff (C) is zero for any party when the percentage of the vote (x*) ranges from 0 to .5. The payoff (C) is one for all x* greater than 5. This relationship is depicted at Figure 7.1.

Figure 7.1 displays an extremely unstable system in which the sole condition for stability is that both parties have an equal chance for electoral victory. (That, in essence, requires that both have a 50 percent chance of gaining the presidency.) Any party having less than a 50 percent chance in the electoral contest will have a payoff (C) of zero. Hence, if the party has any chance of pulling off a successful coup, it will be sorely tempted to do so.

Fortunately, the situation depicted at Figure 7.1 is unlikely, as it assumes perfect information. In other words, each party knows its exact chance of electoral victory (and conversely that of the other party). This is highly unlikely in transitional democracies due to high levels of electoral volatility. Electoral uncertainty is a virtual given. Therefore, we can get a more precise approximation for C if we know the probability of the vote outcome for each party. That will permit us to map the distribution of the probability (p) over the full range of electoral outcomes (x^*). If we assume that the distribution is normally distributed about some point k (an electoral outcome ranging from 0 to 1), then an approximation of that distribution can be modeled. For simplicity sake, we will use equation [13] as an estimate of that function.

$$p = ae^{-x^*} \quad [13]$$

It then follows that,

$$C = ae^{-x^*}(0) \text{ \{for all vote outcomes from 0 to .5\}} + ae^{-x^*}(1) \text{ \{for all vote outcomes greater than .5\}} \quad [14]$$

Since the left hand side of the equation is zero, the equation is simplified to,

$$C = ae^{-x^*} \quad [15]$$

Given equation [15], the relationship between the payoff from electoral victory (C) and the vote outcome (x^*) under conditions of uncertainty is displayed at Figure 7.2. Unlike the situation under the assumption of perfect information depicted at Figure 7.1, there is now a range of electoral outcomes within which democratic stability can be retained. However, the range is rather narrow (between 43 percent and 57 percent of the vote given the 15 percent margin of uncertainty assumed in Figure 7.2). Within this range, both parties have some reasonable expectation of a payoff from an electoral contest. Outside it, one party once again has a payoff of zero, while the other party wins everything. Hence, the democratic regime remains relatively stable only as long as both parties believe that they have some probability of electoral victory. This

134 BEYOND POST-COMMUNIST STUDIES

Figure 7.2 **A Graphic Display of the Relationship between the Payoff (c) and the Proportion of the Vote (x*) for Any Contestant in a Presidential, President-Parliamentary, or Majoritarian Party Parliamentary System under Conditions of Imperfect Information**

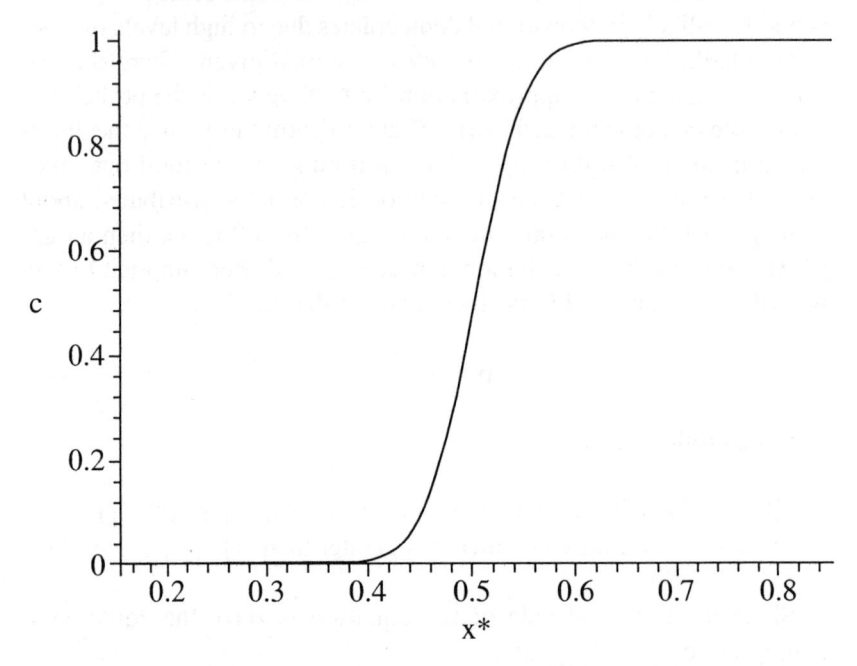

requires that both possess a relatively even degree of electoral strength. In essence, large electoral mandates for any governing party must be avoided in order to assure democratic stability.

A Formal Model of Democratic Consolidation

The fundamental barrier to the emergence of democratic stability in post-communist Europe is the zero-sum, winner-take-all game created by presidential and president-parliamentary systems. If democracy is to consolidate, the theory I developed in chapter four argues that a parliamentary or premier-presidential system must be adopted. Once either system is in place, there are two means for further increasing democratic stability. The first is to increase the number of contestants for political office. This is of no effect if the only salient office is that of the chief executive. It is of great importance, however, in parliamentary and premier-presidential systems, both of which are marked by a politically salient legislature whose position is secured by the fact that the government is accountable to it and not to the president. When the number of contestants to the legislature is increased, a party achieving less than 50 percent of the vote still has a chance to enter a governing coalition. In essence, equation [4] no longer attains, and equations [7] and [8] can be rewritten as follows.

$$T_n = C_n - D_n = p_n - q_n \qquad [16]$$

The probability of the success under the democratic rules for any one party is no longer related to the probability of the success to any other party from either cooperating or defecting from those rules. As long as all sides view the payoff from democracy as higher than that from undemocratic means, the system is stable. This is a much easier condition to achieve.

We can demonstrate this by looking once again at the payoff function (C). In presidential, president-parliamentary, or majoritarian parliamentary systems, this function is related to the proportion of the vote. The party receiving the majority vote wins the presidency. However, in non-majoritarian parliamentary and premier-presidential systems, the relationship of the payoff (C) from electoral victory to the percentage of the vote that any contestant receives (x^*) is related to its chances for winning enough seats in the legislature to enter into a governing coalition. The contest is no longer zero-sum; contestants obtain a payoff for vote totals less than or equal to .5. The equation defining this relationship is,

$$C = ae^{-x^*}(x^{*1/n}) \text{ \{for all vote outcomes from 0 to .5\}}$$
$$+ ae^{-x^*}(1) \text{ \{for all vote outcomes greater than .5\}} \qquad [17]$$

Since the left side of equation [14] is no longer zero, the value of T_n in equation [16] is necessarily larger.

Figure 7.3 graphically portrays the new payoff (C) curve for both parties. There is now a substantial payoff for winning less than 50 percent of the vote. Hence, players are more likely to continue under the democratic rules. However, the problem still remains that if any one player's probability of achieving more than 50 percent of the vote increases, the payoff to all other players decreases to zero (since the first player wins everything).

136 BEYOND POST-COMMUNIST STUDIES

Figure 7.3 **A Graphic Display of the Relationship between the Payoff (c) and the Proportion of the Vote (x*) for Any Contestant in a Premier-Presidential or Non-Majoritarian Parliamentary System**

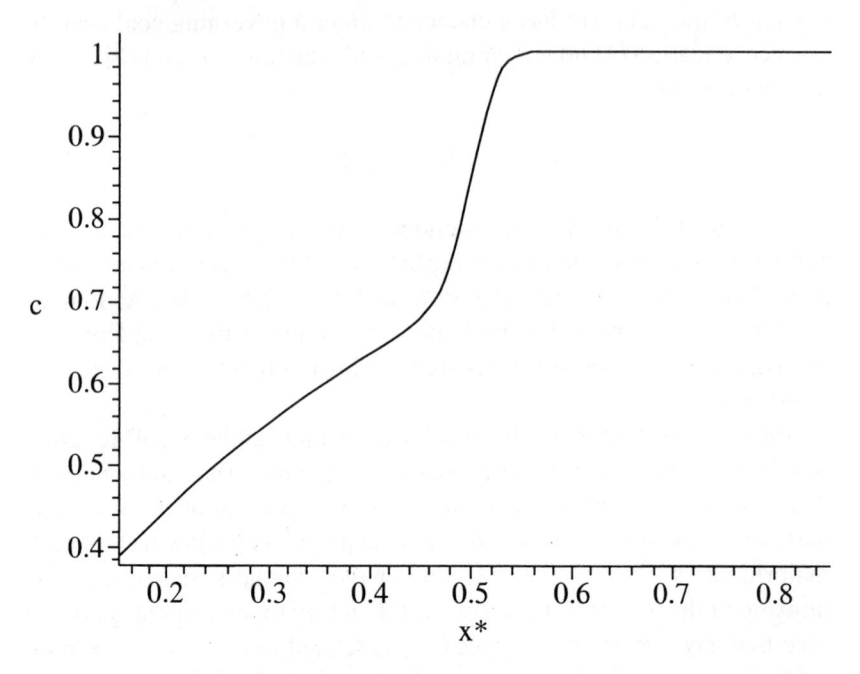

This problem is resolved by the second means for inducing greater democratic stability, increasing the number of institutions to which the contestants vie for political power in democratic elections. (The reader should note that premier-presidentialism, unlike parliamentarism, necessarily increases the number of salient political institutions given that it has both a policy relevant legislature and chief executive.) Much like introducing multiple-party competition to the legislature, the effect of changing the number of institutions that have a meaningful impact on public policy and over which political elites vie for power is to avoid a zero-sum, winner-take-all game. If winning the office of the presidency no longer delivers with it control of the bureaucracy and policy, then calculations concerning the payoff from continuing to play by democratic rules (C) are no longer based on probability of winning or losing one political office. Instead, calculations reflect the probability of gaining any number of political positions, including the legislature (in some cases a bicameral legislature), local governments, or the presidency.

Figure 7.4 **A Graphic Display of the Effect of Requiring Super-Majorities (z > .5) for a One Hundred Percent Payoff (y* = 1) on the Relationship between the Payoff (c) and the Proportion of the Vote (x*) for Any Contestant in a Premier-Presidential or Non-Majoritarian Parliamentary System**

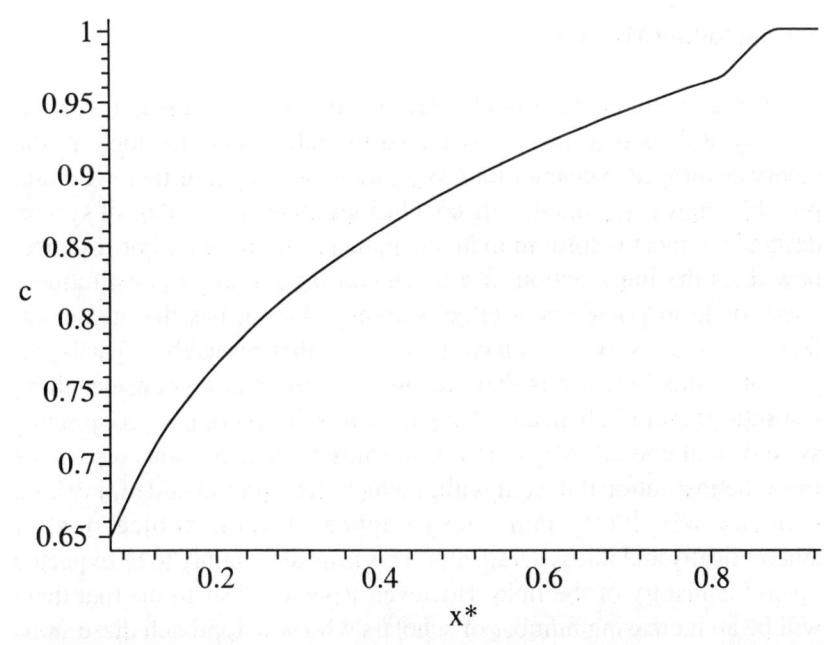

Increasing the number of institutions, however, has the even more important effect of making it harder for any one party to gain control over all salient policy positions. As a consequence, the payoff from electoral victory (C) is no longer assured by gaining merely 50 percent of the vote. Indeed, given that different electoral rules will be used for each institution, a super-majority will be required to assure total control of all political institutions. Figure 7.4 depicts the effect on the payoff (C) for each player in such systems. In essence, contestants can achieve relatively high payoffs from small vote percentages. More important, since no player is likely to achieve the vote threshold necessary for control of all policy-salient institutions, all players will experience substantial payoff from playing by the democratic rules.

The implication is straightforward. Contestants in premier-presidential and non-majoritarian parliamentary systems are less likely to defect from democratic rules than are those in presidential, president-parliamentary, and majoritarian parliamentary systems at the same level of probability of success from an attempted defection. In short, democracy is more stable in the former systems than the latter. This is precisely what the model in chapter four argues. The equations developed here have essentially restated the logic of that model in mathematical form.

A Concluding Word

The formal mathematical model developed to this point is quite primitive, but it does help us to understand the rational-choice logic in the theory developed in chapter four. Were we to develop it further, we could possibly draw some interesting conclusions about what kinds of system designs are most helpful in inducing democratic stability. For instance, how does the introduction of a bicameral legislature, a constitutional court, or local government effect stability? Which has the greater effect? These questions will have to await further research. What is important at this juncture is that our theory permits us to consider these institutions more holistically. A majority of scholars of post-communist systems will undoubtedly continue to study such institutions separately from the institutional design within which they are imbedded, just as a majority will likely continue to approach their subject matter atheoretically and idiosyncratically. This is most certainly to be expected given the history of the field. However, it seems clear to me that there will be an increasing number of scholars who will approach these same tasks more holistically and theoretically. (That will most certainly be the case for political scientists who have yet to achieve tenure.) I am not sure there is a "correct" way. Indeed, the only "right" way is ultimately the one that works. As for me, I am likely, at least at this point in my career, to follow the latter approach, if for no other reason than its amazing elegance.

Notes

Notes to Preface

1. Alexander J. Motyl, *Thinking Theoretically about Soviet Nationalities: History and Comparison in the Study of the USSR*, N.Y.: Columbia University Press, 1992.
2. Philip G. Roeder, "The Revolution of 1989: Postcommunism and the Social Sciences," *Slavic Review* 58, no. 4 (1999): 743–55.
3. See for instance Russell Bova, "Political Dynamics of the Postcommunist Transition: A Comparative Perspective," *World Politics* 44 (1991): 113–58.
4. See for instance Philippe C. Schmitter with Terry Lynn Karl, "Transitologists and Consolidologists," *Slavic Review* 53, no. 1 (1994): 173–85.
5. See Valerie Bunce, "Should Transitologists Be Grounded?" *Slavic Review* 54, no. 1 (1995): 111–27 and Valerie Bunce, "The Political Economy of Postsocialism," Slavic Review 58, no. 4 (1999): 756–93.
6. See M. Steven Fish, "Postcommunist Subversion: Social Science and Democratization in East Europe and Eurasia," *Slavic Review* 58, no. 4 (1999): 794–823.

Notes to Chapter 1

1. Juan J. Linz, "Transitions to Democracy," *The Washington Quarterly* 13, no. 13 (Summer 1990): 143–64; Juan J. Linz and Alfred Stepan, *Problems of Democratic Transition and Consolidation: Southern Europe, South America, and Post-Communist Europe*, Baltimore: The Johns Hopkins University Press, 1996; Adam Przeworski, *Democracy and the Market: Political and Economic Reforms in Eastern Europe and Latin America*, Cambridge: Cambridge University Press, 1991; and Adam Przeworski, et. al., *Sustainable Democracy*, Cambridge: Cambridge University Press, 1995.
2. Terry D. Clark, "The Lithuanian Political Party System: A Case Study of Democratic Consolidation," EEPS: Eastern European Politics and Societies 9 (1995): 41–62.
3. A public opinion survey conducted by "Vilmorius" during the period 4 to 8 November 1999 and reported in "Vilmorius" visuomenes nuomones tyrimas: kam palankus Lietuvos zmones?" *Lietuvos Rytas*, 13 November 1999, p. 3, found that 6.4% express trust in political parties, 10.3% express trust in the *Seimas*, 18.0% trust the government, 17.8% trust the courts, 30.8% trust the police, 32.4% trust the Central Bank, 31.0% express trust in local governments, 42.9% trust the national social security agency (Sodra), 54.7% express trust in the presidency, and 56.5% trust the state health care system.
4. The *New Baltics Barometer II* was conducted in Lithuania in April 1995 by

NOTES TO CHAPTER 1

the University of Strathclyde's Centre for the Study of Public Policy. There were 870 respondents to the survey.

5. *1999 Regular Report from the Commission on Lithuania's Progress towards Accession*, 13 October 1999, p. 15.

6. Samuel P. Huntington, *The Third Wave: Democratization in the Late Twentieth Century*, Norman, Okla.: University of Oklahoma Press, 1991.

7. The classic description of the totalitarian model is provided by Hannah Arendt, *The Origins of Totalitarianism*, 2d ed., N.Y.: World Publishing Company, 1958; and Carl J. Friedrich and Zbigniew K. Brzezinski, *Totalitarian Dictatorship and Autocracy*, 2d ed., revised by Carl J. Friedrich, N.Y.: Praeger, 1965.

8. Jerry F. Hough and Merle Fainsod, *How the Soviet Union is Governed*, Cambridge: Harvard University Press, 1982.

9. H. Gordon Skilling, "Interest Groups and Communist Politics," *World Politics* 18:3 (1966): 435–51.

10. Among the foremost proponents of this view is Alfred Meyer, *The Soviet Political System: An Interpretation*, N.Y.: Random House, 1965.

11. Moshe Lewin, *The Gorbachev Phenomenon: A Historical Interpretation*, Berkeley and Los Angeles: University of California Press, 1988.

12. Valerie Bunce and John M. Echols III, "Soviet Politics in the Brezhnev Era: 'Pluralism' or 'Corporatism?'" in *Soviet Politics in the Brezhnev Era*, edited by Donald R. Kelley, N.Y.: Praeger, 1980.

13. Morris A. McCain, Jr., "Soviet Jurists Divided: A Case for Corporatism in the U.S.S.R?" *Comparative Politics* 15 (1983): 443–60.

14. Charles E. Ziegler, "Issue Creation and Interest Groups in Soviet Environmental Policy: The Applicability of the State Corporatist Model," *Comparative Politics* 18 (1986): 171–92.

15. Valerie Bunce, "The Struggle for Liberal Democracy in Eastern Europe," *World Policy Journal* 7 (1990): 395–430.

16. Samuel P. Huntington, *The Third Wave: Democratization in the Late Twentieth Century*, Norman, Okla.: University of Oklahoma Press, 1991.

17. One of the most extensive of these inventories is provided by Larry Diamond and Juan J. Linz, "Introduction: Politics, Society, and Democracy in Latin America," in Larry Diamond, Juan J. Linz, and Seymour Martin Lipset, eds., *Democracy in Developing Countries: Latin America*, vol. 4, Boulder, Colo.: Lynne Rienner Publishers, pp. 1–57.

18. Seymour Martin Lipset, *Political Man: The Social Bases of Politics*, Garden City, N.Y.: Doubleday, 1960.

19. Guillermo O'Donnell and Philippe C. Schmitter, *Transitions from Authoritarian Rule: Tentative Conclusions from Uncertain Democracies*, Baltimore: The Johns Hopkins University Press, 1986.

20. Juan J. Linz, "Transitions to Democracy," *The Washington Quarterly* 13, no. 13 (Summer 1990): 143–64; Juan J. Linz and Alfred Stepan, *Problems of Democratic Transition and Consolidation: Southern Europe, South America, and Post-Communist Europe*, Baltimore: The Johns Hopkins University Press, 1996; Adam Przeworski, *Democracy and the Market: Political and Economic Reforms in Eastern Europe and Latin America*, Cambridge: Cambridge University Press, 1991; and Adam Przeworski, *Sustainable Democracy*, Cambridge: Cambridge University Press, 1995.

21. See Guillermo O'Donnell and Philippe C. Schmitter, *Transitions from Authoritarian Rule: Tentative Conclusions about Uncertain Democracies*, Baltimore: The Johns Hopkins University Press, 1986.

22. See, for example, Scott Mainwaring, Guillermo O'Donnell, and J. Samuel Valenzuela, eds., *Issues in Democratic Consolidation: The New South American Democracies in Comparative Perspective*, Notre Dame: University of Notre Dame Press, 1992; and Adam Przeworski, *Democracy and the Market: Political and Economic Reforms in Eastern Europe and Latin America*, Cambridge: Cambridge University Press, 1991.

23. See Juan J. Linz, "Presidential or Parliamentary Democracy: Does It Make a Difference?" in Juan J. Linz and A. Valenzuela, eds., *The Failure of Presidential Democracy*, pp. 3–87, Baltimore: The Johns Hopkins University Press, 1994; and Matthew Soberg Shugart and John M. Carey, *Presidents and Assemblies: Constitutional Design and Electoral Dynamic*, Cambridge: Cambridge University Press, 1992.

24. See, for example, Samuel P. Huntington, *The Third Wave: Democratization in the Late Twentieth Century*, Norman, Okla.: University of Oklahoma Press, 1991.

25. A fairly complete inventory of such static factors is provided by Diamond and Linz, "Introduction: Politics, Society, and Democracy in Latin America," in Larry Diamond, Juan J. Linz, and Seymour Martin Lipset, eds., *Democracy in Developing Countries: Latin America*, vol. 4, Boulder, Colo., Lynne Reinner Publishers, pp. 1–57.

26. Samuel P. Huntington, *Political Order in Changing Societies*, New Haven: Yale University Press, 1968.

27. Juan J. Linz and Alfred Stepan, *Problems of Democratic Transition and Consolidation: Southern Europe, South America, and Post-communist Europe*, Baltimore: The Johns Hopkins University Press, 1996.

28. Valerie Bunce, "The Struggle for Liberal Democracy in Eastern Europe," *World Policy Journal* 7 (1990): 395–430.

29. *Ibid.*

Notes to Chapter 2

1. See Valerie Bunce, "Should Transitologists Be Grounded?" *Slavic Review* 54, no. 1 (1995): 111–27; Valerie Bunce, "The Political Economy of Postsocialism," *Slavic Review* 58, no. 4 (1999): 756–93; and Sarah Meiklejohn Terry, "Thinking about Post-communist Transitions: How Different Are They?" *Slavic Review* 52 (1993): 333–37.

2. See the debate on this issue in Valerie Bunce, "Should Transitologists Be Grounded?" *Slavic Review* 54, no. 1 (1995): 111–27; Terry Lynn Karl and Philippe C. Schmitter, "From an Iron Curtain to a Paper Curtain: Grounding Transitologists or Students of Postcommunism?" *Slavic Review* 54 (1995): 965–78; and Valerie Bunce, "Paper Curtains and Paper Tigers," *Slavic Review* 54 (1995): 979–87.

3. Dankwart A. Rustow, "Transitions to Democracy: Toward a Dynamic Model," *Comparative Politics* 2 (1970): 337–64.

4. Juan J. Linz and Alfred Stepan, *Problems of Democratic Transition and Consolidation: Southern Europe, South America, and Post-communist Europe*, Baltimore: The Johns Hopkins University Press, 1996.

5. Robert A. Dahl, *Democracy and Its Critics*, New Haven: Yale University Press, 1989.

6. Claus Offe, "Capitalism by Democratic Design? Democratic Theory Facing the Triple Transition in East Central Europe," *Social Research* 58 (1991): 864–902.

7. See, for example, Dominique Arel, "Ukraine: The Temptation of the Nationalizing State," in Vladimir Tismaneanu, ed., *Political Culture and Civil Society in Russia and the New States of Eurasia*, Armonk, N.Y.: M.E. Sharpe, 1995, pp. 157–88; Arthur H. Miller, Thomas F. Klobucar, William M. Reisinger, and Vicki L. Hesli, "Social Identities in Russia, Ukraine, and Lithuania," *Post-Soviet Affairs* 14 (1998): 248–86; and Zenovia A. Sochor, "Ethnic Politics in Ukraine," in Andreas Klinke, Ortwin Renn, and Jean-Paul Lehners, eds., *Ethnic Conflicts and Civil Society: Proposals for a New Era in Eastern Europe*, Aldershot, UK: Ashgate Publishing Ltd., 1997, pp. 127–50.

8. Milton J. Esman, *Ethnic Politics*, Ithaca: Cornell University Press, 1994.

9. See, for example, Alfred Erich Senn, *Gorbachev's Failure in Lithuania*, N.Y.: St. Martin's Press, 1995; Ursel Schlichting, "Conflicts between Different Nationalities: Chances for and Limits to Their Settlements," in Andreas Klinke, Ortwin Renn, and Jean-Paul Lehners, eds., *Ethnic Conflicts and Civil Society: Proposals for a New Era in Eastern Europe*, Aldershot, UK: Ashgate Publishing Ltd., 1997, pp. 35–52.

10. See Mark R. Beissinger, "Nationalist Violence and the State: Political Authority and Contentious Repertoires in the former USSR," *Comparative Politics* (July 1998): 401–22; Michael E. Brown, "Causes and Implications of Ethnic Conflict," in Michael E. Brown, ed., *Ethnic Conflict and International Security*, Princeton: Princeton University Press, 1993; Walker Connor, *Ethnonationalism: The Quest for Understanding*, Princeton: Princeton University Press, 1994; Karl Deutsch, "Social Mobilization and Political Development," *American Political Science Review* 55 (September 1961); Donald L. Horowitz, *Ethnic Groups in Conflict*, Berkeley: University of California Press, 1985; Rasma Karklins, *Ethnopolitics and Transition to Democracy: The Collapse of the USSR and Latvia*, Washington, D.C.: The Woodrow Wilson Center Press, 1994; Andreas Klinke, Ortwin Renn, and Jean-Paul Lehrners, "Ethnic Conflicts and Cooperation Among and Within States," in Andreas Klinke, Ortwin Renn, and Jean-Paul Lehners, eds., *Ethnic Conflicts and Civil Society: Proposals for a New Era in Eastern Europe*, Aldershot, UK: Ashgate Publishing Ltd., 1997, pp. 3–34; William Pfaff, *The Wrath of Nations: Civilization and the Furies of Nationalism*, N.Y.: Simon and Schuster, 1993; and Anthony Smith, *The Ethnic Origins of Nations*, Oxford: Basil Blackwell, 1986; and Jack Snyder, "Nationalism and the Crises of the Post-Soviet System," in Michael E. Brown, ed., *Ethnic Conflict and International Security*, Princeton: Princeton University Press, 1993; and Zenovia A. Sochor, "Ethnic Politics in Ukraine," in Andreas Klinke, Ortwin Renn, and Jean-Paul Lehners, eds., *Ethnic Conflicts and Civil Society: Proposals for a New Era in Eastern Europe*, Aldershot, UK: Ashgate Publishing Ltd., 1997, pp. 127–50.

11. See, for example, George Schpöflin, "The Problem of Nationalism in the Postcommunist Order," in Peter M. E. Voltan, ed., *Bound to Change: Consolidating Democracy in East Central Europe*, N.Y.: Institute for East-West Studies, 1992.

12. See Rasma Karklins, *Ethnopolitics and Transition to Democracy: The Collapse of the USSR and Latvia*, Washington, D.C.: The Woodrow Wilson Center Press, 1994; and Graham Smith, "Russia, Ethnoregionalism and the Politics of Fed-

eration," *Ethnic and Racial Studies* 19, no. 2 (1996): 391–410.

13. See Carol Skalnik Leff, "Democratization and Disintegration in Multinational States: The Breakup of Communist Federations," *World Politics* 51 (1999): 205–35; and Adam Przeworski et al. *Sustainable Democracy*, Cambridge: Cambridge University Press, 1995.

14. Seymour Martin Lipset, *Political Man: The Social Bases of Politics*, Garden City, N.Y.: Doubleday, 1960; and Joseph Schumpeter, *Capitalism, Socialism and Democracy*, N.Y.: Harper Brothers, 1942.

15. Adam Przeworski, *Democracy and the Market: Political and Economic Reforms in Eastern Europe and Latin America*, Cambridge: Cambridge University Press, 1991; and Richard Rose, "Escaping from Absolute Dissatisfaction: A Trial-and-Error Model of Change in Eastern Europe," *Journal of Theoretical Politics* 4 (1992): 371–93.

16. Lipset, *Political Man.* Seymour Martin Lipset, *Political Man: The Social Bases of Politics*, Garden City, N.Y.: Doubleday, 1960.

17. Samuel P. Huntington, *Political Order in Changing Societies*, New Haven: Yale University Press, 1968; and Mancur Olson, "Rapid Growth as a Destabilizing Force," *Journal of Economic History* 23 (1963): 453–72.

18. Adam Przeworski, Adam Alvarez, Jose Antonio Cheibub, and Fernando Limongi, "What Makes Democracies Endure?" *Journal of Democracy* 7 (January 1996): 39–55; and Adam Przeworski and Fernando Limongi, "Modernization: Theories and Facts," *World Politics* 49 (January 1997): 155–83.

19. Barrington Moore, *Social Origins of Dictatorship and Democracy: Lord and Peasant in the Making of the Modern World*, Boston: Beacon Press, 1966; and Theda Skocpol, *States and social revolutions: a comparative analysis of France, Russia, and China*, Cambridge: Cambridge University Press, 1979.

20. Richard Ahl, "Society and Transition in Post-Soviet Russia," *Communist and Post-Communist Studies* 32 (1999): 175–93.

21. Larry Diamond, "Economic Development and Democracy Reconsidered," in Gary Marks and Larry Diamond, eds., *Reexamining Democracy: Essays in Honor of Seymour Martin Lipset*, Newbury Park, Calif.: SAGE, 1992.

22. Edward N. Muller and Mitchell A. Seligson, "Civic Culture and Democracy: The Question of Causal Relationships," *American Political Science Review* 88, no. 3 (1994): 635–52.

23. Adam Przeworksi, Michael Alvarez, Jose Antonio Cheibub, and Fernando Limongi, "What Makes Democracies Endure?" *Journal of Democracy* 7, no. 1 (January 1996): 39–55.

24. Ross E. Burkart, "Comparative Democracy and Income Distribution: Shape and Direction of the Causal Arrow," *The Journal of Politics* 59 (1997): 148–64.

25. Beverly Crawford, *Markets, States and Democracy: The Political Economy of Post-Communist Transformation*, Boulder, Colo.: Westview Press, 1995; Daniel N. Nelson, "Civil Society Endangered," *Social Research* 63, no. 2 (Summer 1996): 345–68; Adam Przeworski, *Democracy and the Market: Political and Economic Reforms in Eastern Europe and Latin America*, Cambridge: Cambridge University Press, 1991; Adam Przeworski et al., *Sustainable Democracy*, Cambridge: Cambridge University Press, 1995; and Bertram Silverman and Murray Yanowitch, *New Rich, New Poor, New Russia: Winners and Losers on the Russian Road to Capitalism*, Armonk, N.Y.: M. E. Sharpe, 1997.

26. M. Steven Fish, "Democratization's Requisites: The Post-communist Experience," *Post-Soviet Affairs* 14 (1998): 212–47.

27. See Claus Offe, "Capitalism by Democratic Design? Democratic Theory Facing the Triple Transition in East Central Europe," *Social Research* 58 (1991): 864–902.

28. See, for example, Shantayanan Devarajan, "Prescribing Strong Economic Medicine: Revisiting the Myths about Structural Adjustment, Democracy, and Economic Peformance in Developing Countries," *Comparative Politics* 25 (1993): 169–82; Yi Feng, "Democracy, Political Stability and Economic Growth," *British Journal of Political Science* 27 (1997): 391–418; John F. Helliwell, "Empirical Linkages between Democracy and Economic Growth," *British Journal of Political Science* 24 (1994): 225–48; and Marc Lindenberg and Karen L. Remmer, "Democracy and Economic Crisis: The Latin American Experience," *World Politics* 42 (1990): 315–35.

29. Adam Przeworski, *Democracy and the Market: Political and Economic Reforms in Eastern Europe and Latin America*, Cambridge: Cambridge University Press, 1991.

30. Adam Przeworski et al., *Sustainable Democracy*, Cambridge: Cambridge University Press, 1995.

31. M. Steven Fish, "The Determinants of Economic Reform in the Post-communist World," *East European Politics and Societies* 12, no. 1 (Winter 1998): 31–78; Adam Przeworksi et al., *Sustainable Democracy*, Cambridge: Cambridge University Press, 1995; Gordon C. Rausser and S.R. Johnson, "State Market-Civil Institutions: The Case of Eastern Europe and the Soviet Republics," *World Development* 21, no. 4 (1993): 675–89; and Joseph E. Stiglitz, "The Design of Financial Systems for the Newly Emerging Democracies of Eastern Europe," pp. 161–84 in Christopher Clague and Gordon R. Rausser, eds., *The Emergence of Market Economies in Eastern Europe*, Cambridge: Blackwell Publishers, 1992.

32. Raymond M. Duch, "Tolerating Economic Reform: Popular Support for Transitions to a Free Market in the Former Soviet Union," *American Political Science Review* 87 (1993): 590–608.

33. Raymond M. Duch, "Economic Chaos and the Fragility of Democratic Transition in Former Communist Regimes," *Journal of Politics* 57 (1995): 121–58.

34. See David S. Mason, "Attitudes toward the Market and Political Participation in the Post-communist States," *Slavic Review* 54 (1995): 385–406; Mary E. McIntosh, Martha Abele MacIver, Daniel G. Abele, and Dina Smeltz, "Publics Meet Market Democracy in Central and East Europe, 1991–1993, *Slavic Review* 53 (1994): 483–512; and Adam Przeworski, "Public Support for Economic Reforms in Poland," *Comparative Political Studies* 29 (1996): 520–43.

35. Robert J. Brym, "The Ethic of Self-Reliance and the Spirit of Capitalism in Russia," *International Sociology* 11 (1996): 409–26.

36. Matthew Wyman, Stephen White, and Sarah Oates, eds., *Elections and Voters in Post-communist Russia*, Cheltenham, UK: Edward Elgar, 1998.

37. Judith S. Kullberg and William Zimmerman, "Liberal Elites, Socialist Masses, and Problems of Russian Democracy," *World Politics* 51 (April 1999): 323–58.

38. Ada W. Finifter and Ellen Mickiewicz, "Redefining the Political System of the USSR: Mass Support for Political Change," *American Political Science Review* 86 (1992): 857–74.

39. William M. Reisinger, Arthur H. Miller, and Vicki L. Hesli, "Public Behavior and Political Change in Post-Soviet States," *Journal of Politics* 57 (1995): 941–70.

40. Donna Bahry, Cynthia Boaz, and Stacy Burnett Gordon, "Tolerance, Transition, and Support for Civil Liberties in Russia," *Comparative Political Studies* 30 (1997): 484–510.

41. Richard Rose and William T. E. Mishler, "Mass Reaction to Regime Change in Eastern Europe: Polarization or Leaders and Laggards?" *British Journal of Political Science* 24 (1994): 159–82; and William Mishler and Richard Rose, "Trajectories of Fear and Hope: Support for Democracy in Post-communist Europe," *Comparative Political Studies* 28 (1996): 553–81.

42. Pamela Waldron-Moore, "Eastern Europe at the Crossroads of Democratic Transition," *Comparative Political Systems* 32 (1999): 32–62.

43. James L. Gibson, "Political and Economic Markets: Changes in the Connections Between Attitudes Toward Political Democracy and a Market Economy Within the Mass Culture of Russia and Ukraine," *Journal of Politics* 58 (1996): 954–84.

44. Karen Remmer, "The Sustainability of Political Democracy: Lessons from Latin America," *Comparative Political Studies* 29, no. 6 (December 1996): 611–34.

45. Adam Przeworski, et al., *Sustainable Democracy*, Cambridge: Cambridge University Press, 1995.

46. Larry Diamond, "Rethinking Civil Society: Toward Democratic Consolidation," *Journal of Democracy* 5, no. 3 (July 1994): 4–17; and Adam Przeworski et al., *Sustainable Democracy*, Cambridge: Cambridge University Press, 1995.

47. Larry Diamond and Juan J. Linz, "Introduction: Politics, Society, and Democracy in Latin America," in Larry Diamond, Juan J. Linz, and Seymour Martin Lipset, eds., *Democracy in Developing Countries: Latin America*, vol. 4, Boulder, Colo.: Lynne Rienner Publishers, pp. 1–57; and Guillermo O'Donnell and Philippe C. Schmitter, *Transitions from Authoritarian Rule: Tentative Conclusions from Uncertain Democracies*, Baltimore: The Johns Hopkins University Press, 1986.

48. Scott Mainwaring, Guillermo O'Donnell, and J. Samuel Valenzuela, eds., *Issues in Democratic Consolidation: The New South American Democracies in Comparative Perspective*, Notre Dame: University of Notre Dame Press, 1992.

49. James G. March and Johan P. Olson, "New Institutionalism: Organizational Factors in Political Life," *American Political Science Review* 78 (1984): 734–49.

50. Guillermo O'Donnell and Philippe C. Schmitter, *Transitions from Authoritarian Rule: Tentative Conclusions about Uncertain Democracies*, Baltimore: The Johns Hopkins University Press, 1986, p. 37.

51. Russell Bova, "Political Dynamics of the Post-communist Transition: A Comparative Perspective," *World Politics* 44 (1991): 113–58.

52. Helga A. Welsh, "Political Transition Processes in Central and Eastern Europe," *Comparative Politics* (1994): 379–94.

53. Andrew C. Janos, "Continuity and Change in Eastern Europe: Strategies of Post-communist Politics," *East European Politics and Societies* 8 (1994): 1–31.

54. Thomas F. Remington, "Democratization and the New Political Order in Russia," in Karen Dawisha and Bruce Parrott, eds., *Democratic Changes and Authoritarian Reactions in Russia, Ukraine, Belarus, and Moldova*, Cambridge: Cambridge University Press, 1997.

55. Michael McFaul, "Lessons from Russia's Protracted Transition from Communist Rule," *Political Science Quarterly* 114, no. 1 (1999): 103–30.

56. Samuel P. Huntington, *The Third Wave: Democratization in the Late Twentieth Century*, Norman, Okla.: University of Oklahoma Press, 1991.

57. Juan J. Linz and Alfred Stepan, *Problems of Democratic Transition and Consolidation: Southern Europe, South America, and Post-communist Europe*, Baltimore: The Johns Hopkins University Press, 1996.

58. Alexander J. Motyl, "Structural Constraints and Starting Points: The Logic of Systemic Change in Ukraine and Russia," *Comparative Politics* 29 (1997): 433–47.

59. Milada Anna Vachudova and Tim Snyder, "Are Transitions Transitory? Two Types of Political Change in Eastern Europe Since 1989," *East European Politics and Societies* 11 (1997): 1–35.

60. Karen Dawisha and Bruce Parrot, eds., *Politics, Power, and the Struggle for Democracy in South-East Europe*, Cambridge: Cambridge University Press, 1997.

61. Larry Diamond, "Rethinking Civil Society: Toward Democratic Consolidation," *Journal of Democracy* 5, no. 3 (July 1994): 4–17; Larry Diamond and L. Plattner, eds., *The Global Resurgence of Democracy*, Baltimore: The Johns Hopkins University Press, 1996; and Donald L. Horowitz, "Democracy in Divided Societies," *Journal of Democracy* 4, no. 4 (1993): 19–38.

62. Robert A. Dahl, *Pluralist Democracy in the United States*, Chicago: Rand McNally, 1967.

63. Maurice Duverger, *Political Parties*, N.Y.: Wiley and Sons, 1954.

64. Giovanni Sartori, *Parties and Party Systems*, N.Y.: Cambridge University Press, 1976.

65. E. E. Schattschneider, *The Semisovereign People: A Realist's View of Democracy in America*, N.Y.: Harcourt Brace Jovanovich, 1975.

66. Geoffrey Pridham, ed., *Securing Democracy: Political Parties and Democratic Consolidation in Southern Europe*, N.Y.: Routledge, 1990.

67. G. Bingham Powell, *Contemporary Democracies: Participation, Stability, and Violence*, Cambridge: Harvard University Press, 1982.

68. This is what Giovanni Sartori (1976) referred to as the number of "effective" parties.

69. See G. Bingham Powell (1982) for a concise review of the literature surrounding this debate.

70. Arend Lijphart, *Democracies: Patterns of Majoritarian and Consensus Government in Twenty-One Countries*, New Haven: Yale University Press, 1984.

71. See Maurice Duverger, *Political Parties: Their Organization and Activity in the Modern State*, London: Methuen, 1954; Douglas W. Rae, *The Political Consequences of Electoral Laws*, 2d ed., New Haven: Yale University Press, 1971; Rein Taagepera and Matthew S. Shugart, *Seats and Votes: The Effects and Determinants of Electoral Systems*, New Haven: Yale University Press, 1989; and Arend Lijphart, *Electoral Systems and Party Systems: A Study of Twenty-Seven Democracies, 1945–1990*, Oxford: Oxford University Press, 1994.

72. Peter Campbell, *French Electoral Systems and Elections, 1789–1957*, London: Faber and Faber, 1958; Michael Coppedge, "District Magnitude, Economic Performance, and Party-System Fragmentation in Five Latin American Countries," *Comparative Political Studies* 30 (1997): 156–85; Harry Eckstein, "The Impact of Electoral Systems on Representative Government, in Harry Eckstein and D. Apter, eds., *Comparative Politics: A Reader*, N.Y.: Free

Press, 1963; J. G. Grumm, "Theories of Electoral Systems," *Midwest Journal of Political Science* 2 (1958): 357–76; and Seymour Martin Lipset and Stein Rokkan, eds., *Party Systems and Voter Alignments: Cross-National Perspectives*, N.Y.: Free Press, 1967.

73. Gary W. Cox, *Making Votes Count: Strategic Coordination in the World's Electoral Systems*, Cambridge: Cambridge University Press, 1997; Peter Ordeshook and Olga Shvetsova, "Ethnic Heterogeneity, District Magnitude, and the Number of Parties," *American Journal of Political Science* 38 (1994): 100–123; and Rein Taagepera, "The Number of Parties as a Function of Heterogeneity and Electoral System," *Comparative Political Studies* 32, no. 5 (1999): 531–48.

74. Matthew Soberg Shugart and John M. Carey, *Presidents and Assemblies: Constitutional Design and Electoral Dynamics*, N.Y.: Cambridge University Press, 1992.

75. Peter C. Ordeshook and Olga V. Shvetsova, "Ethnic Heterogeneity, District Magnitude, and the Number of Parties," *American Journal of Political Science* 38 (1994): 100–123.

76. Robert G. Moser, "Electoral Systems and the Number of Parties in Post-communist States," *World Politics* 51 (April 1999): 359–84; and Robert G. Moser, "The Impact of Parliamentary Electoral Systems in Russia," *Post-Soviet Affairs* 13 (1997): 284–302.

77. See, for example, Syed Mohsin Hashim, "KPRF Ideology and Its Implications for Democratization in Russia," *Communist and Post-Communist Studies* 32 (1999): 77–89.

78. M. Steven Fish, "The Predicament of Russian Liberalism: Evidence from the December 1995 Parliamentary Elections," *Europe-Asia Studies* 49 (1997): 191–220.

79. Maurice Duverger, *Political Parties: Their Organization and Activity in the Modern State*, London: Methuen, 1954; and Seymour Martin Lipset and Stein Rokkan, *Party Systems and Voter Alignments*, N.Y.: Free Press, 1967.

80. Robert Dahl, *Polyarchy: Participation and Opposition*, New Haven: Yale University Press, 1971.

81. Herbert Kitschelt, "The Formation of Party Systems in East Central Europe," *Politics and Society* 20 (1992): 7–50.

82. Terry D. Clark, "The Lithuanian Political Party System: A Case Study of Democratic Consolidation," *East European Politics and Societies* 9 (Winter 1995): 41–62; and Vello Pettai and Marcus Kreuzer, "Party Politics in the Baltic States: Social Bases and Institutional Context," *East European Politics and Societies* 13 (Winter 1999): 148–89.

83. Alexander C. Pacek, "Macroeconomic Conditions and Electoral Politics in East Central Europe," *American Journal of Political Science* 38 (1994): 723–44; and Joshua A. Tucker, "It's the Economy Comrade! Economic Conditions and Election Results in Russia, Poland, Hungary, the Czech Republic, and Slovakia," a paper presented at the Midwest Political Science Association, 1998.

84. Andras Korosenyi, "Revival of the Past or New Beginning? The Nature of Post-communist Politics," *Political Quarterly* 62 (1991): 52–74; Ivan Szelenyi, Eva Fodor, and Eric Hanley, "Left Turn in Post-communist Politics: Bringing Class Back In?" *East European Politics and Societies* 11 (1997): 190–224; Petr Mateju and Blanka Rehakova, "Turning Left or Class Realignment? Analysis of the Changing

Relationship between Class and Party in the Czech Republic, 1992–1996," *East European Politics and Societies* 11 (1997): 501–42; Kazimierz M. Slomczynski and Goldie Shabad, "Systemic Transformation and the Salience of Class Structure in East Central Europe," *East European Politics and Societies* 11 (1997): 155–89; and Matthew Wyman, Stephen White, and Sarah Oates, eds., *Elections and Voters in Post-communist Russia*, Cheltenham, UK: Edward Elgar, 1998.

85. Geoffrey Evans and Stephen Whitefield, "Identifying the Bases of Party Competition in Eastern Europe," *British Journal of Political Science* 23 (1993): 521–48; and Matthew Wyman, Stephen White, and Sarah Oates, eds., *Elections and Voters in Post-communist Russia*, Cheltenham, UK: Edward Elgar, 1998.

86. Stephen White, Matthew Wyman, and Olga Kryshtanovskaya, "Parties and Politics in Post-communist Russia," *Communist and Post-communist Studies* 28 (1995): 183–202.

87. Juan J. Linz, "Presidential or Parliamentary Democracy: Does It Make a Difference?" in Juan J. Linz and A. Valenzuela, eds., *The Failure of Presidential Democracy*, pp. 3–87, Baltimore: The Johns Hopkins University Press, 1994; Juan J. Linz, "Transitions to Democracy," *The Washington Quarterly* 13, no. 13 (Summer 1990): 143–64; Scott Mainwaring, "Presidentialism, Multipartism, and Democracy: The Difficult Combination," *Comparative Political Studies* 26 (1993): 198–228; and Alfred Stepan and C. Skach, "Constitutional Frameworks and Democratic Consolidation," *World Politics* 46 (1993): 1–22.

88. Timothy J. Power and Mark J. Gasiorowski, "Institutional Design and Democratic Consolidation in the Third World," *Comparative Political Studies* 30, no. 2 (April 1977): 123–55.

89. Matthew Soberg Shugart and John M. Carey, *Presidents and Assemblies: Constitutional Design and Electoral Dynamics*, Cambridge: Cambridge University Press, 1992.

90. *Ibid.*

91. Jan Zielonka, "New Institutions in the Old East Bloc," *Journal of Democracy* 5 (1994): 87–104.

92. Philip Roeder, "Varieties of post-Soviet Authoritarian Regimes," *Post-Soviet Affairs* 10, no. 1 (1994): 61–101.

93. Gerald M. Easter, "Preference for Presidentialism: Post-communist Regime Change in Russia and the NIS," *World Politics* 49 (1997): 184–211.

94. John T. Ishiyama and Matthew Velten, "Presidential Power and Democratic Development in Post-communist Politics," *Communist and Post-Communist Studies* 31 (1998): 217–33.

95. Valerie Bunce, "Presidents and the Transition in Eastern Europe," in Kurt von Mettenheim, ed., *Presidential Institutions and Democratic Politics*, Baltimore: The Johns Hopkins University Press, 1977.

96. Terry M. Nichols, "The Logic of Russian Presidentialism: Institutions and Democracy in Postcommunism," The Carl Beck Papers, no. 1301, University of Pittsburgh, 1998.

97. Matthew Soberg Shugart, "The Inverse Relationship Between Party Strength and Executive Strength: A Theory of Politicians' Constitutional Choices," *British Journal of Political Science* 28 (1998): 1–29.

98. Timothy Frye, "A Politics of Institutional Choice: Post-communist Presidencies," *Comparative Political Studies* 30 (1997): 523–52.

99. See, for example, Jerry F. Hough, Evelyn Davidheiser, and Susan Goodrich Lehmann, *The 1996 Russian Presidential Election*, Washington, D.C.: Brookings Institution Press, 1996; and Jerry F. Hough and Susan Goodrich Lehmann, "The Mystery of Opponents of Economic Reform among the Yeltsin Voters," in Matthew Wyman, Stephen White, and Sarah Oates, eds., *Elections and Voters in Post-communist Russia*, Cheltenham, UK: Edward Elgar, 1998, pp. 190–227.

100. John T. Ishiyama, "The Sickle or the Rose? Previous Regime Types and the Evolution of the Ex-Communist Parties in Post-communist Politics," *Comparative Political Studies* 30 (1997): 299–330; and John T. Ishiyama, "Communist Parties in Transition: Structures, Leaders, and Processes of Democratization in Eastern Europe," *Comparative Politics* 27 (1995): 147–66.

101. Bryon Moraski and Gerhard Loewenberg, "The Effect of Legal Thresholds on the Revival of Former Communist Parties in East-Central Europe," *The Journal of Politics* 61, no. 1 (1999): 151–70.

102. See Alison Mahr and John Nagle, "Resurrection of the Successor Parties and Democratization in East-Central Europe," *Communist and Post-communist Studies* 28 (1995): 393–409.

103. David S. Mason, "Attitudes toward the Market and Political Participation in the Post-communist States," *Slavic Review* 54 (1995): 385–406; and Alexander C. Pacek, "Macroeconomic Conditions and Electoral Politics in East Central Europe," *American Journal of Political Science* 38, no. 3. (1994): 723–44.

104. See, for example, Voytek Zubek, "The Phoenix Out of the Ashes: The Rise to Power of Poland's Post-communist SdRP," *Communist and Post-communist Studies* 28 (1995): 275–306.

105. John T. Ishiyama, "The Sickle or the Rose? Previous Regime Types and the Evolution of the Ex-Communist Parties in Post-communist Politics," *Comparative Political Studies* 30 (1997): 299–330; John T. Ishiyama, "The Communist Successor Parties and Party Organizational Development in Post-Communist Politics," *Political Research Quarterly* 52, no. 1 (1999): 87–112; and John T. Ishiyama, "Communist Parties in Transition: Structures, Leaders, and Processes of Democratization in Eastern Europe," *Comparative Politics* 27 (1995): 147–66.

106. Evelyn Davidheiser, "The CPRF: Towards Social Democracy or National Socialism?" in Matthew Wyman, Stephen White, and Sarah Oates, eds., *Elections and Voters in Post-communist Russia*, Cheltenham, UK: Edward Elgar, 1998, pp. 240–76.

107. Syed Mohsin Hashim, "KPRF Ideology and Its Implications for Democratization in Russia," *Communist and Post-Communist Studies* 32 (1999): 77–89.

108. Joan Barth Urban and Valerii D. Solovei, *Russia's Communists at the Crossroads*, Boulder, Colo.: Westview Press, 1997.

109. Jean Blondel, *Comparative Legislatures*, Englewood Cliffs, N.J.: Prentice-Hall, Inc., 1973; Michael L. Mezey, *Comparative Legislatures*, Durham, N.C.: Duke University Press, 1979; Joel Smith and Lloyd D. Musolf, eds., *Legislatures in Development: Dynamics of Change in New and Old States*, Durham, N.C.: Duke University Press, 1979; and Gerhard Loewenberg and Samuel C. Patterson, *Comparing Legislatures*, Boston: Little, Brown and Company, 1979.

110. Fred W. Riggs, "Bureaucrats and Political Development: A Paradoxical View," in Joseph J. LaPalombara, ed., *Bureaucracy and Political Development*, Princeton: Princeton University Press, 1963; Fred W. Riggs, *Legislative Origins: A Compara-*

tive and Contextual Approach, International Studies Association, Occasional Paper No. 7, Pittsburgh: International Studies Association, 1975.

111. Michael L. Mezey, "The Functions of Legislatures in the Third World," *Legislative Studies Quarterly* 8, no. 4 (1983): 511–50; Fred W. Riggs, "Bureaucrats and Political Development: A Paradoxical View," in Joseph J. LaPalombara, ed., *Bureaucracy and Political Development*, Princeton: Princeton University Press, 1963; and Fred W. Riggs, *Legislative Origins: A Comparative and Contextual Approach*, International Studies Association, Occasional Paper No. 7, Pittsburgh: International Studies Association, 1975.

112. See David M. Olson and Philip Norton, eds., *The New Parliaments of Central and Eastern Europe*, London: Frank Cass, 1996; and Thomas F. Remington, ed., *Parliaments in Transition: The New Legislative Politics in the Former USSR and Eastern Europe*, Boulder, Colo.: Westview Press, 1994.

113. See, for example, Terry D. Clark, "A House Divided: A Roll-call Analysis of the First Session of the Moscow City Soviet," *Slavic Review* 51, no. 4 (Winter 1992): 674–90; and Terry D. Clark, "Voting Patterns in the Russian Federation Council," *The Journal of Communist Studies and Transition Politics* 11, no. 4 (December 1995): 372–83.

114. See Terry D. Clark, Stacy J. Holscher, and Lisa Hyland, "The LDLP Faction in the Lithuanian Seimas, 1992–1996," *Nationalities Papers* (1999); and Moshe Haspel, Thomas F. Remington, and Steven S. Smith, "Electoral Institutions and Party Cohesion in the Russian Duma," *The Journal of Politics* 60, no. 2 (1998): 417–39.

115. See, for example, Terry D. Clark, Stacy J. Holscher, and Lisa Hyland, "The LDLP Faction in the Lithuanian Seimas, 1992–1996," *Nationalities Papers* (1999); Terry D. Clark, "Coalitional Behavior in the Lithuanian Parliament: The First Four Years," *Demokratizatsiya: The Journal of Post-Soviet Democratization* 3, no. 1 (Winter 1995): 61–75; and Terry D. Clark, "Coalition Realignment in the Supreme Council of the Republic of Lithuania and the Fall of the Vagnorius Government," *Journal of Baltic Studies* 24, no. 1 (Spring 1993): 53–66.

116. For a concise summary of this literature see David P. Baron, "Comparative Dynamics of Parliamentary Governments," *American Political Science Review* 92, no. 3 (1998): 593–609.

117. David M. Olson and Philip Norton, eds., *The New Parliaments of Central and Eastern Europe*, Portland, Ore.: Frank Cass, 1996.

118. David M. Olson, "Paradoxes of Institutional Development: The New Democratic Parliaments of Central Europe," *International Political Science Review* 18, no. 4 (1997): 401–16.

119. Giuseppe DiPalma, *To Craft Democracies: An Essay on Democratic Transition.* Berkeley: University of California Press, 1990; and Guillermo O'Donnell and Philippe C. Schmitter, *Transitions from Authoritarian Rule: Tentative Conclusions from Uncertain Democracies*, Baltimore: The Johns Hopkins University Press, 1986.

120. Dankwart A. Rustow, "Transitions to Democracy: Toward a Dynamic Model," *Comparative Politics* 2 (1970): 337–64.

121. Adam Przeworski, *Democracy and the Market: Political and Economic Reforms in Eastern Europe and Latin America*, Cambridge: Cambridge University Press, 1991.

122. Dimitar Mircev, "Ethnocentrism and Strife Among Political Elites: The End of Yugoslavia," in Hans Derlien and George Szablowski, eds., *Regime Transition,*

Elites and Bureaucrats in Eastern Europe, special edition of *Governance* 6, no. 3 (July 1993): 372–85.

123. Judith Kullberg, John Higley, and Jan Pakulski, "Elites, Institutions and Democratisation in Russia and East Europe," in Graeme Gill, ed., *Elites and Leadership in Russian Politics*, N.Y.: St. Martin's Press, Inc., 1998, pp. 106–33.

124. Judith S. Kullberg, "The Ideological Roots of Elite Political Conflict in Post-Soviet Russia," *Europe-Asia Studies* 46, no. 6 (1994): 929–53.

125. Arthur H. Miller, Vicki L. Hesli, and William M. Reisinger, "Conceptions of Democracy among Mass and Elite in Post-Soviet Societies," *British Journal of Political Science* 27 (1997): 157–90; and William M. Reisinger, Andrei Yu. Melville, Arthur H. Miller, and Vicki L. Hesli, "Mass and Elite Political Outlooks in Post-Soviet Russia: How Congruent?" *Political Research Quarterly* 49, no. 1 (1996): 77–101.

126. Eric Hanley, Natasha Yershova, and Richard Anderson, "Old Wine in a New Bottle? The Circulation and Reproduction of Russian Elites," *Theory and Society* 24, no. 5 (1995): 639–68; Olga Kryshtanovskaya and Stephen White, "From Power to Property: The *Nomenklatura* in Post-Communist Russia," in Graeme Gill, ed., *Elites and Leadership in Russian Politics*, N.Y.: St. Martin's Press, Inc., 1998, pp. 81–105; Olga Kryshtanovskaya and Stephen White, "From Soviet Nomenclatura to Russian Elite," *Europe-Asia Studies* 48 (1996): 711–33; Liliia F. Shevtsova, "Dilemmy postkommunisticheskogo obshchestva," *Polis (Politicheskie issledovaniia)*, no. 5 (1996): 80–90; and Ivan Szelenyi and Szonja Szelenyi, "Circulation or Reproduction of Elites during the Post-Communist Transformation of Eastern Europe: Introduction," *Theory and Society* 24, no. 5 (1995): 615–38.

127. T. H. Rigby, "New Top Elites for Old in Russian Politics," *British Journal of Political Science* 23 (1999): 323–43.

128. David Lane and Cameron Ross, *The Transition from Communism to Capitalism: Ruling Elites from Gorbachev to Yeltsin*, N.Y.: St. Martin's Press, Inc., 1999.

Notes to Chapter 3

1. Steven M. Fish, "Rethinking Civil Society: Russia's Fourth Transition," *Journal of Democracy* 5, no. 3 (July 1994): 31–42; Alberto Gasparini and Vladimir Yadov, eds., *Social Actors and Designing the Civil Society of Eastern Europe*, London: JAI Press, Inc., 1995; Jeffrey W. Hahn, "Changes in Contemporary Russian Political Culture," in Vladimir Tismaneanu, ed., *Political Culture and Civil Society in Russia and the New States of Eurasia*, Armonk, N.Y.: M. E. Sharpe, Inc., 1995; and Geoffey Pridham and Tatu Vanhanen, "Introduction," in Geoffrey Pridham and Tatu Vanhanen, eds., *Democratization in Eastern Europe: Domestic and International Perspectives*, N.Y.: Routledge, 1994, pp. 1–14.

2. Robert D. Putnam, *Making Democracy Work: Civic Traditions in Modern Italy*, Princeton: Princeton University Press, 1993.

3. *Ibid.*

4. Fritz Plasser, Peter A. Ulram, and Harald Waldrauch, *Democratic Consolidation in East-Central Europe*, N.Y.: St. Martin's Press, Inc., 1998.

5. Ronald Inglehart, "The Renaissance of Political Culture," *American Political Science Review* 82 (1988): 1203–30; and Ronald Inglehart, *Culture Shift in Advanced Industrial Society*, Princeton: Princeton University Press, 1990.

6. Edward N. Muller and Mitchell A. Seligson, "Civic Culture and Democracy: The Question of Causal Relationships," *American Political Science Review* 88 (1994): 635–52.

7. The contours of this debate are laid out in Stephen Whitefield and Geoffrey Evans, "Political Culture Versus Rational Choice: Explaining Responses to Transition in the Czech Republic and Slovakia," *British Journal of Political Science* 29 (1999): 129–54.

8. Stephen White, "Political Culture in Communist States," *Comparative Political Studies* 16 (1984): 351–65.

9. Walter Laqueur, *The Long Road to Freedom*, N.Y.: Scribner's, 1989.

10. Harry Eckstein, Frederic J. Fleron, Jr., Erik P. Hoffmann, and William M. Reisinger, with Richard Ahl, Russell Bova, and Philip G. Roeder, *Can Democracy Take Root in Post-Soviet Russia? Explorations in State-Society Relations*, N.Y.: Rowman & Littlefield Publishers, Inc., 1998.

11. Nicolai N. Petro, *The Rebirth of Russian Democracy: An Interpretation of Political Culture*, Cambridge: Harvard University Press, 1995.

12. For an excellent review of the transition from a generally pessimistic assessment of the effects of political culture on change in the Soviet era to the relatively more optimistic assessments in the post-Soviet era, see Frederic J. Fleron, Jr., "Post-Soviet Political Culture in Russia: An Assessment of Recent Empirical Investigations," *Europe-Asia Studies* 48 (1996): 225–60.

13. Jeffrey W. Hahn, "Continuity and Change in Russian Political Culture," pp. 299–330 in Frederic J. Fleron, Jr., and Erik P. Hoffmann, eds., *Post-communist Studies and Political Science: Methodology and Empirical Theory in Sovietology*, Boulder, Colo.: Westview Press, 1993.

14. James Alexander, "Surveying Attitudes in Russia: A Representation of Formlessness," *Communist and Post-communist Studies* 30 (1997): 107–27.

15. See, for example, Donna Bahry and Lucan Way, "Citizen Activism in the Russian Transition," *Post-Soviet Affairs* 10 (1994): 330–66; Raymond M. Duch, "Tolerating Economic Reform: Popular Support for Transitions to a Free Market in the Former Soviet Union," *American Political Science Review* 87 (1993): 590–608; Ada W. Finifter and Ellen Mickiewicz, "Redefining the Political System of the USSR: Mass Support for Political Change," *American Political Science Review* 86 (1992): 857–74; James L. Gibson, "Perceived Political Freedom in the Soviet Union," *Journal of Politics* 55 (1993): 936–74; James L. Gibson, "The Resilience of Mass Support for Democratic Institutions and Processes in the Nascent Russian and Ukrainian Democracies," in Vladimir Tismaneanu, ed., *Political Culture and Civil Society in Russia and the New States of Eurasia*, Armonk, N.Y.: M. E. Sharpe, 1995; James L. Gibson, Raymond M. Duch, and Kent L. Tedin, "Democratic Values and the Transformation of the Soviet Union," *Journal of Politics* 54 (1992): 329–71; Jeffrey W. Hahn, "Changes in Contemporary Russian Political Culture," in Vladimir Tismaneanu, ed., *Political Culture and Civil Society in Russia and the New States of Eurasia*, Armonk, N.Y.: M. E. Sharpe, 1995; David S. Mason, "Attitudes toward the Market and Political Participation in the Post-communist States," *Slavic Review* 54 (1995): 385–406; Ian McAllister and Stephen White, "Political Participation in Post-communist Russia: Voting, Activism, and the Potential for Mass Support," *Political Studies* 42 (1994): 593–615; William M. Reisinger, Arthur H. Miller, and Vicki L. Hesli, "Public Behavior and Political Change in Post-Soviet States," *Journal of*

Politics 57 (1995): 941–70; William M. Reisinger, Arthur H. Miller, and Vicki L. Hesli, eds., *Public Opinion and Regime Change: The New Politics of Post-Soviet Societies*, Boulder, Colo.: Westview Press, 1993; and Richard Rose, "Rethinking Civil Society: Postcommunism and the Problem of Trust," *Journal of Democracy* 5 (July 1994): 18–30.

16. Robert J. Brym, "Re-evaluating Mass Support for Political and Economic Change in Russia," *Europe-Asia Studies* 48 (1996): 751–66; Frederic J. Fleron, Jr., "Post-Soviet Political Culture in Russia: An Assessment of Recent Empirical Investigations," *Europe-Asia Studies* 48 (1996): 225–60; and Robert D. Grey, William L. Miller, Stephen White, and Paul Heywood, "The Structure of Russian Political Opinion," *Coexistence* 32 (1995): 183–215.

17. James L. Gibson and Raymond M. Duch, "Political Intolerance in the USSR: The Distribution and Etiology of Mass Opinion," *Comparative Political Studies* 26 (1993): 286–329; James L. Gibson, Raymond M. Duch, and Kent L. Tedin, "Democratic Values and the Transformation of the Soviet Union," *The Journal of Politics* 54 (1992): 329–71; and James L. Gibson, "Putting Up with Fellow Russians: An Analysis of Political Tolerance in the Fledgling Russian Democracy," *Political Research Quarterly* 51 (1998): 37–68.

18. Thomas M. Nichols, "Russian Democracy and Social Capital," *Social Science Information*, London: SAGE, 1996, pp. 629–42.

19. E. E. Schattschneider, *The Semisovereign People: A Realist's View of Democracy in America*, Hinsdale, Ill.: Dryden Press, 1975.

20. Joel S. Migdal, *Strong Societies and Weak States: State-Society Relations and State Capabilities in the Third World*, Princeton: Princeton University Press, 1988.

21. For the contours of this debate see Vaclav Havel and Vaclav Klaus, with commentary by Petr Pithart, "Civil Society after Communism: Rival Visions," *Journal of Democracy* 7, no. 1 (1996): 12–23.

22. Robert A. Dahl, *Democracy and Its Critics*, New Haven: Yale University Press, 1989.

23. See Michael Bernhard, "Civil Society and Democratic Transition in East Central Europe," *Political Science Quarterly* 108 (1993): 307–26.

24. Larry Diamond, "Rethinking Civil Society: Toward Democratic Consolidation," *Journal of Democracy* 5, no. 3 (July 1994): 4–17; and William Kornhauser, *The Politics of Mass Society*, N.Y.: Free Press, 1959.

25. Larry Diamond, "Rethinking Civil Society."

26. Valerie Bunce, "The Struggle for Liberal Democracy in Eastern Europe," *World Policy Journal* 7 (1990): 396–430.

27. Jane L. Curry, "A Reconsideration of the Realities of 'Civil Society' in the Light of the Post-Communist Society," in Adolph Bibic and Gigi Graziano, eds., *Civil Society, Political Society, Democracy*, Ljubljana: Slovenian Political Science Association, 1994, pp. 231–48;Wolfgang Merkel, "Democratic Consolidation and Civil Society: Problems of Democratic Consolidation in East Central Europe," in Adolph Bibic and Gigi Graziano, eds., *Civil Society, Political Society, Democracy*, Ljubljana: Slovenian Political Science Association, 1994, pp. 325–51; and George Schopflin, "Obstacles to Liberalism in Post-communist Politics," *East European Politics and Society* 5 (1991): 189–94.

28. Andrzej Korbonski, "Civil Society and Democracy in Poland: Prospects and Problems," in Adolph Bibic and Gigi Graziano, eds., *Civil Society, Political Society,*

Democracy, Ljubljana: Slovenian Political Science Association, 1994, pp. 215–30; and Mate Szabo, "The State of Political Institutions, Political Society, and Civil Society in Hungary," in Adolph Bibic and Gigi Graziano, eds., *Civil Society, Political Society, Democracy*, Ljubljana: Slovenian Political Science Association, 1994, pp. 265–86.

29. William M. Reisinger, Arthur H. Miller, and Vicki L. Hesli, "Public Behavior and Political Change in Post-Soviet States," *The Journal of Politics* 57 (1995): 941–70.

30. See the essays in Alberto Gasparini and Vladimir Yadov, eds., *Social Actors and Designing the Society of Eastern Europe*, London: JAI Press, Inc., 1995.

31. Lisa A. Baglione and Carol L. Clark, "Transforming Russian Unions," *Problems of Post-Communism* 45, no. 1 (1998): 43–53.

32. Oleg Yanitsky, "Ecological Movements and Fears of Environmental Disasters," in Alberto Gasparini and Vladimir Yadov, eds., *Social Actors and Designing the Society of Eastern Europe*, London: JAI Press, Inc., 1995, pp. 193–204.

33. Robert F. Goeckel, "The Baltic Churches and the Democratization Processes," in Michael Bourdeaux, ed., *The Politics of Religion in Russia and the New States of Eurasia*, Armonk, N.Y.: M. E. Sharpe, Inc., 1995, pp. 202–25.

34. Edward K. Snajdr, "The Children of the Greens: New Ecological Activism in Post-Socialist Slovakia," *Problems of Post-Communism* 45, no. 1 (1998): 54–62.

35. Klaus von Beyme, *Transition to Democracy in Eastern Europe*, N.Y.: St. Martin's Press, Inc., 1996; and David W. Lovell, "Nationalism, Civil Society, and the Prospects for Freedom in Eastern Europe," *Australian Journal of Politics and History* 45, no. 1 (1999): 65–77.

36. David W. Lovell, "Nationalism, Civil Society, and the Prospects for Freedom in Eastern Europe," *Australian Journal of Politics and History* 45, no. 1 (1999): 65–77.

37. One exception is Jan Kubik, "Institutionalization of Protest during Democratic Consolidation in Central Europe," in David S. Meyer and Sidney Tarrow, eds., *The Social Movement Society: Contentious Politics for a New Century*, N.Y.: Rowman & Littlefield Publishers, Inc., 1998, pp. 131–52.

38. Joe Foweraker and Todd Landman, "Individual Rights and Social Movements: A Comparative and Statistical Inquiry," *British Journal of Political Science* 29 (1999): 291–322.

39. See Anne N. Costain and Andrew S. McFarland, eds., *Social Movements and American Political Institutions*, N.Y.: Rowman & Littlefield Publishers, Inc., 1998; and David S. Meyer and Sidney Tarrow, eds., *The Social Movement Society: Contentious Politics for a New Century*, N.Y.: Rowman & Littlefield Publishers, Inc., 1998.

40. Alberto Gasparini and Vladimir Yadov, eds., *Social Actors and Designing the Civil Society of Eastern Europe*, London: JAI Press, Inc., 1995.

41. Georgina Waylen, "Women and Democratization: Conceptualizing Relations in Transition Politics," *World Politics* 46, no. 3 (1994): 327–53.

42. Donald Barry, *Toward the "Rule of Law" in Russia?* Armonk, N.Y.: M. E. Sharpe, Inc., 1992; A. E. Dick Howard, ed., *Constitution Making in Eastern Europe*, Washington, D.C.: The Johns Hopkins University Press, 1993; John Reitz, "Progress in Building Institutions for the Rule of Law," in Robert D. Grey, ed., *Democratic Theory and Post-Communist Change*, Upper Saddle River, N.J.: Prentice-Hall, Inc., 1997, pp. 144–89; and Bruce L. R. Smith and Gennady M. Danilenko, eds., *Law in Democracy in the New Russia*, Washington, D.C.: The Brookings Institution, 1993.

43. Eugene Huskey, "Russian Judicial Reform after Communism," in Peter H. Solomon, Jr., ed., *Reforming Justice in Russia, 1864–1996*, Armonk, N.Y.: M. E. Sharpe, Inc., 1997, pp. 325–47; Gordon B. Smith, "The Struggle over the Procuracy," in Peter H. Solomon, Jr., ed., *Reforming Justice in Russia, 1864–1996*, Armonk, N.Y.: M. E. Sharpe, Inc, 1997, pp. 348–73; and Gordon B. Smith, *Reforming the Russian Legal System*, Cambridge: Cambridge University Press, 1996.

44. Eugene Huskey, "Russian Judicial Reform after Communism," in Peter H. Solomon, Jr., ed., *Reforming Justice in Russia, 1864–1996*, Armonk, N.Y.: M. E. Sharpe, Inc., 1997, pp. 325–47; Michael Newcity, "Russian Legal Tradition and the Rule of Law," in Jeffrey D. Sachs and Katharina Pistor, eds., *The Rule of Law and Economic Reform in Russia*, Boulder, Colo.: Westview Press, 1997, pp. 41–54; and John Reitz, "Constitutionalism and the Rule of Law: Theoretical Perspectives," in Robert D. Grey, ed., *Democratic Theory and Post-Communist Change*, Upper Saddle River, N.J.: Prentice-Hall, Inc., 1997, pp. 111–43.

45. Pedro C. Magalhaes, "The Politics of Judicial Reform in Eastern Europe," *Comparative Politics* 32, no. 1 (1999): 43–62.

46. Shannon Ishiyama Smithey and John Ishiyama, "Judicious choices: designing courts in post-communist politics," *Communist and Post-Communist Studies* 33 (2000): 163–82.

47. Adam Przeworski et al., *Sustainable Democracy*, Cambridge: Cambridge University Press, 1995.

48. Juan J. Linz and Alfred Stepan, *Problems of Democratic Transition and Consolidation: Southern Europe, South America, and Post-Communist Europe*, Baltimore: The Johns Hopkins University Press, 1996.

49. Exceptions are Hans Derlien and George Szablowski, eds., *Regime Transitions, Elites and Bureaucrats in Eastern Europe*, special edition of *Governance* 6, no. 3 (July 1993); and Tamas L. Fellegi, "Regime Transformation and the Mid-Level Bureaucratic Forces in Hungary," in Peter M. E. Volten, ed., *Bound to Change: Consolidating Democracy in East Central Europe*, N.Y.: Institute for East-West Studies, 1992, pp. 119–15.

50. See, for example, George M. Guess, "Transformation of Bureaucratic States in Eastern Europe: Public Expenditure Lessons from Latin America," *International Journal of Public Administration* 20, no. 3 (1997): 621–41; Joachim Jens Hesse, "From Transformation to Modernization: Administrative Change in Central and Eastern Europe," *Public Administration* 71 (1993): 219–57; and Eric M. Rice, "Public Administration in Post-Socialist Eastern Europe," *Public Administration Review* 52, no. 2 (1992): 116–24.

51. Massimo Balducci, "Training Civil Servants in the Administrations of Central and Eastern Europe: A Missed Opportunity?" *International Review of Administrative Sciences* 61 (1995): 61–72; George M. Guess, "Transformation of Bureaucratic States in Eastern Europe"; Eric M. Rice, "Public Administration in Post-Socialist Eastern Europe"; and Mark Sanna, "Public Management in Russia: Failures of the Old System," *The Public Manager*, Summer 1993, pp. 35–38.

52. Stephen Handelman, "The Russian 'Mafiya,'" *Foreign Affairs* 73, no. 2 (1994): 83–96; and Tony Verheijen and Antoaneta Dimitrova, "Private Interests and Public Administration: The Central and East European Experience," *International Review of Administrative Sciences* 62 (1996): 197–218.

53. Ase Grodeland, Tatyana Koshechkina, and William L. Miller, "Alternative

Strategies for Coping with Officials in Different Post-communist Regimes: The Worm's Eye View," *Public Administration and Development* 17 (1997): 511–28.

54. See Kenneth A. Shepsle and Barry R. Weingast, *Positive Theories of Congressional Institutions*, Ann Arbor: The University of Michigan Press, 1998, for an overview of the research agenda on congressional committee systems.

55. See Melissa P. Collie and Joseph Cooper, "Multiple Referral and the 'New' Committee System in the House of Representatives," in Lawrence Dodd and Bruce Oppenheimer, eds., *Congress Reconsidered*, 4th ed., Washington, D.C.: Congressional Quarterly Press, 1989.

56. See, for example, Randall G. Holcombe and Glenn R. Parker, "Committees in legislatures: A property rights perpective," *Public Choice* 70 (1991): 11–20; and Kenneth A. Shepsle and Barry R. Weingast, "The Institutional Foundations of Committee Power," *American Political Science Review* 81 (1987): 85–104.

57. See, for example, D. Roderick Kiewit and Matthew D. McCubbins, *The Logic of Delegation: Congressional Parties and the Appropriations Process*, Chicago: University of Chicago Press, 1991.

58. David Austen-Smith, "Information Transmission in Debate," *American Journal of Political Science* 34 (1990): 124–52; Thomas W. Gilligan and Keith Krehbiel, "Asymmetric Information and Legislative Rules with a Heterogeneous Committee," *American Journal of Political Science* 33 (1989): 459–90; and Thomas W. Gilligan and Keith Krehbiel, "Organization of Informative Committees by a Rational Legislature," *American Journal of Political Science* 34 (1990): 531–64.

59. Thomas F. Remington and Steven S. Smith, "Theories of Legislative Institutions and the Organization of the Russian Duma," *American Journal of Political Science* 42 (1998): 545–72.

60. Matthew Soberg Shugart and John M. Carey, *Presidents and Assemblies: Constitutional Design and Electoral Dynamic*, Cambridge: Cambridge University Press, 1992; Juan J. Linz, "Presidential or Parliamentary Democracy: Does It Make a Difference?" in Juan J. Linz and A. Valenzuela, eds., *The Failure of Presidential Democracy*, pp. 3–87, Baltimore: The Johns Hopkins University Press, 1994; Juan J. Linz, "Transitions to Democracy," *The Washington Quarterly* 13, no. 13 (Summer 1990): 143–64; Scott Mainwaring, "Presidentialism, Multipartism, and Democracy: The Difficult Combination," *Comparative Political Studies* 26 (1993): 198–228; and Alfred Stepan and C. Skach, "Constitutional Frameworks and Democratic Consolidation," *World Politics* 46 (1993): 1–22.

61. D. Roderick Kiewit and Matthew D. McCubbins, *The Logic of Delegation: Congressional Politics and the Appropriations Process*, Chicago: University of Chicago Press, 1991; and Matthew D. McCubbins, Roger G. Noll, and Barry R. Weingast, "Administrative Procedures as Instruments of Political Control," *Journal of Law, Economics, and Organization* 3 (1987): 243–77.

62. Adam Przeworski et al., *Sustainable Democracy*, Cambridge: Cambridge University Press, 1995.

63. See Floyd Hunter, *Community Power Structure*, Chapel Hill, N.C.: University of North Carolina Press, 1953.

64. See Robert Dahl, *Who Governs? Democracy and Power in an American City*, New Haven: Yale University Press, 1961.

65. John R. Logan and Harvey L. Molotch, *Urban Fortunes: The Political Economy of Place*, Berkeley: University of California Press, 1987.

66. Todd Swanstrom, *The Crisis of Growth Politics: Cleveland, Kucinich, and the Challenge of Urban Populism*, Philadelphia, Temple University Press, 1985; and S. L. Elkins, "State and Market in City Politics: Or, the Real Dallas," in *The Politics of Urban Development*, eds. Clarence Stone and H. T. Sanders, Lawrence, Kans.: University Press of Kansas, 1987.

67. For example, Kathryn Stoner-Weiss, "Central Weakness and Provincial Autonomy: Observations on the Devolution Process in Russia," *Post-Soviet Affairs* 15 (1999): 87–106, argues that it does, while Mikhail Filippov and Olga Shvetsova, "Asymmetric Bilateral Bargaining in the New Russian Federation: A Path-Dependence Explanation," *Communist and Post-Communist Studies* 32 (1999): 61–76, argue that it does not.

68. See, for example, Theodore H. Friedgut and Jeffrey W. Hahn, eds., *Local Power and Post-Soviet Politics*, Armonk, N.Y.: M. E. Sharpe, 1994; and Jeffrey W. Hahn, ed., *Democratization in Russia: The Development of Legislative Institutions*, Armonk, N.Y.: M. E. Sharpe, 1996.

69. Fred Warren Riggs, *Legislative origins; a comparative and contextual approach*, International Studies Association Occasional Paper, no. 7, Pittsburgh: University of Pittsburgh Press, 1975.

70. See, for example, Robert Axelrod, *Conflict of Interest: A Theory of Divergent Goals with Applications to Politics*, Chicago: Markham Publishing Company, 1970; Michael Taylor and V. Herman, "Party Systems and Government Stability," *American Political Science Review* 65 (1971): 28–37; Michael Laver, "Dynamic Factors in Government Coalition Formation," *European Journal of Political Research* 2 (1974): 259–70; Paul Warwick, "The Durability of Coalition Governments in Parliamentary Democracies," *Comparative Political Studies* 11 (1979): 465–98; Eric Browne and John Dreijmanis, eds., *Government Coalitions in Western Democracies*, N.Y.: Longman, Inc., 1982; Bernard Grofman, "The Comparative Analysis of Coalition Formation and Duration: Distinguishing Between-Country and Within-Country Effects," *British Journal of Political Science* 2 (1989): 291–302; John D. Robertson, "The Political Economy and the Durability of European Coalition Cabinets: New Variations on a Game Theoretic Perspective," *Journal of Politics* 45 (1983): 932–57; Eric Browne, John P. Frendreis, and Dennis W. Gleiber, "An 'Events' Approach to the Problem of Cabinet Stability," *Comparative Political Studies* 17 (1984): 167–97; John D. Robertson, "Toward a Political-Economic Accounting of the Endurance of Cabinet Administrations: An Empirical Assessment of Eight European Democracies," *American Journal of Political Science* 28 (1984): 693–709; Eric Browne, John P. Grendreis, and Dennis W. Gleiber, "The Study of Cabinet Dissolutions in Parliamentary Democracies," *Legislative Studies Quarterly* 11 (1986): 619–28; John D. Robertson, "Economic Polarization and Cabinet Formation in Western Europe," *Legislative Studies Quarterly* 11 (1986): 533–49; and Peter Van Roozendaal, "The Effect of Dominant and Central Parties on Cabinet Composition and Durability," *Legislative Studies Quarterly* 17 (1992): 5–36.

Notes to Chapter 4

1. Frederic J. Fleron, ed., *Communist Studies and the Social Sciences: Essays on Methodology and Empirical Theory*, Chicago: Rand McNally, 1969.

2. Alexander J. Motyl, *Thinking Theoretically about Soviet Nationalities: His-*

tory and Comparison in the Study of the USSR, N.Y.: Columbia University Press, 1992.

3. Fredric J. Fleron, Jr. and Erik P. Hoffmann explicitly call upon scholars to begin to employ theory in *Post-communist Studies and Political Science: Methodology and Empirical Theory in Sovietology*, Boulder, Colo.: Westview Press, 1993.

4. Joseph A. Schumpeter, *Capitalism, Socialism, and Democracy*, 3d ed., N.Y.: Harper Brothers, 1950.

5. Scott Mainwaring, Guillermo O'Donnell, and J. Samuel Valenzuela, eds., *Issues in Democratic Consolidation: The New South American Democracies in Comparative Perspective*, South Bend, Ind.: University of Notre Dame Press, 1992, and Guillermo O'Donnell and Philippe Schmitter, *Transitions from Authoritarian Rule: Tentative Conclusions about Uncertain Democracies*. Baltimore: The Johns Hopkins University Press, 1989.

6. Russell Bova, "Political Dynamics of the Post-communist Transition: A Comparative Perspective," *World Politics* 44 (1991): 113–58.

7. Robert A. Dahl, Polyarchy, New Haven: Yale University Press, 1971.

8. Larry Diamond, "Is the Third Wave Over?" *Journal of Democracy* 7, no. 3 (July 1996): 20–37.

9. Samuel P. Huntington, "After Twenty Years: The Future of the Third Wave," *Journal of Democracy* 8 (October 1997): 3–12.

10. Adam Przeworski, *Democracy and the Market: Political and Economic Reforms in Eastern Europe and Latin America*, Cambridge: Cambridge University Press, 1991.

11. *Ibid.*

12. *Ibid.*

13. Dankwart A. Rustow, "Transitions to Democracy: Toward a Dynamic Model," *Comparative Politics* 2 (1970): 337–64.

14. Adam Przeworski, *Democracy and the Market*.

15. Juan J. Linz and Alfred Stepan, *Problems of Democratic Transition and Consolidation: Southern Europe, South America, and Post-communist Europe*, Baltimore: The Johns Hopkins University Press, 1996.

16. Linz and Stepan, *Problems of Democratic Transition and Consolidation*.

17. Andreas Schedler, "What is Democratic Consolidation?" *Journal of Democracy* 9, no. 2 (April 1998): 91–107.

18. Adam Przeworski, *Democracy and the Market*.

19. Matthew Soberg Shugart and John M. Carey, *Presidents and Assemblies: Constitutional Design and Electoral Dynamics*, Cambridge: Cambridge University Press, 1992, identify four constitutional designs for executive-legislative relations: parliamentarism, presidentialism, premier-presidentialism, and president-parliamentarism. Parliamentarism is distinguished by having a single popular mandate (resident in the legislature), a split executive (a separate head of government and head of state, with the latter performing a largely representational, versus political, role), and governmental accountability to the legislature. Presidentialism is marked by two competing popular mandates (one possessed by the president, the other by the legislature), a single executive (combining the roles of head of state and head of government), and governmental accountability to the president. Shugart and Carey argue that premier-presidentialism and president-parliamentarianism are often confused with presidentialism. However, they are qualitatively different sys-

tems. Similarly to presidentialism, they both have dual popular mandates, but the similarities stop there. In contrast to presidentialism, premier-presidential and president-parliamentary systems have a split executive in which the president exercises significant political powers. The government is accountable to the legislature in premier-presidential systems, but it is accountable to either the president or both the president and legislature in president-parliamentarism. It is this latter aspect that Shugart and Carey identify as being particularly problematic for president-parliamentary systems.

20. Adam Przeworski et al., *Sustainable Democracy*, Cambridge: Cambridge University Press, 1995.

21. Linz and Stepan, *Problems of Democratic Transition and Consolidation*.

22. Adam Przeworski et al., *Sustainable Democracy*, Cambridge: Cambridge University Press, 1995.

23. Linz and Stepan, *Problems of Democratic Transition and Consolidation*.

24. Douglass North, *Private Security and the Law*, Cincinnati: Anderson Publishing, 1989; and Douglass North, *Institutions, Institutional Change, and Economic Performance*, N.Y.: Cambridge University Press, 1990.

Notes to Chapter 5

1. Duncan Black, *The Theory of Committees and Elections*, Cambridge: Cambridge University Press, 1958.

2. D. Roderick Kiewiet and Matthew D. McCubbins, "Presidential Influence on Congressional Appropriations Decisions," *American Journal of Political Science* 32 (1988): 131–43.

3. Kenneth A. Shepsle and Mark S. Bonchek, *Analyzing Politics: Rationality, Behavior, and Institutions*, N.Y.: W. W. Norton & Company, Inc., 1997, p. 422.

4. See the examples given by Kenneth A. Shepsle and Mark S. Bonchek, *Analyzing Politics: Rationality, Behavior, and Institutions*, N.Y.: W. W. Norton & Company, Inc., 1997, pp. 422–28.

5. Local government elections in Lithuania are contested on the basis of a party list vote in which voters cast their ballots for the party of their choice, not individual candidates. Parties are then allotted the number of deputies in the local councils proportional to the vote they receive, provided they pass the electoral threshold, following which Mayors are elected by the city councils.

6. Anthony Downs, *An Economic Theory of Democracy*, New York: Harper 1957.

7. See Maurice Duverger, *Political Parties: Their Organization and Activity in the Modern State*, London: Methuen, 1954; Arend Lijphart, *Electoral Systems and Party Systems: A Study of Twenty-Seven Democracies, 1945–1990*, Oxford: Oxford University Press, 1994; Douglas W. Rae, *The Political Consequences of Electoral Laws*, 2d ed., New Haven: Yale University Press, 1971; William H. Riker, *Liberalism Against Populism: A Confrontation Between the Theory of Democracy and the Theory of Social Choice*, San Francisco: W.H. Freeman 1982; Giovanni Sartori, *Parties and Party Systems*, Cambridge: 1976; and Rein Taagepera and Matthew S. Shugart, *Seats and Votes: The Effects and Determinants of Electoral Systems*, New Haven: Yale University Press, 1989.

8. John D. Huber and Charles R. Shipan, "The Costs of Control: Legislators, Agencies, and Transaction Costs," *Legislative Studies Quarterly* 25 (2000): 25–52.

9. See, for example, Vitalis Nakrosis, "Lithuanian Public Administration: A Usable State Bureaucracy," *Journal of Baltic Studies* 32 (2001): 170–81.

Notes to Chapter 6

1. William H. Riker, *Liberalism Against Populism*, San Francisco: W.H. Freeman, 1982.
2. Kenneth A. Shepsle, "Institutional Arrangements and Equilibrium in Multidimensional Voting Models," *American Journal of Political Science* 23 (1979): 27–59; and Kenneth A. Shepsle and Barry R. Weingast, "The Institutional Foundations of Committee Power," *American Political Science Review* 81 (1987): 85–104.
3. See Richard D. McKelvey, "Intransitivities in Multidimensional Voting Models," *Journal of Economic Theory* 12 (1976): 472–82.
4. Arthur T. Denzau and Robert J. Mackay, "Gatekeeping and Monopoly Power of Committees: An Analysis of Sincere and Sophisticated Behavior," *American Journal of Political Science* 27 (1983): 740–61; and Keith Krehbiel, "Sophisticated and Myopic Behavior in Legislative Committees: An Experimental Study," *American Journal of Political Science* 30 (1986): 542–61.
5. One exception is Terry D. Clark, Stacy Holscher, and Lisa Hyland, "The LDLP Faction in the Lithuanian Seimas, 1992–1996," *Nationalities Papers* 27 (1999): 227–46.
6. Michael Laver and Kenneth A. Shepsle, *Making and Breaking Governments: Cabinets and Legislatures in Parliamentary Governments*, Cambridge: Cambridge University Press, 1996.
7. The size principle argues that parties will form coalitions of the smallest size possible in order to maximize the gains in ministerial portfolios accruing to each participant in the coalition. Such minimum-winning coalitions are discussed in William H. Riker, *The Theory of Political Coalitions*, New Haven: Yale University Press, 1962.
8. Many scholars have argued that coalition building is constrained by ideological affinity. Potential coalition partners must be close enough programmatically to permit them to cooperate. See Robert Axelrod, *Conflict of Interest: A Theory of Divergent Goals with Applications to Politics*, Chicago: Markham Publishing Company, 1970; Abram De Swaan, *Coalition Theories and Cabinet Formations*, San Francisco: Jossey-Bass, Inc., 1973; and Lawrence C. Dodd, *Coalitions in Parliamentary Governments*, Princeton: Princeton University Press, 1976.
9. Michael Laver and Kenneth A. Shepsle, *Making and Breaking Governments: Cabinets and Legislatures in Parliamentary Governments*, Cambridge: Cambridge University Press, 1996.
10. This is in line with the theoretical propositions underlying Robert Axelrod, *Conflict of Interest: A Theory of Divergent Goals with Applications to Politics*, Chicago: Markham Publishing Company, 1970; Abram De Swaan, *Coalition Theories and Cabinet Formations*, San Francisco: Jossey-Bass, Inc., 1973; Lawrence C. Dodd, *Coalitions in Parliamentary Governments*, Princeton: Princeton University Press, 1976, in contrast to that of Anthony Downs, *An Economic Theory of Democracy*, N.Y.: Harper and Row Publishers, 1957, who adopted the premise that parties are motivated by the desire to win political office.

11. Michael Laver and Kenneth A. Shepsle, *Making and Breaking Governments: Cabinets and Legislatures in Parliamentary Governments*, Cambridge: Cambridge University Press, 1996.

12. If the status quo cabinet is the generalized median cabinet with an empty win set, the cabinet remains.

13. Michael Laver and Kenneth A. Shepsle, *Making and Breaking Governments: Cabinets and Legislatures in Parliamentary Governments*, Cambridge: Cambridge University Press, 1996.

A Short Bibliography of Rational-Choice Literature Arranged by Subject

General Literature on Rational Choice

Adams, James F., and Ernest W. Adams. "The Geometry of Voting Cycles." *Journal of Theoretical Politics* 12 (2000): 131–53.

Bianco, William T. "Doing the Politically Right Thing: Results, Behavior, and Vote Trading." *Journal of Politics* 51 (1989): 886–99.

Coase, R. H. "The Problem of Social Cost." *The Journal of Law and Economics* 3 (1960): 1–44.

Fiorina, Morris, P., and Charles R. Plott. "Committee Decisions under Majority Rule: An Experimental Study." *The American Political Science Review* 72 (1978): 575–95.

Hirshleifer, Jack, and Juan Carlos Marinez Coll. "What Strategies Can Support the Evolutionary Emergence of Cooperation?" *Journal of Conflict Resolution* 32 (1988): 367–93.

Johnson, James. "Is Talk Really Cheap? Prompting Conversation Between Critical Theory and Rational Choice." *American Political Science Review* 87 (1993): 74–86.

McKelvey, Richard D., and Peter C. Ordeshook. "An Experimental Study of the Effects of Procedural Rules on Committee Behavior." *Journal of Politics* 46 (1984): 182–205.

Parker, Glenn R. "Looking Beyond Reelection: Revising Assumptions about the Factors Motivating Congressional Behavior." *Public Choice* 63: 237–52.

Quattrone, George A., and Amos Tversky. "Contrasting Rational and Psychological Analyses of Political Choice." *The American Political Science Review* 82 (1988): 719–36.

Runge, Carlisle Ford. "Institutions and the Free Rider: The Assurance Problem in Collective Action." *Journal of Politics* 46 (1984): 155–81.

Shepsle, Kenneth A. "Institutional Equilibrium and Equilibrium Institutions." In Herbert Weisberg, ed., pp. 51–81, *Political Science: The Science of Politics*. New York: Agathon Press, 1986.

Shepsle, Kenneth A., and Barry R. Weingast. "Positive Theories of Congressional Institutions." *Legislative Studies Quarterly* 19 (1994): 5–35.

Shepsle, Kenneth A., and Barry R. Weingast. "When Do Rules of Procedure Matter?" *Journal of Politics* 46 (1984): 207–21.

The New Institutionalism

March, James, and Johan P. Olsen. "The New Institutionalism: Organizational Factors in Political Life." *The American Political Science Review* 78 (1984): 734–49.

Remington, Thomas F., and Steven S. Smith. "Political Goals, Institutional Context, and the Choice of an Electoral System: The Russian Parliamentary Election Law." *American Journal of Political Science* 40 (1996): 1253–79.

Riker, William H. "Implications from the Disequilibrium of Majority Rule for the Study of Institutions." *The American Political Science Review* 74 (1980): 432–46.

Shepsle, Kenneth A. "Institutional Arrangements and Equilibrium in Multidimensional Voting Models." *American Journal of Political Science* 23 (1979): 27–59.

Shepsle, Kenneth A., and Barry Weingast. "Uncovered Sets and Sophisticated Voting Outcomes with Implications for Agenda Institutions." *American Journal of Political Science* 28 (1984): 49–74.

Median Voter Theorem

Black, Duncan. "Arrow's Work and the Normative Theory of Committees." *Journal of Theoretical Politics* 3 (1991): 259–76.

Moraski, Byron J., and Charles R. Shipan. "The Politics of Supreme Court Nominations: A Theory of Institutional Constraints and Choices." *American Journal of Political Science* 43 (1999): 1069–95.

Spatial Modeling

Adams, James, and Samuel Merrill III. "Modeling Party Strategies and Policy Representation in Multiparty Elections: Why Are Some Strategies So Extreme?" *American Journal of Political Science* 43 (1999): 765–91.

Bottom, William P., et al. "The Institutional Effect on Majority Rule Instability: Bicameralism in Spatial Policy Decisions. *American Journal of Political Science* 44 (2000): 523–40.

Brams, Steven J., and Peter C. Fishburn. "When Is Size a Liability? Bargaining Power in Minimal Winning Coalitions." *Journal of Theoretical Politics* 7 (1995): 301–16.

Hinich, Melvin J., Valeri Khmelko, and Peter C. Ordeshook. "Ukraine's 1998 Parliamentary Elections: A Spatial Analysis." *Post-Soviet Affairs* 15 (1999): 149–85.

Kiewiet, D. Roderick, and Matthew D. McCubbins. "Presidential Influence on Congressional Appropriations Decisions." *American Journal of Political Science* 32 (1988): 131–43.

Kollman, Ken, John H. Miller, and Scott E. Page. "Political Parties and Electoral Landscapes." *British Journal of Politics* 28 (1998): 139–58.

Quinn, Kevin M., Andrew D. Martin, and Andrew B. Whitford. "Voter Choice in Multi-Party Democracies: A Test of Competing Theories and Models." *American Journal of Political Science* 43 (1999): 1231–47.

Remington, Thomas F., et al. "Transitional Institutions and Parliamentary Alignments in Russia." *Parliaments in Transition: The New Politics in the Former*

USSR and Eastern Europe. Ed. Remington, Thomas F. Boulder, Colo.: Westview Press, 1994. 159–80.

Schofield, Norman. "Coalition Politics: A Formal Model and Empirical Analysis." *Journal of Theoretical Politics* 7 (1995): 245–81.

Warwick, Paul V. "Policy Distance and Parliamentary Government." *Legislative Studies Quarterly* 23 (1998): 319–45.

Legislative Analysis

Dyson, James W., and John W. Soule. "Congressional Committee Behavior on Roll Call Votes: The U.S. House of Representatives." *Midwest Journal of Political Science* (1970): 626–47.

Eulau, Heinz, and Very McCluggage. "Standing Committees in Legislatures: Three Decades of Research." *Legislative Studies Quarterly* 9 (1984): 195–270.

Francis, Wayne L., and James W. Risslesperger. "U.S. State Legislative Committees: Structure, Procedural Efficiency, and Party Control." *Legislative Studies Quarterly* 7 (1982): 453–71.

Hamm, Keith E., and Gary Moncrief. "Effects of Structural Change in Legislative Committee Systems on Their Performance in U.S. States. *Legislative Studies Quarterly* 3 (1982): 383–98.

Kiewiet, D. Roderick, and Mathew D. McCubbins. *The Logic of Delegation: Congressional Parties and the Appropriations Process.* Chicago: University of Chicago Press, 1991. 207–37.

Kim, Young C. "The Committee System in the Japanese Diet: Recruitment, Orientation, and Behavior." *Legislative System in Developing Countries*. Eds. Boynton, G.R., and Chon Lim Kim. Durham: Duke University Press, 1975. 69–84.

Lewis, Anne L. "Floor Success as Measure of Committee Performance in the House." *The Journal of Politics* 40 (1978): 460–67.

Parker, Glenn R., and Suzanne L. Parker. "Factions in Committees: The U.S. House of Representatives." *The American Political Science Review* 73 (1979): 85–102.

Polsby, Nelson W. "The Institutionalization of the U.S. House of Representatives." *The American Political Science Review* 62 (1968): 144–68.

Riker, William H., and Steven J. Brams. "The Paradox of Vote Trading." *The American Political Science Review* 67 (1973): 1235–47.

Unekis, Joseph K., and Leroy N. Rieselbach. "Congressional Committee Leadership 1971–1978." *Legislative Studies Quarterly* 2 (1983): 251–70.

Unekis, Joseph K., "From Committee to the Floor: Consistency in Congressional Voting." *The Journal of Politics* 40 (1978): 761–69.

Committee Systems

Adler, Scott E., and John S. Lapinski. "Demand-Side Theory and Congressional Committee Composition: A Constituency Characteristics Approach. *American Journal of Political Science* 41 (1997): 896–918.

Austen-Smith, David. "Information Transmission in Debate." *American Journal of Political Science* 34 (1990): 124–52.

Bawn, Kathleen. "Strategic Responses to Institutional Change: Parties, Committees, and Multiple Referral." *Public Choice* 88 (1996): 239–58.

Gilligan, Thomas W., and Keith Krehbiel. "Asymmetric Information and Legislative Rules with a Heterogeneous Committee." *American Journal of Political Science* 33 (1989): 459–90.
Gilligan, Thomas W., and Keith Krehbiel. "Organization of Informative Committees by a Rational Legislature." *American Journal of Political Science* 34 (1990): 531–64.
Hall, Richard L., and Bernard Grofman. "The Committee Assignment Process and the Conditional Nature of Committee Bias." *American Political Science Review* 84 (1990): 1149–66.
Holocombe, Randall G., and Glenn R. Parker. "Committees in Legislatures: A Property Rights Perspective." *Public Choice* 70 (1991): 11–20.
Krehbiel, Keith. "Sophisticated and Myopic Behavior in Legislative Committees: An Experimental Study." *American Journal of Political Science* 30 (186): 542–61.
Remington, Thomas F., and Steven S. Smith. "Theories of Legislative Institutions and the Organization of the Russian Duma." *American Journal of Political Science* 42 (1998): 545–72.
Shepsle, Kenneth A. "Institutional Arrangements and Equilibrium in Multidimensional Voting Models." *American Journal of Political Science* 23 (1979): 27–59.
Shepsle, Kenneth A., and Barry R. Weingast, "The Institutional Foundations of Committee Power." *American Political Science Review* 81 (1987): 85–104.
Weingast, Barry R., and William J. Marshall. "The Industrial Organization of Congress; or, Why Legislatures, Like Firms, Are Not Organized as Markets." *Journal of Political Economy* 96 (1988): 132–63.
Wilkerson, John. "Analyzing Committee Power: A Critique." *American Journal of Political Science* 35 (1991): 613–23.

Principal-Agent Analysis

Bendor, Jonathan, Serge Taylor, and Roland Van Gaalan. "Politicians, Bureaucrats, and Asymmetric Information." *American Journal of Political Science* 31 (1987): 796–828.
Huber, John D., and Charles R. Shipan. "The Costs of Control: Legislators, Agencies, and Transaction Costs." *Legislative Studies Quarterly* 25 (2000): 25–52.
Kiewiet, D. Roderick, and Matthew D. McCubbins. *The Logic of Delegation: Congressional Parties and the Appropriations Process.* Chicago: University of Chicago Press, 1991. 1–38.
Maltzman, Forrest, and Steven S. Smith. "Principles, Goals, Dimensionality, and Congressional Committees." *Legislative Studies Quarterly* 19 (1994): 457–76.
McCubbins, Mathew D., Roger G. Noll, and Barry R. Weingast. "Administrative Procedures as Instruments of Political Control. *Journal of Law, Economics, and Organization* 3 (1987): 243–77.
McCubbins, Matthew D., and Thomas Schwartz. "Congressional Oversight Overlooked: Police Patrols versus Fire Alarms." *American Journal of Political Science* 28 (1984): 165–79.
Spiller, Pablo T. "Agency and the Role of Political Institutions." *Information and Democratic Processes.* Eds. Ferejohn, John A., and James H. Kuklinski. Urbana: University of Illinois Press, 1990. 269–78.

The Portfolio Allocation Model

Laver, Michael L., and Kenneth A. Shepsle. "Cabinet Ministers and Government Formation in Parliamentary Democracies." *Cabinet Ministers and Parliamentary Government.* Cambridge: Cambridge University Press, 1994.

Laver, Michael L., Colin Rallings, and Michael Thrasher. "Policy Payoffs in Local Government." *British Journal of Political Science* 28 (1998): 333–53.

Laver, Michael L., and Kenneth A. Shepsle. "Events, Equilibria, and Government Survival." *American Journal of Political Science* 42 (1998): 28–54.

Laver, Michael L., and Kenneth A. Shepsle. "Understanding Government Survival: Empirical Exploration or Analytical Models?" *British Journal of Political Science* 29 (1999): 395–415.

Warwick, Paul V. "Ministerial Autonomy or Ministerial Accommodation? Contested Bases of Government Survival in Parliamentary Democracies." *British Journal of Political Science* 29 (1999): 309–94.

Formal Theory

Crawford, Sue E.S., and Elinor Ostrom. "A Grammar of Institutions." *American Political Science Review* 89 (1995): 582–60.

Ferejohn, John A., and Morris P. Fiorina. "Optimizing Models of Public Decision Making: Purposive Models of Legislative Behavior." *American Economics Review* 65 (1975): 407–14.

Fiorina, Morris P. "Formal Models in Political Science." *American Journal of Political Science* 19 (1975): 133–59.

Shepsle, Kenneth A. "Prospects for Formal Models of Legislatures." *Legislative Studies Quarterly* 10 (1985): 5–19.

Index

Abele, Daniel G. 23n
Adamkus, Valdas 96–98
Ahl, Richard 21
Alexander, James 45n
amendments
  presidential 96
Anderson, Richard 40n
Appointments
  presidential 16, 96
area studies *ix*, 3
Arel, Dominique 19n
Arrow, Kenneth 109
asymmetric information 54, 106
Austen-Smith, David 53n
Authoritarian 3, 7, 11–14, 22, 28, 34, 40, 43, 59, 60, 66–68, 74, 78, 83
Axelrod, Robert 57n, 118n

B

Baglione, Lisa A. 47
Bahry, Donna 24, 45n
Balducci, Massimo 51n
Baron, David P. 39n
Barry, Donald 49n
Beissinger, Mark R. 20n
behavioralism 20, 33, 35
  and definitions of democracy 62
  influence on post-communist studies 4, 18, 29, 39, 43, 50
Bernhard, Michael 46n

Black, Duncan 88
Blondel, Jean 38n
Boaz, Cynthia 24
Bonchek, Mark S. 97, 98n
Bova, Russell *x*, 51, 61
Brazauskas, Algirdas 96
Brown, Michael E. 20n
Browne, Eric 57n
Brym, Robert J. 23, 46n
Bunce, Valerie *x*, 10, 11, 14n, 18n, 34, 47n
bureaucracy 69–70, 78–79, 80, 129, 136
  usable state bureaucracy 14, 50–51, 76
  and legislatures 38, 54–55
  principal-agent problems 105–106
  reform 71, 74, 76, 77, 81
bureaucratic model 9
Burkart, Ross 21

C

cabinets
  durability 39, 106
  formation 118
  at the generalized median 120
  portfolio allocation model 118–121
Campbell, Peter 31n
Carey, John M. 13n, 31, 33, 34, 54n, 70n
case studies 6

Chechnya 79
civil society 12, 15, 28, 32, 36, 52,
    63, 67, 69, 74, 79, 80
  arena of democracy 14, 42–43,
    46–49, 76
  resurgent society 60–61, 62, 63,
    78
Clark, Carol L. 47
Clark, Terry D. 33n, 39n, 118n
class
  class system 21, 33, 69, 80
  middle class 21
Collie, Melissa P. 52n
communism 11
  communist era 45–47, 72
communist studies 8, 59
Connor, Walker 20n
constitutional courts 72, 79, 82, 97–99
contextualism 20
Cooper, Joseph 52n
Coppedge, Michael 31n
corporatism 10–11
corruption 51
cost-benefit analysis 26, 27, 39
Costain, Anne N. 49n
counter-elites 61, 63, 67, 69, 74, 76,
    78, 80
Cox, Gary W. 31n
Crawford, Beverly 22
Curry, Jane L. 47n

D

Dahl, Robert A. 19n, 30, 32n, 46,
    55n, 61
Danilenko, Gennady M. 49n
Davidheiser, Evelyn 36n, 37n
Dawisha, Karen 29
democracy x, 5, 11
  arenas 14, 15, 18, 20, 22, 25, 28,
    32, 36

democracy
  arenas *(continued)*
    civil society 14, 42–43, 46–48,
      76
    economic society 14, 20–25, 76
    political society 14, 52, 76–77
    rule of law 14, 49–50, 66, 76, 77
    usable state bureaucracy 14,
      50–51, 76
    interactions across arenas 36,
      48, 76–77
  consolidated democracy 74–75, 77,
    78 (Lithuania), 80, 82
  equilibrium 68, 78, 82
  definitions 60, 61–62
  human rights 48
  norms 5, 7, 19, 32, 43, 66
  precondition
    stateness 14
  stable 133–134, 135, 137–138
  unstable 74, 75, 77, 131
democratic consolidation x, 11, 12,
    14–15
  definition 64, 66
  democracy in equilibrium 68, 82,
    129
    weakening competing forces 68,
      69–71, 82
    increasing institutional
      involvement 68, 71–72, 82,
      134, 136
  issues not covered 52, 57
  paradigm 5, 14–15, 18, 40–41, 42,
    83, 128
  second stage of democratization 60
  theory 65–68
democratization 5, 6, 8, 11–16, 18,
    19, 21, 22, 25, 26, 28, 29, 43,
    44, 47–50, 57, 59, 60, 62,
    64–67, 71, 75, 128, 129
  and women 49
  reversal 59

democratization *(continued)*
  stages 60
Denzau, Arthur T. 116n
Derlien, Hans 51n
De Swaan, Abram 118n
Deutsch, Karl 20n
Devarajan, Shantayanan 22n
Diamond, Larry 12n, 13n, 21, 25n, 26n, 29n, 46n, 47n, 61
Dimitrova, Antoaneta 51n
DiPalma, Giuseppe 39n
Dodd, Lawrence C. 118n
Downs, Anthony 99, 118n
Dreijmanis, John 57n
Duch, Raymond M. 23, 24, 45n, 46n
Duverger, Maurice 30, 31n, 32n, 102n
Duverger's Law 31

E

East Central Europe 5
Easter, Gerald M. 34
Eckstein, Harry 31n, 44
economic growth 12, 21, 22, 90, 91
economic reform 21–25, 33, 36, 69
economic society
  arena of democracy 14, 15, 20–25, 36, 76
electoral systems 31, 34, 38
  impact on political outcomes 102–103
  proportional representation (PR) 31, 36, 39, 102
  single mandate district system 31, 34, 39, 103
elites 4, 8, 11, 12, 15, 17, 21, 22, 25–28, 30–32, 34, 35, 38–40, 42, 43, 49, 55, 60–61, 63–64, 66–72, 76, 77, 130, 136
  bargaining 27, 28
  contest for power 67–68, 78

elites *(continued)*
  divided 67, 73, 78, 79, 80, 81
  hegemonic 74, 77, 78 (Russia), 80
  pacts 27, 28, 61, 64
  theory 55
Elkins, S.L. 56n
Esman, Milton J. 20n
essentialism 20
ethnic conflict 19–20
  contextualism 20
  essentialism 20
Evans, Geoffrey 33n, 44n
executive
  executive-legislative relations 13, 33–35, 38, 53–55, 57, 70, 76, 77, 94–97
  parliamentarism 33–34, 70, 71, 73
  premier-presidentialism 33–34, 70, 71, 73
  president-parliamentarism 33, 54, 70, 72
  presidentialism 33–35, 54, 70, 72
  presidential appointments 96–97
  presidential vetoes 94–96

F

federalism 20, 56
Fellegi, Tamas L. 51n
Feng, Yi 22n
Filippov, Mikhail 56n
Finifter, Ada W. 24, 45n
Fish, M. Steven *x*in, 22, 23n, 32n, 43n
Fleron, Frederic J., Jr. 45n, 46n, 59, 59n
Fodor, Eva 33n
formal modeling 129, 138
Foweraker, Joe 48n

fragmentation 19–20, 30, 31, 51, 55, 57, 60, 67, 82
Friedgut, Theodore H. 57n
Frye, Timothy 35

G

Gasiorowski, Mark J. 33n
Gasparini, Alberto 43n, 47n, 49n
generalized median 120
Gibson, James L. 25, 45n, 46n
Gilligan, Thomas W. 53n
Gleiber, Dennis W. 57n
global capital 56, 70, 71, 74, 78, 80
Goeckel, Robert F. 47
Gordon, Stacy Burnett 24
Grendreis, John P. 57n
Grey, Robert D. 46n
Grodeland, Ase 51n
Grofman, Bernard 57n
growth machine 56
Grumm, J.G. 31n
Guess, George M. 51n

H

Hahn, Jeffrey W. 43n, 45, 45n, 57n
Handelman, Stephen 51n
Hanley, Eric 33n, 40n
Hashim, Syed Mohsin 32n, 37n
Haspel, Moshe 39n
Havel, Vaclav 46n
Helliwell, John F. 22n
Herman, V. 57n
Hesli, Vicki L. 19n, 24, 40n, 45n, 47
Hesse, Joachim Jens 51n
Heywood, Paul 46n
Higley, John 40
Hoffmann, Erik P. 59n
Holcombe, Randall G. 53n
Holscher, Stacy 118n
Horowitz, Donald L. 20n, 29n

Hough, Jerry 9, 36n
Howard, A.E. Dick 49n
Huber, John D. 106n
Hunter, Floyd 55n
Huntington, Samuel P. 7n, 12, 13n, 14, 14n, 16, 21n, 28, 61
Huskey, Eugene 50n
Hyland, Lisa 118n

I

Inglehart, Richard 44
institutionalism 12, 18, 26, 29
 New Institutionalism 4, 13
institutionalized pluralism 9
institutions 4, 5, 12–16, 18, 21, 23, 25, 26, 29, 36, 39, 42–43, 45, 47–50, 52, 57, 60, 62, 66–68, 71, 75–77, 79, 86, 88, 92, 95, 98, 99, 104, 107–110, 136, 137
 democratic institutions 7, 12, 22, 45, 60, 67, 68, 86, 88
interest groups 30, 32, 48–49
 theory 9
Ishiyama, John T. 34, 36n, 37n, 50

J

Janos, Andrew C. 27
Johnson, S.R. 23n
judiciary 49, 77
 constitutional courts 97
 independence 72
 reform 72, 79, 82
 spatial analysis 97–99

K

Karklins, Rasma 20n
Karl, Terry Lynn xn, 18n
Kiewit, D. Roderick 53n, 54n, 94
Kitschelt, Herbert 32n

Klaus, Vaclav 46n
Klinke, Andreas 20n
Klobucar, Thomas F. 19n
Korbonski, Andrzej 47n
Kornhauser, William 46n
Korosenyi, Andras 33n
Koshechkina, Tatyana 51n
Krehbiel, Keith 53n, 116n
Kreuzer, Marcus 33n
Kryshtanovskaya, Olga 33n, 40n
Kubik, Jan 48n
Kullberg, Judith S. 23, 39

L

Landman, Todd 48n
Lane, David 40
Lapinskas, Kestutis 97
Laqueur, Walter 44
Laver, Michael 57n, 118, 119, 119n, 120n, 121
Leadership 8, 9 12, 37, 40, 47, 53, 57, 97, 102, 104, 105, 117
legislature 38–40, 78, 80, 136
  agenda 110–117
  committee systems 52–53, 92–93, 111
  principal agent analysis 104–106
  executive-legislative relations 13, 33–35, 38, 53–55, 57, 70, 76, 77, 94–97
    parliamentarism 33–34, 70, 71, 73
    premier-presidentialism 33–34, 70, 71, 73
    president-parliamentarism 33, 70, 72
    presidentialism 33–35, 70, 72
  factional system 39
  legislative oversight 105–106
  legislative rules 92, 104–105, 111

legislature
  legislative rules *(continued)*
    closed rule 92
    open rule 93
  Lithuanian legislature (see *Seimas*)
  and party systems 38
  quorum 92
  roll-call analysis 16, 39, 89–92
  sincere voting 116
  strategic voting 116
Lehmann, Susan Goodrich 36n
Lewin, Moshe 9n
Lijphart, Arend 30, 102n
Lindenberg, Marc 22n
Linz, Juan J. 7n, 12n, 13n, 14, 19n, 26n, 28, 33n, 51, 54n, 64n, 76, 77n
Lipset, Seymour Martin 12, 20n, 21, 31n, 32n
Lithuania 6–8, 16, 79–83, 86–87, 89–92, 94–97, 98–99, 99–102, 102–103, 104–106, 116–117, 121–127
  local government 43, 52, 55–57, 81, 136, 138
  autonomy 72, 75, 79
  reform 72, 75–76, 82
Loewenberg, Gerhard 36n, 38n
Logan, John R. 55, 56n
Lovell, David W. 48n

M

MacIver, Martha Abele 23n
Mackay, Robert J. 116n
Magalhaes, Pedro C. 50
Mahr, Alison 36n
Mainwaring, Scott 13n, 26n, 33n, 60n

majority cycling problem 108–113, 115, 116, 118, 119
majority, single mandate district system 103
market reform 22–25, 51
marketization 19, 22, 44, 102
March, James G. 26n
Mason, David S. 23n, 36n, 45n
Mateju, Petr 33n
McAllister, Ian 45n
McCain, Morris A., Jr. 11n
McCubbins, Matthew D. 53n, 54n, 94
McFarland, Andrew S. 49n
McFaul, Michael 27
McIntosh, Mary E. 23n
McKelvey, Richard D. 116n
median voter theorem 16, 87, 88–89, 95, 97, 114–115
Melville, Andrei Yu. 40n
Merkel, Wolfgang 47n
Meyer, Alfred 10n
Meyer, David S. 49n
Michael L. Mezey 38n
Mickiewicz, Ellen 24, 45n
Migdal, Joel S. 46
Miller, Arthur H. 19n, 24, 40n, 45n, 47
Miller, William L. 46n, 51n
Mircev, Dimitar 40
mode of transition (path dependency) 28–29
modernization and development theory 10
Mishler, William 25
Molotch, Harvey L. 55, 56n
Moore, Barrington 21
Moraski, Bryon 36n
Moser, Robert G. 31
Motyl, Alexander *ix*n, 28, 59
Muller, Edward 21, 44
Musolf, Lloyd D. 38n

N

Nagle, John 36n
Nakrosis, Vitalis 106n
nationalism 19, 29, 48, 75
NATO 85–87, 124–125
Nelson, Daniel N. 22
new institutionalism 4, 13, 26, 107, 128
Newcity, Michael 50n
Nichols, Terry M. 34, 46
Noll, Roger G. 54n
North, Douglass, 77n
Norton, Philip 38n, 39n

O

Oates, Sarah 23n, 33n
O'Donnell, Guillermo 12n, 13n, 26n, 27n, 39n, 60n
Offe, Claus 19n, 22n
Olson, David M. 38n, 39n
Olson, Johan P. 26n
Olson, Mancur 21n
Ordeshook, Peter 31, 31n

P

Pacek, Alexander A. 33n, 36n
Pakulski, Jan 40
paradigm 3–4, 8, 11, 13–14, 15, 18, 26, 35, 40–41, 42, 48, 57, 83, 84, 128
  Thomas Kuhn 11
Parker, Glenn R. 53n
parliamentarism 13, 33–34, 70, 71, 73, 129, 132, 134, 135, 136, 137–138
Parrot, Bruce 29
path dependency 13, 26, 28–29

INDEX 175

Patterson, Samuel P. 38n
Petro, Nicolai 45
Pettai, Nicolai 33n
Pfaff, William 20n
Plasser, Fritz 44n
pluralism
  theory 9, 55
political culture 43–45
political parties 30
  anti-systemic parties 7, 32
  communist party 3, 9–10, 32, 36–37
  Lithuanian political parties 86–87, 89–90, 102
  party systems 13, 31–33, 57, 76, 80
  and legislatures 38, 81
  and spatial analysis 99–102
  strong parties 120, 121, 127
political science 3, 5, 6, 13, 18, 19, 83, 128
political society
  arena of democracy 14, 76–77
  issues not covered 52, 57
portfolio allocation model 118–121, 124–127
post-communist studies 3–4, 6, 8, 15, 18–19, 26, 28, 29, 35, 36, 39–41, 42, 47, 50, 52, 59, 61, 65, 83, 84, 121, 128
  issues not covered 52
Powell, G. Bingham 30
Power, Timothy J. 33n
preferences
  group 85
  individual 84, 108
  transitive 109
premier-presidentialism 33–34, 70, 71, 73, 80, 94, 134, 135, 136, 137–138

president-parliamentarism 33, 54, 70, 72, 78, 129, 131, 132, 134, 135, 137–138
presidentialism 33–35, 54, 70, 72, 129, 131, 132, 134, 135, 137–138
Pridham, Geoffrey 30, 43n
principal-agent
  analysis 104–106
  issues not covered in post-communist studies 52–55
  principal-agent problems 104
privatization 25, 37, 69–70, 73–76, 78–80, 102, 110, 112, 115
procuracy 11, 49, 50
proportional representation (PR) 31, 36, 39, 102
Przeworski, Adam 7n, 12n, 13n, 20n, 21, 22n, 23n, 25, 39, 50, 55, 61, 62, 62n, 63, 66, 75, 76n
public administration 51, 57, 71, 74–79, 81, 82
Putnam, Robert D. 43

R

Rae, Douglas W. 31n, 102n
rational-choice *xi*, 4, 6, 16–20, 26, 35, 39, 44, 50, 58, 62, 63, 66, 83, 84, 87, 88, 98, 102, 107, 108, 111, 116, 121, 128, 138
  reformulation of democratization 62, 66
  theory 84–85, 87, 88–89, 98, 121
Rausser, Gordon C. 23n
regime survival 64
Rehakova, Blanka 33n
Reisinger, William M. 19n, 24, 40n, 45n, 47
Reitz, John 49n, 50n

Remington, Thomas F. 27, 38n, 39n, 53n
Remmer, Karen L. 22n, 25n
replacement 28
Rice, Eric M. 51n
Rigby, T.H. 40
Riggs, Fred W. 38n, 57
Riker, William H. 102n, 111, 118n
Robertson, John D. 57n
Roeder, Philip G. *ix*n, 34
Rokkan, Stein 31n, 32n
roll-call analysis 16, 39, 89–92
Rose, Richard 20n, 25, 45n
Ross, Cameron 40
rule of law
  arena of democracy 14, 49–50, 76, 77
  confused with democratic consolidation 66
Rustow, Dankwart A. 19n, 39, 62

S

Sajudis 8, 80, 81, 86
Sanna, Mark 51n
Sartori, Giovanni 30, 102n
Schattschneider, E.E. 30, 46
Schedler, Andreas 64–65
Schmitter, Philippe C. *x*n, 12n, 13n, 18n, 26n, 27n, 39n, 60n
Schopflin, George 20n, 47n
Schumpter, Joseph 20n, 60
Seimas 7, 8, 81, 88, 91, 92, 94, 95, 97–99, 102, 105, 111, 114–116, 125
  agenda control 111
  factional system 121–124
  rules 91, 94, 96, 104–105
Seligson, Mitchell A. 21, 44

Senn, Alfred Erich 20n
Shabad, Goldie 33n
Shepsle, Kenneth A. 52n, 53n, 97, 98n, 111n, 118, 119, 119n, 120n, 121
Shevtsova, Liliia F. 40n
Shipan, Charles R. 106n
Shugart, Matthew Soberg 13n, 31, 31n, 33, 34, 35, 54n, 70n, 102n
Shvetsova, Olga 31, 31n, 56n
Silverman, Bertram 22n
sincere voting 116
Skach, C. 33n, 54n
Skalnik-Leff, Carol 20n
Skilling, H. Gordon 9
Skocpol, Theda 21n
Slomczynski, Kazimierz M. 33n
Smeltz, Dina 23n
Smith, Bruce L.R. 49n
Smith, Gordon R. 50n
Smith, Graham 20n
Smith, Joel 38n
Smith, Steven S. 39n, 53n
Smithey, Shannon Ishiyama 50
Snajdr, Edward K. 47
Snyder, Jack 20n
Snyder, Tim 29
Sochor, Zenovia A. 19n, 20n
social capital 43
social-democratic party 32, 80, 86, 90
social differentiation 69, 70, 80
social movements 48–49
socialist 24, 33, 36
society. *See* civil society
Solovei, Valerii D. 37n
Soviet Union 5, 28, 32–36, 40, 46, 51

spatial analysis 16
  demonstrated 86–89, 92–93, 94–97, 97–99, 99–102
state 25
state controller 97
State Duma 102
stateness
  precondition for democracy 14, 19–20, 48, 55, 75
Stepan, Alfred 7n, 12n, 14, 19n, 28, 33n, 49, 51n, 54n, 64n, 76, 77n
Stiglitz, Joseph E. 23n
Stoner-Weiss, Kathryn 56n
strategic choice 4, 12, 26–27, 39, 42, 62
strategic voting 116
strong parties 120, 121, 127
structuralism 36
Sueiga 104
Swanstrom, Todd 56n
Szablowski, George 51n
Szabo, Mate 47n
Szelenyi, Ivan 33n, 40n
Szelenyi, Szonja 40n

T

Taagapera, Rein 31n, 102n
Tarrow, Sidney 49n
Taylor, Michael 57n
Tedin, Kent L. 45n, 46n
Terry, Sarah Meiklejohn 18n
theory *ix*, *x*, 59–60, 84, 129, 138
  deductive theory 84
Third Wave 12
totalitarian model 8–11
transformation 5, 28, 35, 45
transition to democracy
  first stage of democratization 60

transition to democracy *(continued)*
  theory 60–64
transitive preference 109
transplacement 28
Tucker, Joshua A. 33n

U

Ulram, Peter A. 44n
Urban, Joan Barth 37n
urban regimes
  theory 56

V

Vachudova, Milada Anna 29
Valenzuela, Samuel J. 26n, 60n
Van Roozendaal, Peter 57n
Vanhanen, Tatu 43n
Velten, Matthew 34
Verheijen, Tony 51n
vetoes
  presidential 16, 94–96
von Beyme Klaus 48n

W

Waldron-Moore, Pamela 25
Waldrauch, Harald 44n
Warwick, Paul 57n
Way, Lucan 45n
Waylen, Georgina 49n
Weingast, Barry R. 52n, 53n, 54n, 111n
Welsh, Helga A. 27
White, Stephen 23n, 33n, 40n, 44, 45n, 46n
Whitefield, Stephen 33n, 44n
winner-take-all 31, 130, 132, 134, 136

Woodrow Wilson Center 12, 60
Wyman, Matthew 23n, 33n

Y

Yadov, Vladimir 43n, 47n, 49n
Yanitsky, Oleg 47
Yanowitch, Murray 22n
Yershova, Natasha 40n

Z

zero-sum 129, 134, 136
 outcome of democratization 74, 77
Ziegler, Charles E. 11
Zielonka, Jan 34
Zimmerman, William 23
Zubek, Voytek 37n

About the Author

Terry D. Clark is associate professor of political science and international studies at Creighton University. His research focuses on institutional development in post-communist Europe. He has published in *Slavic Review*, *EEPS*, *Nationality Studies*, *Policy Studies Journal*, and *PS*, among other journals. A past recipient of three IREX grants, he was a Senior Fulbright Scholar in Lithuania in academic year 1999–2000.

WITHDRAWN